British Social Attitudes

Attitudes

The 25th
REPORT

The **National Centre for Social Research** (NatCen) is an independent, non-profit social research organisation. It has a large professional staff together with its own interviewing and coding resources. Some of NatCen's work – such as the survey reported in this book – is initiated by NatCen itself and grant-funded by research councils or charitable foundations. Other work is initiated by government departments or quasi-government organisations to provide information on aspects of social or economic policy. NatCen also works frequently with other institutes and academics. Founded in 1969 and now Britain's largest social research organisation, NatCen has a high reputation for the standard of its work in both qualitative and quantitative research.

The contributors

Simon Anderson
Director of the *Scottish Centre for Social Research*, part of NatCen

John Appleby
Chief Economist at the King's Fund

Rossy Bailey
Senior Researcher at the *National Centre for Social Research* and Co-Director of the *British Social Attitudes* survey series

Julie Brownlie
Senior Lecturer in Sociology, Department of Applied Science, Stirling University

Sarah Butt
Senior Researcher at the *National Centre for Social Research* and Co-Director of the *British Social Attitudes* survey series

Elizabeth Clery
Senior Researcher at the *National Centre for Social Research* and Co-Director of the *British Social Attitudes* survey series

John Curtice
Research Consultant at the *Scottish Centre for Social Research*, part of NatCen and Professor of Politics at Strathclyde University

Geoff Dench
Fellow of the Young Foundation and Visiting Professor at Greenwich University

Ingrid Esser
Assistant Professor of Sociology, Swedish Institute for Social Research (SOFI), Stockholm University

Lisa Given
Senior Researcher at the *Scottish Centre for Social Research*, part of NatCen

Oliver Heath
Lecturer in Politics, Royal Holloway, University of London; formerly Research Fellow in Politics, Strathclyde University

Alison Park
Research Group Director at the *National Centre for Social Research* and Co-Director of the *British Social Attitudes* survey series

Miranda Phillips
Research Director at the *National Centre for Social Research* and Co-Director of the *British Social Attitudes* survey series

Andrew Shaw
Research Group Director at the *National Centre for Social Research*

Janet Stockdale
Senior Lecturer in Social Psychology at the London School of Economics and Political Science (LSE)

Katarina Thomson
Formerly Research Director at the *National Centre for Social Research* and Co-Director of the *British Social Attitudes* survey series

British Social Attitudes

Attitudes

The 25th
REPORT

EDITORS
Alison Park
John Curtice
Katarina Thomson
Miranda Phillips
Elizabeth Clery

Los Angeles • London • New Delhi • Singapore • Washington DC

National Centre *for* Social Research

© National Centre for Social Research 2009

First published 2009

Apart from any fair dealing for the purposes of research or private study, or criticism or review, as permitted under the Copyright, Designs and Patents Act, 1988, this publication may be reproduced, stored or transmitted in any form, or by any means, only with the prior permission in writing of the publishers, or in the case of reprographic reproduction, in accordance with the terms of licences issued by the Copyright Licensing Agency. Enquiries concerning reproduction outside those terms should be sent to the publishers.

SAGE Publications Ltd
1 Oliver's Yard
55 City Road
London EC1Y 1SP

SAGE Publications Inc.
2455 Teller Road
Thousand Oaks, California 91320

SAGE Publications India Pvt Ltd
B 1/I 1 Mohan Cooperative Industrial Area
Mathura Road
New Delhi 110 044

SAGE Publications Asia-Pacific Pte Ltd
33 Pekin Street #02-01
Far East Square
Singapore 048763

Library of Congress Control Number: 2008937948

British Library Cataloguing in Publication data

A catalogue record for this book is available from the British Library

ISBN 978-1-84860-639-5

Printed in Great Britain by The Cromwell Press Ltd, Trowbridge, Wiltshire
Printed on paper from sustainable resources

Contents

6   Pay more, fly less? Changing attitudes to air travel
Sarah Butt and Andrew Shaw   **129**

**7   Therapy culture? Attitudes towards emotional support
     in Britain**
Simon Anderson, Julie Brownlie and Lisa Given   **155**

8   Britain at play: should we 'do' more and view less?
Rossy Bailey and Alison Park   **173**

List of tables and figures

Chapter 3

Chapter 4

Chapter 5

Chapter 6

Chapter 7

Introduction

The *British Social Attitudes* survey series began a quarter of a century ago, in 1983. In his foreword to the report on the first survey, Sir Claus Moser observed:

> What makes the series so important is precisely that it is a series. It is from the monitoring and understanding of trends in attitudes that one can learn most about what is happening in a society … (Moser, 1984)

We hope that, 25 years on, this report lives up to this prediction. In it, we focus on the results of the 2007 survey and assess what they tell us about the attitudes and behaviour of the British public.

Four chapters demonstrate the value of monitoring trends in attitudes over time. Chapter 1 examines attitudes to devolution in England, as well as feelings of 'Englishness', and assesses how these have changed since the advent of devolution elsewhere in the UK. In Chapter 2, we examine how satisfaction with the NHS has changed over the last 25 years and explore the reasons behind satisfaction and dissatisfaction. In Chapter 4 we focus upon employment commitment in different countries across the world, and the extent to which there is any relationship between levels of commitment and welfare state arrangements. In particular, we ask whether there is any evidence that the most generous welfare states contain the laziest and least motivated workers. And in Chapter 6 we examine the increasingly topical subject of air travel, focusing particularly upon how the public are likely to react to any increases in the cost of flying.

The remaining five chapters consider new topics in the survey series, thus helping ensure that the survey's content remains up to date and relevant. Public services 'reform' has been a key priority of the current UK Labour government; Chapter 3 examines the extent to which choice and diversity in the provision of public services is important to the public. Chapter 5 examines whether, and how, parenthood has an impact on people's attitudes and values, focusing particularly on attitudes to family relationships, work and family life. In Chapter 7, we describe the use that people make of emotional support networks, whether these are informal (such as friends and family) or formal (such as counsellors, GPs and therapists). In Chapter 8 we explore leisure patterns, focusing on how these vary between different groups and the extent to which individual leisure choices appear to be linked to happiness, health and social capital. Finally, in Chapter 9, we examine whether Britain is witnessing a decline in levels of social trust, and assess the extent to which people feel that they are the victims (or perpetrators) of inconsiderate or disrespectful behaviour in public.

Most of the tables in the report are based on *British Social Attitudes* data from 2007 and earlier years. Conventions for reading the tables are set out in Appendix II of this report. Full details of all the questions included in the 2007 survey can be found at www.natcen.ac.uk/bsaquestionnaires.

Our thanks

British Social Attitudes could not take place without its many generous funders. The Gatsby Charitable Foundation (one of the Sainsbury Family Charitable Trusts) has provided core funding on a continuous basis since the survey's inception and in doing so has ensured the survey's security and independence. A number of government departments have regularly funded modules of interest to them, while respecting the independence of the study. In 2007 we gratefully acknowledge the support of the Departments for Health, Transport, and Work and Pensions. We also thank the Department for Children, Schools and Families, the Department for Business, Enterprise and Regulatory Reform and the Respect Task Force (now the Youth Taskforce). Our thanks are also due to the Hera Trust.

The Economic and Social Research Council (ESRC), the body primarily responsible for funding academic social science research in Britain, has regularly provided the funds needed to field modules on the survey. In 2007 it funded the module about public services described in Chapter 3 (via the ESRC's *Public Services Programme*) as well as questions about English devolution (Chapter 1) and emotional support (Chapter 7). The ESRC *Public Services Programme* also funded work in Scotland, Wales and Northern Ireland, and Chapter 3 includes data from these countries. In Scotland, the module was carried on our sister survey, *Scottish Social Attitudes*; questions from that survey are also reported on in Chapter 1. Further details about the *Scottish Social Attitudes* survey can be found in Ormston (2008).

The ESRC also continued to support the participation of Britain in the *International Social Survey Programme* (ISSP), a collaboration whereby surveys in over 40 countries field an identical module of questions in order to facilitate comparative research. The British results from 2007 are described in Chapter 8, while Chapter 4 uses ISSP data from 2005 to compare thirteen different countries. The 2007 survey was also part of another international research project about mental health stigma, funded by Indiana University as part of work for the US National Institutes of Health.

We would also like to thank Professor Richard Topf of London Metropolitan University for all his work in creating and maintaining access to an easy to use website that provides a fully searchable database of all the questions that have ever been carried on a *British Social Attitudes* survey, together with details of the pattern of responses to every question. This site provides an invaluable resource for those who want to know more than can be found in this report. It is located at www.britsocat.com.

The *British Social Attitudes* survey is a team effort. The research group that designs, directs and reports on the study is supported by complementary teams who implement the survey's sampling strategy and carry out data processing. The researchers in turn depend on fieldwork controllers, area managers and field interviewers who are responsible for all the interviewing, and without whose efforts the survey would not happen at all. The survey is heavily dependent too on staff who organise and monitor fieldwork and compile and distribute the survey's extensive documentation, for which we would pay particular thanks to Pauline Burge and her colleagues in NatCen's administrative office in Brentwood. We are also grateful to Sandra Beeson and Sue Corbett in our computing department who expertly translate our questions into a computer assisted questionnaire, and to Roger Stafford who has the unenviable task of editing, checking and documenting the data. Meanwhile the raw data have to be transformed into a workable SPSS system file – a task that has for many years been performed with great care and efficiency by Ann Mair at the Social Statistics Laboratory at the University of Strathclyde. Many thanks are also due to David Mainwaring and Kate Wood at our publishers, Sage.

Finally, we must praise the people who anonymously gave up their time to take part in our 2007 survey. They are the cornerstone of this enterprise. We hope that some of them might come across this volume and read about themselves and the story they tell of modern Britain with interest.

The Editors

References

Ormston, R. (2008), *Scottish Social Attitudes Survey 2007 Core Module – Report 1: Attitudes to Government in Scotland*, Scottish Government Social Research, available at http://www.scotland.gov.uk/Publications/2008/05/16095134/0

1 Is there an English backlash? Reactions to devolution

John Curtice[*]

One of the principal claims of those who had doubts about the merits of creating the Scottish Parliament and the Welsh Assembly was that the change would provoke an 'English backlash' (Marr, 2000). People in England would become resentful that Scotland and Wales had been accorded a measure of self-government denied to themselves (Wright, 2000). Indeed, MPs from Scotland would continue to have a say in laws that apply only to England, whereas MPs from England would no longer have the ability to influence laws that apply only to Scotland (Dalyell, 1977). Meanwhile, people in Scotland and Wales would continue to enjoy higher average public spending per head than their counterparts in England. It was unrealistic, critics argued, to expect people in England to be willing to tolerate such unfairness for much longer (McLean, 2005; McLean *et al.*, 2008).

Arguably, however, some of the potential tensions created by the devolution settlement were masked during the first eight years of devolution because the same political party, Labour, both ran the UK government at Westminster and was either the senior or the sole partner in government in both Edinburgh and Cardiff. Potential disputes between the UK government and the devolved administrations could be managed informally via party channels (Trench, 2007). But after the 2007 devolved elections, the Scottish National Party (SNP) secured power in Edinburgh. Although only a minority administration, the new SNP government has not been reticent in criticising the UK government in defence of what it feels are Scotland's interests. Meanwhile in Wales too, Plaid Cymru, the Welsh nationalist party, has entered office for the first time, albeit as a junior coalition partner to Labour. In short, the arguments and differences between England and her neighbours are now being exposed to public view – and people in England can be expected to want to see their interests being defended too.

The potential forms of any English backlash are, however, many and varied (Hazell, 2006). At one extreme England might feel so discontented with the

---

[*] John Curtice is Research Consultant at the *Scottish Centre for Social Research*, part of NatCen, and Professor of Politics at Strathclyde University.

advantages accorded to Scotland and Wales that it decides to sue for divorce; that is, to demand independence for itself, leaving Scotland and Wales to look after themselves (and Northern Ireland either to become independent or to unite with the Irish Republic) (Nairn, 1981, 2000; Heffer, 1999). At the other extreme, England might simply want to adjust the existing devolution settlement, removing the apparent inequity in the distribution of public expenditure and reducing or eliminating the ability of Scottish MPs to vote on English laws (Conservative Party, 2000; Russell and Lodge, 2006; Conservative Democracy Task Force, 2008). In between these two positions – or perhaps in contrast to them – England might decide to embrace devolution for itself – either in the form of a parliament for the whole of England or, as the UK Labour government once envisaged, assemblies in each of England's regions (Stoker, 2000; Cabinet Office, 2002).

Any of these developments might be expected to be associated with deeper attitudinal changes. The creation of separate political institutions in Scotland and Wales, institutions that symbolise those countries' distinctive sense of national identity, might stimulate in England an appreciation of and adherence to a distinctive English national identity instead of a more all-embracing British identity (Paxman, 1998; Thatcher, 1998). Moreover, whereas the difference between 'being English' and 'being British' might hitherto have been indistinct and fuzzy (Cohen, 1995), it might now become sharper. As a result those who feel English might come to feel that their country's distinctive national identity should be reflected in distinctive political institutions (Gellner, 1983). Alternatively, perhaps, regional identities within England could become stronger (Mitchell, 2000). Either way the emotional glue that previously has helped to keep the United Kingdom together might begin to come unstuck in the wake of Scottish and Welsh devolution.

This chapter examines whether these fears or expectations of an English backlash have proved to be justified. The *British Social Attitudes* survey series is uniquely capable of addressing this task. Although a number of commercial opinion polls have periodically asked questions about attitudes in England towards devolution, none have consistently and regularly asked the same survey questions over an extended period of time. They are thus unable to provide clear evidence on whether there has been any change in attitudes since the devolved institutions were established in 1999, and it is only with the aide of such evidence, which *British Social Attitudes* does provide, that we can establish whether or not there has been any English backlash.

We begin by looking at trends in national identity. Is there any evidence that people in England are becoming more aware of having a distinctive sense of 'Englishness' that they might feel sets them apart from the rest of the UK, and which they might want recognised through distinctive English political institutions? We also consider (more briefly) people's strength of attachment to their region of England. We then turn to attitudes towards devolution and the Union. Does England now want devolution for itself? Is it unhappy about the degree of devolution accorded to Scotland and Wales? Is there, indeed, a wish to end the Union? Thereafter, we consider attitudes in England towards some of the alleged unfairness of the current devolution settlement, such as the ability of Scottish MPs to vote on English laws, and the financial advantages enjoyed by Scotland and Wales. Finally, we try to account for the results that we uncover, and in so doing examine whether there is any evidence that people's sense of identity now makes more difference to their views about how they should be governed.

Identity

One way of ascertaining people's sense of national identity is to ask them to choose which one or more amongst a list of possible identities describe how they think of themselves. The question we have asked regularly in this vein in recent years reads as follows:

> *Please say which, if any, of the words on this card describes the way* ***you*** *think of* ***yourself.*** *Please choose as many or as few as apply*

and the options presented to respondents are:

> *British, English, European, Irish, Northern Irish, Scottish, Ulster, Welsh,* and *other answer*

Since respondents are able to choose as many or as few answers as they wish, we shall refer to this as 'multiple choice' national identity.

As we might anticipate, most people in England give one of two answers to this question – "British" or "English" – or else say they are both (Table 1.1).

Table 1.1 Trends in multiple choice national identity, England 1996–2007

	1996	1997[+]	1998	1999	2000	2001	2002	2003	2004	2005	2006	2007
	%	%	%	%	%	%	%	%	%	%	%	%
British	71	76	70	71	67	67	73	70	69	70	68	68
English	52	54	55	65	59	63	57	59	55	60	67	57
Both	29	36	34	44	35	39	37	38	33	38	45	34
Base	*1019*	*3150*	*2695*	*2718*	*2887*	*2761*	*2897*	*3709*	*2684*	*3643*	*3666*	*3517*

[+]Source: British Election Study
Base: respondents living in England
'Both' refers to those stating they are both British and English
Percentages do not add up to 100 because respondents could give more than one answer. Answers other than "British" or "English" not shown

Two points are immediately apparent. First, while the proportion saying they are English rose somewhat between 1996 and 1999 from 52 per cent to 65 per cent,[1] thereafter it has simply fluctuated trendlessly; indeed in our most recent survey it is no more than 57 per cent. Second, there is little sign of any secular decline over the last decade in the proportion saying they are British. At 68 per cent our most recent reading is, for example, little different from that in 2000. We might note, too, that in every single year the proportion saying they are British has outnumbered the proportion saying they are English, albeit not necessarily by very much. Both identities are popular, but there is little sign people's sense of Englishness has supplanted their sense of Britishness.

But what of the little over a third or so – and sometimes rather more – who say they are *both* English and British? Where do they feel their loyalties lie if we force them to choose between these two identities? Perhaps – increasingly – their sense of being English is felt more intensely than that of being British. Maybe in saying they are British they are doing no more than stating a fact about their citizenship, whereas in saying they are English they are revealing where their emotional loyalties lie. If this is so, the picture suggested by Table 1.1 might be misleading.

To establish whether or not this might be the case we can examine what happens when those who gave more than one answer to our initial question were subsequently asked to state which one identity "**best** describes the way you think of yourself" and their answers then combined with the responses of those who initially only named one identity. Doing so enables us to identify the proportion who regard British and English as their only or more important identity, a measure that we can regard as 'forced choice' identity. As it happens, we also have an additional reading for this measure in 1992 (when respondents were only allowed to choose one identity) as well as for 1996 onwards.

In practice, as Table 1.2 reveals, this forced choice measure also fails to uncover any evidence of a growing sense of English national identity in recent years. Since 1999 the proportion choosing British as their sole or more important identity has continued to outnumber the proportion choosing English. The one occasion when this was not the case – in 2006 – may have been occasioned by the fact that the survey coincided with England's participation in that year's football World Cup. There certainly is not any evidence of a consistent secular increase in the proportion choosing to say they are English since Scottish and Welsh devolution has been in place – the most recent reading of 39 per cent is below that obtained on three occasions between 1999 and 2001. However, we should note that in the years leading up to and including 1999 there was an increase in the proportion saying they are English. Before 1999 typically only around a third or so gave top priority to feeling English, a level that has never subsequently been repeated.[2] So while we may not have any evidence of a consistent secular increase in people's sense of Englishness since the advent of devolution, we do appear to have *prima facie* evidence that the initial creation of the new institutions may have induced some people to feel distinctively English, a change that has not subsequently been reversed.

Table 1.2 Trends in forced choice national identity, England 1992–2007

	1992[+]	1996	1997[+]	1998	1999	2000	2001	2002	2003	2004	2005	2006	2007
	%	%	%	%	%	%	%	%	%	%	%	%	%
British	63	58	55	51	44	47	44	51	48	51	48	39	47
English	31	34	33	37	44	41	43	37	38	38	40	47	39
Base	2125	1019	3150	2695	2718	2887	2761	2897	3709	2684	3643	3666	3517

[+]Sources: British Election Studies
Base: respondents living in England
Answers others than "British" or "English" not shown

We can, however, take another approach in recognition of the fact that some people may have a dual identity. This is explicitly to acknowledge its existence and present survey respondents with the following question, which is often known as the 'Moreno scale' (Moreno, 1988):

Some people think of themselves first as British. Others may think of themselves first as English. Which, if any, of the following best describes how you see yourself?

English not British

More English than British

Equally English and British

More British than English

British not English

Other description

The answers obtained in response to this question in recent years are shown in Table 1.3. Typically just over three in five state they are some mixture of British and English, considerably more than spontaneously choose both identities when presented with a list of multiple options. So it seems that most people in England have some sense of being both British and English. But crucially for our argument so far, there is no evidence of a secular increase since 1999 in the proportion saying they are "English, not British". On the other hand the proportion giving that response has been consistently higher since 1999 than it was in 1997, once again suggesting that a sense of Englishness did awaken in some people in the immediate wake of the creation of the devolved institutions in Scotland and Wales.

Table 1.3 Trends in national identity (Moreno scale), England 1997–2007

	1997[+]	1999	2000	2001	2003	2007
	%	%	%	%	%	%
English not British	7	17	18	17	17	19
More English than British	17	14	14	13	19	14
Equally English and British	45	37	34	42	31	31
More British than English	14	11	14	9	13	14
British not English	9	14	12	11	10	12
Base	*3150*	*2718*	*1928*	*2761*	*1917*	*859*

[+]Source: British Election Study
Base: respondents living in England

But perhaps instead of gradually making people more aware of their sense of Englishness, the advent of devolution has encouraged people in England to feel more strongly attached to their particular region of England. On a number of occasions since 2001 we have asked respondents:

> *How much pride do you have in being someone who lives in (government office region[3]) or do you not think of yourself in that way at all?*

As seen in Table 1.4, the proportion saying they are "very proud" of their region has stubbornly remained at just below one in four. True, the proportion saying they "do not think of themselves in that way" at all has fallen from the very high figure of 52 per cent in 2001 to 44 per cent now, but this drop has simply been accompanied by an increase in the proportion saying they are "not very" or are "not at all" proud of their region.[4]

Table 1.4 Regional pride, England 2001–2007

	2001	2002	2003	2007
Degree of pride in government office region	%	%	%	%
Very proud	22	24	22	23
Somewhat proud	22	20	25	25
Not very proud	2	2	4	5
Not at all proud	1	1	1	2
Don't think of self in that way	52	52	48	44
Base	*2761*	*2897*	*3709*	*859*

Base: respondents living in England

While we do not know what the position was before 1999, there is clearly little evidence of an increase in attachment to the English regions since Scottish and Welsh devolution has been in place. Equally, there is certainly no evidence here to support Storry and Childs' claim (1997: 6) that "Regional identities … are very strong".[5]

So we have identified just one potentially important change in the pattern of identities in England over the last decade. Although still no less likely than before to describe themselves as British, since 1999, people have apparently become more likely to give priority to their sense of feeling English. But this development was seemingly a once and for all change that has not been fuelled further by any backlash against the actual operation of the devolution settlement. Moreover, despite the change it still remains the case that more people readily acknowledge a British identity than do an English one.

Constitutional preferences

But what of more explicit evidence of an English backlash? Is there any evidence that people in England wish to change radically the way they are governed? As we indicated earlier, the most extreme form that such a possible backlash might take would be a demand to end England's links with the rest of the UK and become independent. However, when for the first time in our 2007 survey we asked people which of two options would be "better for England", just 16 per cent said "for England to become an independent country, separate from the rest of the United Kingdom", while no less than 77 per cent preferred "for England to remain part of the United Kingdom, along with Scotland, Wales and Northern Ireland". This suggests that for the most part there is an overwhelming preference to maintain the Union.

Moreover, it seems that there has been little change in the level of support for dismembering the United Kingdom. Although the question about what would be better for England was only asked for the first time in 2007, we have, as detailed in Tables 1.5a and 1.5b, asked people in England on a regular basis their views about how both Scotland and Wales should be governed, including the option of those two countries becoming independent.[6] As can be seen in the tables, only around one in five say that Scotland should become independent, somewhat fewer Wales, figures that are largely similar to the proportion advocating independence for England.[7] Moreover, although here there does seem to have been an increase in support for Scottish and Welsh independence between 1997 and 1999, thereafter there has not been any secular trend. So apart from the possibility that the initial creation of the devolved institutions may have persuaded some people in England of the merits of independence for Scotland and Wales, there seems little reason to think that the experience of devolution elsewhere in the UK has given rise to sufficient resentment to cause more people in England to want to sue for independence.

Table 1.5a Attitudes in England towards how Scotland should be governed, 1997–2007

	1997[+]	1999	2000	2001	2002	2003	2007
Scotland should …	%	%	%	%	%	%	%
… become independent, separate from UK and EU or separate from UK but part of EU	14	21	19	19	19	17	19
… remain part of UK, with its own elected parliament which has **some** taxation powers	38	44	44	53	41	50	36
… remain part of UK, with its own elected parliament which has **no** taxation powers	17	13	8	7	11	8	12
… remain part of UK, **without** an elected parliament	23	14	17	11	15	13	18
Don't know	8	8	11	10	14	11	15
Base	3150	902	1928	2761	1924	1917	859

[+]Source: British Election Study
Base: respondents living in England

Table 1.5b Attitudes in England towards how Wales should be governed, 1997–2007

	1997[+]	1999	2000	2001	2003	2007
Wales should …	%	%	%	%	%	%
… become independent, separate from UK and EU or separate from UK but part of EU	13	20	16	17	16	17
… remain part of UK, with its own elected parliament which has law-making **and** taxation powers	37	33	35	39	37	29
… remain part of UK, with its own elected assembly which has limited law-making powers **only**	18	22	17	19	20	18
… remain part of UK **without** an elected assembly	25	15	20	14	15	20
Don't know	8	9	12	11	12	16
Base	3150	902	1928	2761	1917	859

[+]Source: British Election Study
Base: respondents living in England

Still, the absence of much support for breaking up the United Kingdom does not necessarily mean that people's preference to maintain the Union is strongly felt. When asked:

*If in the future England, Scotland and Wales were all to **become** **separate independent countries**, rather than all being part of the United Kingdom together, would you be pleased, sorry, or, neither pleased nor sorry?*

no more than 44 per cent said they would be "sorry". True, only eight per cent said they would be "pleased"; instead the most common response, given by 46 per cent, was that they would be "neither pleased nor sorry". Moreover, the proportion saying they would be sorry has fallen somewhat since 2003, when 49 per cent indicated that they would feel that way. For many people in England, perhaps, the United Kingdom is simply a fact of life that they do not question rather than an institution they are keen to preserve.

Meanwhile we might also note from Tables 1.5a and 1.5b that there appears to be considerable support in England for the existence of devolution (as opposed to either independence or reintegration) for Scotland and Wales. Over the last 10 years a majority have usually supported one of the two devolution options with which they were presented, while no more than one in five have opposed the existence of any kind of separate parliament or assembly in Scotland and Wales. True, there is some evidence that this support may have tailed off somewhat more recently; only 48 per cent now support some kind of devolution for Scotland, 47 per cent for Wales, compared with 60 per cent and 57 per cent respectively in 2003. But this seems in part to be the result of a growth in the proportion saying "don't know" – and thus perhaps growing indifference rather than outright hostility. Certainly it would still seem to be the case that if England has reacted at all to the experience of devolution it is more likely that this reaction has taken the form of demanding devolution for itself rather than wishing to see it brought to an end elsewhere in the UK.

Of course, as we have already noted, one of the complications of the devolution debate within England – in contrast to the position in Scotland and Wales – is that more than one proposal has been put forward as to what should be the territorial scope of any devolved institutions in England. Organisations such as the Campaign for an English parliament argue that England should have her own devolved parliament, thereby mirroring the position in Scotland. Others prefer a form of devolution to the nine official regions of England, perhaps running some services in their region but not having the ability to pass legislation. This was the form of devolution promoted by the UK Labour government until its proposals were defeated in a referendum in the North East of England in November 2004.

So in asking people about devolution for England we asked respondents to choose between three options. These are:

i.   the *status quo* whereby laws for England are made by the UK Parliament,
ii.   establishing an English parliament similar to the Scottish Parliament in Edinburgh, and
iii. a form of regional devolution to bodies whose powers and responsibilities are similar to those of the Welsh Assembly prior to the implementation of the Government of Wales Act (2006).[8]

Despite the relatively high level of support for devolution for Scotland and Wales, Table 1.6 shows that since 1999 consistently over half of respondents in England have supported the *status quo* of no devolution in England. Moreover, there does not appear to be any evidence that this figure is in secular decline. Only around a third favour some form of devolution, with support divided more or less evenly between the two options. Support for regional devolution in particular seems to have fallen away in the wake of its defeat in the 2004 referendum, but the most recent reading for 2007 does not suggest that a coalition of support is building around the idea of an English parliament instead.

Table 1.6 Constitutional preferences for England, 1999–2007

	1999	2000	2001	2002	2003	2004	2005	2006	2007
Which would be best for England?[9]	%	%	%	%	%	%	%	%	%
England governed as it is now, with laws made by the UK Parliament	62	54	57	56	50	53	54	54	57
Each region of England to have its own assembly that runs services like health	15	18	23	20	26	21	20	18	14
England as a whole to have its own new parliament with law-making powers	18	19	16	17	18	21	18	21	17
Base	*2718*	*1928*	*2761*	*2897*	*3709*	*2684*	*1794*	*928*	*859*

Base: respondents living in England

It seems, then, that even after nearly a decade of devolution elsewhere in the UK, England still does not want devolution for itself. True, we should bear in mind that there is far from unanimous support for the current constitutional arrangements in England – the level of demand for some degree of change is in danger of being understated because it is fragmented between different options. But the existing arrangements nevertheless continue to have the support of a majority.[10]

Still, people's answers to survey questions about constitutional change often depend on their precise wording (Curtice and Jowell, 1998). As a way of trying to assess the possibility that a differently worded question might present a very different picture, we have in recent years also occasionally asked respondents a second question that is deliberately designed to tap into the possible feeling that England should be treated in a similar way to Scotland and Wales. We asked respondents whether they agree or disagree that:

> Now that Scotland has its own Parliament and Wales its own Assembly, every English region should have its own elected assembly too.

But, as Table 1.7 shows, even when asked in this way, the demand for devolution still continues to appear muted. Just 22 per cent now believe that every region should have its own assembly in order to match the position in Scotland and Wales, while no less than 41 per cent are opposed. Moreover, on this measure, support for English devolution is now at its lowest ebb yet.[11]

Table 1.7 Attitudes in England towards regional government, 2001–2007

	2001	2002	2003	2007
Every region of England should have its own elected assembly	%	%	%	%
Agree	29	27	30	22
Neither	25	23	25	23
Disagree	32	37	33	41
Base	*2341*	*2419*	*3024*	*739*

Base: respondents living in England

So it seems there is little demand in England for radical change to the territorial arrangements under which it is governed. Few want to see England become independent of the rest of the UK, while only a minority want some form of devolution for themselves. At the same time there appears to be considerable willingness to accept the existence of separate institutions in Scotland and Wales. Moreover, the state of public opinion on these issues seems to be little different now to what it was in 1999 when the devolved institutions in Scotland

and Wales were first created. Evidence of a growing backlash against the advantages accorded to Scotland and Wales has so far proven hard to find indeed.

Constitutional grumbles

Still, England's apparent lack of interest in either devolution or independence does not necessarily mean that it is willing to accept any perceived unfairness of the current devolution settlement. After all, nothing in the data we have presented so far gives reason to believe that people in England are necessarily happy about the division of public spending between England and the rest of the UK. And even if they do not want their own separate parliament, they may still wonder why Scottish MPs can vote on English legislation. Perhaps it is in examining these milder potential sources of discontent that we might find evidence of a backlash in recent years.

When commercial opinion polls attempt to ascertain whether people in England are happy about the level of public expenditure in Scotland they usually preface their question by telling their respondents that government spending per head in Scotland is about 120 per cent of the level in England (Curtice, 2008). It is hardly surprising that they then typically find that most people believe Scotland's share is unfair. However, to ask the question in this way is rather to miss the point: it can only be argued that there is real discontent in England about the level of public expenditure in Scotland if people say that the level is unfair or too generous without being told what the level is. Thus the *British Social Attitudes* series has consistently asked people simply whether they believe that Scotland's share of government spending is fair or unfair, without providing any further information. Our question reads:

> *Would you say that compared with other parts of the United Kingdom, Scotland gets **pretty much** its fair share of government spending, **more** than its fair share, or **less** than its fair share of government spending?*

Despite the sometimes strident criticisms that have been voiced about the current generous level of funding enjoyed by Scotland,[12] when the question is posed in this way, still only around one in three people in England feel that Scotland gets more than its fair share of government spending (see Table 1.8). Moreover, consistently more than one in five say they "don't know" whether Scotland's share of public spending is fair or not, an indication that for many the issue is still far from being a prominent one. Nevertheless, there are some signs of growing discontent. Between 2000 and 2003 less than a quarter of people in England felt that Scotland secured more than its fair share of spending; around a third now do so. So the criticisms of the current funding arrangements that have been voiced do in fact seem to have had some impact on public opinion, giving us the first discernible evidence of some kind of backlash.

Table 1.8 Attitudes in England towards the financial relationship between England and Scotland, 2000–2007

	2000	2001	2002	2003	2007
Compared with other parts of the UK, Scotland's share of government spending is …	%	%	%	%	%
… much more than its fair share	8	9	9	9	16
… little more than its fair share	13	15	15	13	16
… pretty much its fair share	42	44	44	45	38
… little less than its fair share	10	8	8	8	6
… much less than its fair share	1	1	1	1	1
Don't know	25	23	22	25	22
Now Scotland has its own parliament, it should pay for its services out of taxes collected in Scotland	%	%	%	%	%
Strongly agree	n/a	20	n/a	22	28
Agree	n/a	53	n/a	52	47
Neither agree nor disagree	n/a	12	n/a	12	14
Disagree	n/a	11	n/a	10	5
Strongly Disagree	n/a	1	n/a	*	1
Base	*1928*	*2761*	*2897*	*1917*	*859*

n/a = not asked
Base: respondents living in England

Moreover, as Table 1.8 also shows, there is clear support for the idea that "now that Scotland has its own parliament, it should pay for its services out of taxes collected in Scotland". This view has also, if anything, strengthened more recently; 28 per cent now say they "strongly agree" with this proposition compared with 20 per cent in 2001. The funding of public spending in Scotland may not be as salient an issue in the public's mind as many a commentator is inclined to assume, but it is an issue about which resentment does seem to have grown somewhat in recent years.

Meanwhile, as Table 1.9 shows, around three in five people in England agree with the following statement, which refers to the so-called 'West Lothian' question:

Now that Scotland has its own parliament, Scottish MPs should no longer be allowed to vote in the House of Commons on laws that only affect England.

However, people are more inclined simply to "agree" with this proposition than they are to "strongly agree", casting some doubt on how deeply this feeling is held. Certainly, there is little evidence that support for this demand has increased over recent years.[13] The pattern of responses in 2007 is much the same as it was in 2003. Evidently, the occasional instances since 1999 of Scottish MPs casting votes in the House of Commons which were decisive in securing the passage of legislation that was not applicable in Scotland (such as the introduction of foundation hospitals and university 'top-up' fees) have not given rise to any discernible public reaction.[14]

Table 1.9 Attitudes in England towards the 'West Lothian' question, 2000–2007

	2000	2001	2003	2007
Scottish MPs should no longer be allowed to vote on English legislation	%	%	%	%
Strongly agree	18	19	22	25
Agree	46	38	38	36
Neither agree nor disagree	19	18	18	17
Disagree	8	12	10	9
Strongly disagree	1	2	1	1
Base	*1695*	*2341*	*1530*	*739*

Base: respondents living in England

So while England may not want devolution for itself, some of the apparent anomalies thrown by the asymmetric devolution settlement may still be a potential source of discontent. It seems that people in England do wonder why Scottish MPs can still vote on English laws given that English MPs no longer have any say in Scottish legislation. And while unprompted concern about the financial advantages enjoyed by Scotland may still only be the preserve of a minority, the size of that minority has grown. Indeed, it is that last trend that is the first evidence we have of some kind of growing backlash in England against the devolution settlement.

Why no backlash?

Clearly we are left with an important question. Why is there so little evidence of an English backlash since the creation of the devolved institutions in Scotland and Wales? One presumption behind the expectation of a backlash is that people in England would come to the view that devolution to Scotland and Wales constituted a major change in the way the United Kingdom is governed – either for good or for ill – and would react accordingly. Yet, however momentous the advent of devolution in Scotland and Wales may seem to be in the eyes of constitutional scholars, there never was any guarantee that it would be regarded in the same way by the ordinary public in England. After all, as has often been remarked, England dominates the Union and as a result it is very easy for developments in the rest of the UK to be ignored by or seem unimportant to its population.

Certainly, when people in England have been asked whether creating the Scottish Parliament or the Welsh Assembly has improved the way Britain as a whole is governed, or made it worse, a majority have consistently said it had not made any difference. When we have asked:

> *Do you think that so far **creating the Scottish Parliament** has improved the way Britain as a whole is governed, made it worse, or has it made no difference?*

followed by a similarly worded question about "creating the Welsh Assembly", there has never been more than a third who reckoned that either form of devolution had either improved matters or made them worse. Moreover, a relatively large proportion of people – no less than 15–16 per cent in 2007 – are unable to say what difference the devolved institutions have made, suggesting that the issue does indeed have little salience for many people in England (Table 1.10). But above all we should note that the devolved institutions are no more likely now to be thought to have made a difference (either way) than was the case in 2000, just 12 months after their creation.

Table 1.10 Perceived impact of devolution on how Britain is governed, England 2000–2007

	2000	2001	2002	2003	2007
Impact of Scottish Parliament on how Britain is governed	%	%	%	%	%
Improved	18	15	19	12	12
Made no difference	54	62	54	64	55
Made worse	13	9	10	6	14
Don't know	12	12	14	16	15
Impact of Welsh Assembly on how Britain is governed	%	%	%	%	%
Improved	15	11	n/a	8	11
Made no difference	57	65	n/a	66	58
Made worse	12	7	n/a	6	11
Don't know	13	14	n/a	18	16
Base	*1928*	*2761*	*1924*	*1917*	*859*

n/a = not asked
Base: respondents living in England

England may not, then, have exhibited a growing backlash to devolution simply because devolution is not thought to have made much difference – and is no more likely to be thought to have done so now than it was in its early days. But there is a further feature of public opinion in England that needs to be considered. Nationalism has at its heart the belief that a nation has the right to govern itself through its own distinctive political institutions (Gellner, 1983). Yet hitherto at least it has not been apparent that most people who say they are English feel the need for their identity to be recognised in the form of separate political institutions (Curtice, 2006). In other words, English national identity seems to make little difference to people's constitutional preference. And it would seem unlikely that any backlash could occur in the absence of an English nationalist sentiment.

Table 1.11 shows the weakness of the link between national identity and constitutional preference. Those whose 'forced choice' national identity is English rather than British are only a little more likely to favour the creation of an English parliament; in 2003, for example, they were just seven percentage points more likely to do so. However, in the most recent survey this difference has increased to 16 points.[15] So, perhaps, here is a sign that at last feeling English is beginning to make some difference to people's views?

Table 1.11 Constitutional preferences for England by forced choice national identity, England 2003, 2006 and 2007

	2003		2006		2007	
	British	English	British	English	British	English
Which would be best for England?	%	%	%	%	%	%
England governed as it is now, with laws made by the UK Parliament	52	49	59	54	69	50
Each region of England to have its own assembly that runs services like health	28	24	18	16	12	16
England as a whole to have its own new parliament with law-making powers	16	23	17	25	11	27
Base	1785	1447	362	431	408	347

Base: respondents living in England

Certainly, the difference between the strength of the relationship between national identity and constitutional preference in 2007 and that in 2006 is statistically significant, albeit only at the 95 per cent level.[16] To that degree the finding cannot simply be dismissed. But, equally, not too much should be made of a change registered in just one year. Certainly, the change between 2006 and 2007 in the strength of the relationship between national identity and constitutional preference is not replicated if we look at attitudes towards any other aspect of the devolution settlement.[17] It is thus difficult to argue that there has been a systematic increase in English nationalist sentiment.

In particular, there is no significant evidence of a change in the strength of the relationship between national identity and perceptions of the fairness of Scotland's share of public expenditure. As Table 1.12 shows, the increase between 2003 and 2007 in the proportion stating that Scotland receives more than its fair share of public spending amongst those who say they are English is, at 11 points, matched almost exactly by a 10-point increase amongst those who say they are British. The overall increase in the proportion feeling that Scotland gets more than its fair share – the strongest evidence we have uncovered so far of an English backlash – does not seem to have been based on a resentment fuelled by English national feeling.[18]

Table 1.12 Perceptions of Scotland's share of spending by forced choice national identity, England 2000, 2003 and 2007

	2000		2003		2007	
	British	**English**	**British**	**English**	**British**	**English**
Compared with other parts of UK, Scotland's share of govt spending is …	%	%	%	%	%	%
… more than fair	22	23	19	26	29	37
… pretty much fair	43	42	46	45	43	35
… less than fair	10	11	8	8	6	8
Base	*877*	*822*	*898*	*760*	*408*	*347*

Base: respondents living in England

One reason why those who feel English are only somewhat more supportive of an English parliament could be that they regard the existing UK Parliament as an English institution anyway. After all, what is now the UK Parliament was originally just England's parliament; representatives from Wales, Scotland and Ireland subsequently simply joined this body when they became part of the Union. To assess whether parliament is regarded as an English institution we asked people to describe it using the five-point 'Moreno' scale. As can be seen in Table 1.13, in 1999 only three-quarters as many people felt that parliament was wholly or predominantly an English institution as believed it was a British one. That imbalance still exists. Now 38 per cent say that parliament is predominantly or wholly British, while only 21 per cent consider it predominantly or wholly English.

This is not what we would expect to find if an English backlash has failed to occur because parliament is already considered to be an English institution. Moreover, those who think of parliament as wholly or predominantly an English institution are actually less likely to favour the constitutional status quo. Amongst this group, 50 per cent are happy for England's laws to continue to be made by the House of Commons, compared with 65 per cent of those who consider parliament to be wholly or mostly British. Perceptions of parliament thus fail to explain the lack of a backlash.

Table 1.13 Perceptions in England of the Houses of Parliament, 1999 and 2007

	1999	2007
Houses of Parliament are ...	%	%
... English, not British	11	8
... more English than British	18	13
... equally English and British	27	29
... more British than English	18	26
... British, not English	22	12
... neither	2	7
Base	*2718*	*859*

Base: respondents living in England

Instead it may be more fruitful to examine people's perceptions of whether the UK government can be trusted to look after England's interests. Perhaps England feels the UK government already does enough to look after its interests within the Union, and this helps explain why relatively few feel it is necessary for England to mimic the devolution granted to Scotland and Wales. So, we reminded respondents that the UK government has responsibility for Scotland, Wales and Northern Ireland along with England and then asked them how much they trusted the government to look after England's interests in particular:

> *The United Kingdom government at Westminster has responsibility for England, Scotland, Wales and Northern Ireland. How much do you trust the UK government at Westminster to work in the best long-term interest of England?*
>
> *[Just about always, Most of the time, Only some of the time, Almost never]*

Table 1.14 shows that, although there has been some drop in the level of trust since 2001, as many as 50 per cent still say that they trust the government either "just about always" or "most of the time". This is notably higher than the 35 per cent of people in Scotland who trust the UK government to look after Scotland's interests and the equivalent figure of 36 per cent for people in Wales.[19]

Table 1.14 Trust in the UK government to look after long-term interests of England, 2001, 2003 and 2007

	2001	2003	2007
	%	%	%
Just about always	9	7	7
Most of the time	48	46	43
Only some of the time	33	35	34
Almost never	6	9	10
Base	2761	975	859

Base: respondents living in England

Importantly, these perceptions of trust are strongly linked (in the expected direction) to people's constitutional preferences: among those who trust the UK government to look after England always or most of the time, 70 per cent favour the constitutional *status quo*. In contrast, among those who do not trust the UK government, only 47 per cent do so. Perhaps in focusing on the implications of asymmetric devolution for how parliament operates, devolution's critics have failed to appreciate that what governments do matters more to the public than parliamentary process. In any event it seems that, despite some fall in the perception, the UK government is still regarded as sufficiently English to limit the extent of any English backlash.

Conclusions

For the most part we have uncovered relatively little evidence of an English 'backlash'. An apparent initial trend in 1999 towards feeling more English and less British has not been sustained. Moreover, eight years' experience of seeing devolution in action seems to have done little to persuade people in England to embrace devolution for themselves, while they still appear willing to accept its existence in Scotland and Wales. Meanwhile that experience certainly seems to have done nothing to reduce public support for the continuance of the Union. This is, at least, in part because most people in England do not think that devolution has made much difference to how Britain is governed, while they are still inclined to feel that the UK government looks after England's interests.

But while the current constitutional configuration of the UK still seems to fit the contours of public opinion in England reasonably well, it would be a mistake to assume the match is perfect. Only just over half of people in England prefer the current arrangements to either a separate English parliament or regional devolution – if the debate between those two options were to be resolved one way or another, the demand for constitutional change in England might seem more pressing than it currently does. The merits of allowing Scottish MPs to vote on laws that apply only to England are not immediately apparent to most people in England, albeit not to any greater degree now than in 1999. But perhaps most significantly, there are some signs of a growing reaction against the levels of public spending enjoyed by Scotland, an issue that strictly speaking predates the current devolution settlement but one which has become more prominent in the wake of its introduction. True, at the moment the issue is still one that only exercises a minority – but perhaps it could yet prove to be a flashpoint for the Union unless it is seen to be satisfactorily addressed.

Notes

1. We quote the 1997 British Election Study figure here rather than that for the 1997 *British Social Attitudes* survey because the latter had a much smaller sample size of 1153. However, at 68 per cent "British" and 50 per cent "English" (and 26 per cent both), the figures for that year's *British Social Attitudes* survey do not give reason to question our argument here that the pattern of responses has changed little since 1996. It simply suggests some caution needs to be exercised in respect of the rather high figure of 76 per cent "British" recorded by the election study. Note that the unweighted sample size for the election study includes a deliberate oversample of ethnic minority respondents; the weighted sample size is notably smaller, 2492.
2. In the 1997 *British Social Attitudes* survey 36 per cent had an "English" 'forced choice' identity, 53 per cent "British".
3. Details of these regions may be found at www.statistics.gov.uk.
4. In sharp contrast to these figures, when asked how much pride they have in being British just seven per cent say they do not think of themselves in that way. Equally, the equivalent figure when asked about pride in being English is just 15 per cent.
5. It is, of course, possible that there are some regional identities that are strong but that these either do not coincide with the government office regions or are not captured by the terms used to describe those regions. However, the only proposals for regional devolution that have been seriously considered in Westminster have been ones related to the government office regions.
6. In the two questions presented in Tables 1.5a and 1.5b, the first row (the 'independence' category) was presented to respondents as two separate options: "Scotland/Wales should become independent, separate from the UK and the European Union" and "Scotland/Wales should become independent, separate from the UK but part of the European Union".
7. Those favouring independence for England overlap considerably with those who indicate a preference for Scotland and Wales to become independent, though the overlap is not perfect. Amongst those who believe it would be better for England to

become an independent country, 60 per cent state that they would prefer Scotland to become independent, while 58 per cent say the same of Wales.

8. Under this Act, Westminster can grant the Welsh Assembly the right to pass primary legislation in specific defined areas.

9. The precise question text was "With all the changes going on in the way different parts of Great Britain are run, which of the following do you think would be best for England?" Note that in 2004–2006 the second option read "that makes decisions about the region's economy, planning and housing". The 2003 survey carried both versions of this option and demonstrated that the difference of wording did not make a material difference to the pattern of response. Throughout this chapter the figures quoted for 2003 are those for the two versions combined.

10. Note that this remains true even if we take into account support for England becoming independent. A few of those who in response to the question detailed in Table 1.6 said that they favoured the *status quo* indicated that they thought it would be better for England to become an independent country. Even if we eliminate them, the level of support for the *status quo* is still 52 per cent.

11. The question does, of course, refer to regional devolution rather than an English parliament. It may well be that the particularly low level of agreement with the proposition in 2007 reflects the decline in support for regional assemblies in particular since 2003 as shown in Table 1.6. Nevertheless, given that the levels of support for the two forms of devolution have typically been (and still are) similar to each other, it is not self-evident that a similarly worded question in respect of an English parliament would evince substantially higher levels of support

12. For examples of some of the critical popular commentary on Scotland's share of spending see Heathcoat Amory (2007) and Heffer (2007).

13. We might note, too, that because the question was not asked before the introduction of devolution we cannot be sure that some people in England have always wondered why Scottish MPs could vote on laws that only applied in England.

14. For further details see Russell and Lodge (2006).

15. As we might anticipate, there is also a relationship between national identity and support for English independence. But again the relationship is only a modest one. Amongst those who choose British as their identity, 11 per cent favour independence for England, compared with 22 per cent of those who state they are English.

16. We undertook a loglinear analysis of the combined data for the two years. In the absence of an interaction term for constitutional preference by national identity by year, the residual chi-square was 8.86, which with two degrees of freedom is significant at $p=.012$.

17. Apart from the informal analysis presented in the next paragraph, we also used loglinear analysis to test for evidence of a statistically significant change between 2000 and 2007 in the relationship between national identity and (i) attitudes towards Scottish MPs voting on English laws, and (ii) Scotland's share of spending. We also used the same technique to assess whether there was significant change between 2001 and 2007 in the relationship between national identity and whether services in Scotland should be paid for out of taxes raised in Scotland. None of these analyses suggested a significant change has occurred.

18. Readers will, however, note that in contrast to the position in 2003 and 2007 there was no difference at all in 2000 between the attitudes of those who chose British as their identity and those who chose English. However, as reported in the previous note, loglinear analysis indicates that there was not a significant change between 2000 and 2007 in the strength of the relationship between national identity and Scotland's share of spending. In the absence of the relevant interaction term, the residual chi-square was 2.48, which with two degrees of freedom is only significant at p=.289.
19. These figures come from the 2007 *Scottish Social Attitudes* survey and the 2007 *Wales Life and Times Survey*. See also Curtice (2006: 133).

References

Cabinet Office/Department for Transport, Local Government and the Regions (2002), *Your region, your choice: Revitalising the English regions*, White paper Cm 5511, London: The Stationery Office

Cohen, R. (1995), 'Fuzzy frontiers of identity: the British case', *Social Identities*, **1**: 35–62

Conservative Democracy Task Force (2008), *Answering the question: Devolution, the West Lothian question and the future of the Union*, London: Conservative Party

Conservative Party (2000), *Strengthening Parliament: Report of the Commission to Strengthen Parliament* (Chair: Lord Norton of Louth), London: Conservative Party

Curtice, J. (2006), 'What the people say – if anything', in Hazell, R. (ed.), *The English question*, Manchester: Manchester University Press

Curtice, J. (2008), *Where stands the Union now? Lessons from the 2007 Scottish Parliament election*, London: Institute for Public Policy Research

Curtice, J. and Jowell, R. (1998), 'Is there really a demand for constitutional change?', *Scottish Affairs – Special Issue on Constitutional Change*, 61–93

Dalyell, T. (1977), *Devolution: the end of Britain?*, London: Jonathan Cape

Gellner, E. (1983), *Nations and nationalism*, Oxford: Blackwell

Hazell, R. (ed.) (2006), *The English question*, Manchester: Manchester University Press

Heathcoat Amory, E. (2007), 'The new apartheid', *Daily Mail*, 16 June

Heffer, S. (1999), *Nor shall my sword: the reinvention of England*, London: Weidenfeld & Nicolson

Heffer, S. (2007), 'The Union of England and Scotland is over', *Daily Telegraph*, 14 November

McLean, I. (2005), *The fiscal crisis of the United Kingdom*, London: Palgrave

McLean, I., Lodge, G. and Schmuecker, K. (2008), *Fair shares? Barnett and the politics of public expenditure*, London: Institute for Public Policy Research

Marr, A. (2000), *The day that Britain died*, London: Profile Books

Mitchell, A. (2000), 'A manifesto for the North', in Wright, A. and Chen, S. (eds.), *The English question*, London: Fabian Society

Moreno, L. (1988) 'Scotland and Catalonia: The Path to Home Rule', in McCrone, D. and Brown, A. (eds.), *The Scottish Government Yearbook 1988*, Edinburgh: Unit for the Study of Government in Scotland

Nairn, T. (1981), *The break-up of Britain: crisis and neo-nationalism*, London: Verso

Nairn, T. (2000), *After Britain: New Labour and the return of Scotland*, London: Granta Books

Paxman, J. (1998), *The English: portrait of a people*, London: Michael Joseph

Russell, M. and Lodge, G. (2006), 'Government by Westminster', in Hazell, R. (ed.), *The English question*, Manchester: Manchester University Press

Stoker, G. (2000), 'Is regional government the answer to the English question?', in Wright, A. and Chen, S. (eds.), *The English question*, London: Fabian Society

Storry, M. and Childs, P. (1997), *British cultural identities*, London: Routledge

Trench, A. (ed.) (2007), *Devolution and power in the United Kingdom*, Manchester: Manchester University Press

Thatcher, M. (1998), 'Don't wreck the heritage we all share', reprinted in Paterson, L. (ed.), *A diverse assembly: the debate on the Scottish Parliament*, Edinburgh: Edinburgh University Press

Wright, A. (2000), 'England, Whose England?', in Wright, A. and Chen, S. (eds.), *The English question*, London: Fabian Society

Acknowledgements

The *National Centre for Social Research* is grateful to the Economic and Social Research Council (ESRC) for their financial support which enabled us to ask the questions fielded in 2007 (research contract no. T0063.GH.P&S). Previous waves of data collection between 1999 and 2006 were funded by various grants from both the ESRC and the Leverhulme Trust. Neither body is responsible for the interpretations and opinions expressed here.

2 The NHS: satisfied now?

John Appleby and Miranda Phillips[*]

The year 2007 was significant for the NHS. It heralded the last year of a funding boost that started at the turn of the century and saw NHS cash spending nearly double and real spending rise by over 60 per cent, taking funding from 5.6 to 7.6 per cent of GDP. Clearly, such growth was never intended to continue indefinitely. The comprehensive spending review in November 2007 announced much reduced growth in NHS funding from 2008 to 2011: on average around three per cent per annum in real terms or about half the growth rate in previous years and a reversion to the long-term trend (Wanless *et al.*, 2007). Still, this is a reduction in *growth* not in absolute levels. The bigger and, hopefully, better NHS is here to stay.

Politically, 2007 was also significant, with a change in prime minister, a new ministerial team at the Department of Health in England and increasing signs of a policy divergence in Scotland and Wales. In policy terms, that year saw a continuation of the main government themes – in England at least – of devolution of power and budgets within the NHS and the promotion of the 'third phase' in reform. This involves a 'self-improving' NHS where quality and efficiency improvements are to be driven by patient choice and competition, coupled with greater use of financial incentives, not only for organisations but also for individuals (Stevens, 2004).

Importantly, given its centrality in government health policy over the last eight years – arising from its importance to the public – waiting times hit a historic low. Furthermore, the prospect of hitting the 'final' waiting times target – that no one should wait longer than 18 weeks from GP referral to treatment in hospital – was on course to become a reality by the end of 2008.

Of course, 2008 – the year we are writing this chapter – provides, perhaps, an even more resonant occasion: the sixtieth year of the inception of the NHS. As it turned out, this anniversary generated much analysis and thought about the evolutionary (and occasionally revolutionary) journey of the NHS itself since

---

[*] John Appleby is Chief Economist at the King's Fund. Miranda Phillips is a Research Director at the *National Centre for Social Research* and is Co-Director of the *British Social Attitudes* survey series.

1948, debate about its sustainability – both financially and politically – and arguments about its future; did it even have one? Are the pressures it bears too great? Will public expectations always exceed its capacity to respond? Have we reached the point of tax resistance? Can, frankly, the NHS ever satisfy its customers?

The *British Social Attitudes* survey provides a unique source of data with which to answer these questions. In this, the twenty-fifth year of the survey series, we take the long view and not only report on trends in overall NHS satisfaction since 1983, but explore variations by satisfaction with individual NHS services, views of different groups and attitudes towards choice and how these might explain why people are satisfied or dissatisfied with the NHS.

Paying for the NHS

Before we look in detail at satisfaction with the NHS, we start by reviewing the evidence on attitudes towards paying taxes to fund public services like health. Since the survey series began in 1983, we have asked respondents for their views on the level of taxation and spending in relation to three public services:

> *Suppose the government had to choose between the three options on this card. Which do you think it should choose?*
>
> *Reduce taxes and spend less on health, education and social benefits*
>
> *Keep taxes and spending on these services at the same level as now*
>
> *Increase taxes and spend more on health, education and social benefits*

Figure 2.1 shows the responses to this question since 1983. The first point to note is that, throughout the period, the proportion wanting to cut taxes and spending has been very small, now standing at just seven per cent. The issue has always been whether to *increase* taxes and spending or to keep things as they are. In the late 1980s, the later Thatcher years, the public came to perceive insufficient levels of government spending and the proportion wanting to increase taxes rose. It levelled off at about 60 per cent where it stayed for most of the 1990s. As recently as 2002, the year Gordon Brown increased national insurance to pay for increases in health spending, as many as 63 per cent said that taxes and spending should go up and just 34 per cent thought they should stay the same or be reduced. However, since then, a growing proportion of the public seem to have had their appetite for greater spending sated. The proportion saying they want to keep things as they are has risen and has now overtaken the proportion wanting more spending for the first time since the mid-1980s. In fact, support for increasing taxes and spending is now lower than at any time since 1984.

Figure 2.1 Attitudes to tax and spend, 1983–2007

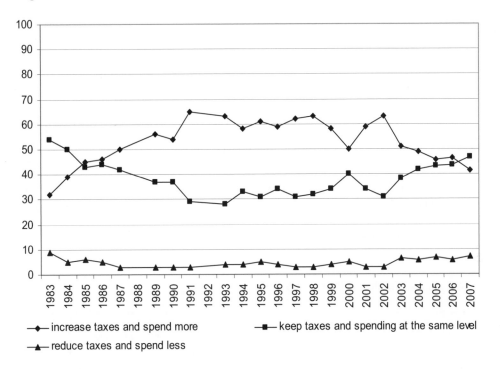

—◆— increase taxes and spend more   —■— keep taxes and spending at the same level

—▲— reduce taxes and spend less

Where does this leave the NHS? Of course, the survey question refers to wider government spending than just the NHS, but health is mentioned and it is bound to be an important consideration in the public's mind. Two possible NHS-related explanations can be offered for the decline in support for more taxation and spending (though, of course, there may be other factors, not necessarily related to views about the NHS). One reason could be that an increasing proportion of the public do not feel the need for higher spending on the NHS, because they are satisfied with the service it provides. After all, a massive investment has already been made and no one is proposing cutting NHS budgets. If this is the case, we would expect to see an increase in public satisfaction with the NHS in recent years. If so, Figure 2.1 implies a rather rosy picture of public attitudes towards the NHS. Still, the absence of further expansion removes a vehicle for easy improvements in health services so may leave the NHS with a harder task of fulfilling expectations in the years to come.

But we should also consider another possibility. A decline in support for increased taxation may be due to a view that spending more (as the government has done over the last seven years) has not improved the NHS. Why throw good money after bad? If this is the case, we would expect to see declining satisfaction with the NHS. To establish whether either of these explanations holds true, we need to examine how satisfaction with the NHS has changed over time, and the *British Social Attitudes* survey series provides us with the data to do so.

Trends in satisfaction with the NHS

The NHS as a whole

It is a quarter of a century since *British Social Attitudes* first asked a question about satisfaction with the overall running of the NHS:

> *All in all, how satisfied or dissatisfied would you say you are with the way in which the National Health Service runs nowadays?*

The full results are shown in Table 2.1. To make the interpretation of these results easier, the proportion expressing satisfaction is also shown graphically in Figure 2.2a, with the net satisfaction level (calculated as very/quite satisfied minus very/quite dissatisfied) shown in Figure 2.2b.

Table 2.1 Satisfaction with the NHS, 1983–2007[1]

	83	84	86	87	89	90	91	93	94	95	96	97	98	99	00	01	02	03	04	05	06	07
	%	%	%	%	%	%	%	%	%	%	%	%	%	%	%	%	%	%	%	%	%	%
Very satisfied	11	11	6	7	6	7	7	9	10	8	7	7	8	8	8	7	8	6	7	10	10	10
Quite satisfied	44	40	34	34	30	30	33	35	34	29	29	28	33	39	34	32	32	38	36	38	39	41
Neither	20	19	19	20	18	15	19	18	17	18	14	15	21	20	19	20	18	18	20	20	16	19
Quite dis-satisfied	18	19	23	24	25	27	23	23	22	25	28	28	26	23	26	27	26	24	23	21	22	20
Very dis-satisfied	7	11	16	15	21	20	18	15	16	20	22	22	11	11	13	14	14	13	14	10	12	10

Question not asked/survey not conducted in 1985, 1988 and 1992

In 1983 more than half (55 per cent) of those surveyed said they were "very" or "quite" satisfied with the NHS. Since then the trend has fluctuated – reaching lows of 36 or 37 per cent in 1989/1990 and again in 1995/1996. But since 2001 there has been the longest overall period of increases since the survey began in the proportion saying they were satisfied, albeit chiefly as a result of an increase in those saying they were "quite satisfied". The latest results reveal satisfaction to be at its highest level, dissatisfaction at its lowest, and net satisfaction at its highest since 1984 (51 per cent, 30 per cent and 21 points respectively).

Figure 2.2a Satisfaction with the NHS, 1983–2007

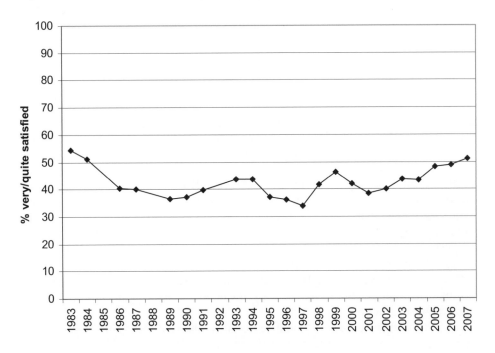

Figure 2.2b Net satisfaction with the NHS, 1983–2007

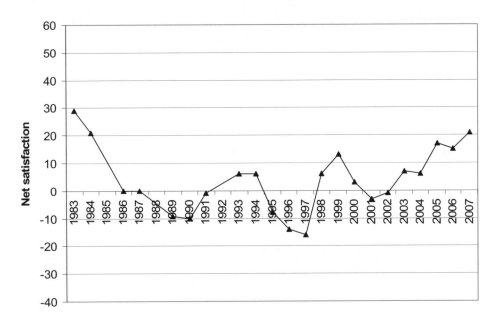

Cause for the NHS to celebrate? Well, perhaps; while getting back to early 1980s' levels of satisfaction may not seem much of an achievement, we should bear in mind that it has happened against a background of considerable (and controversial) policy change. It also seems reasonable to assume that this has been a period of rising public expectations. With this in mind, the improvement starts to look much more impressive.

On the other hand, should we be at all surprised that over a period when the NHS has received an unprecedented boost in funding and waiting times (historically the public's number one complaint about the NHS) have reached their shortest for many decades, these improvements have been noticed and appreciated by the public? Previous findings in *The 20th Report* had suggested that survey respondents were relatively insensitive to changes in the level of NHS funding over time (Appleby and Alvarez-Rosete, 2003). Nevertheless, in the five years since, funding has continued to increase so substantially that it would have been extraordinary if satisfaction had not also improved.

On waiting times, *The 22nd Report* (Appleby and Alvarez-Rosete, 2005) suggested that views on the need to improve outpatient waiting times and waiting time in accident and emergency departments were strongly associated with satisfaction with the NHS overall. It may therefore not be unreasonable to assume that actual improvements in these areas have gone some way to improving satisfaction.

Either way, there appears to be a reasonably happy picture for the NHS. The money has been spent, the targets have largely been met, the public have noticed and responded with greater satisfaction. However, future funding growth will be more limited. And if future funding is achieved without increases in taxes perhaps the voting and taxpaying public will not mind.[2] But before we conclude that all is fine with the NHS, we need to look at satisfaction with the individual parts of the service and particularly consider the prospect of rising expectations outstripping achievements.

Different attitudes to different parts of the service

While satisfaction with the NHS overall may provide a useful barometric guide to public opinion about the service, it is by definition a very general question. Such a *gestalt* view of the whole health care system can hide as much as it reveals. For this reason we also ask for opinions about some of the main services provided by the NHS:

> *From your own experience, or from what you have heard, please say how satisfied or dissatisfied you are with the way in which each of these parts of the National Health Service runs nowadays:*
>
>   ... *local doctors or GPs?*
>   ... *National Health Service dentists?*
>   ... *being in hospital as an in-patient?*
>   ... *attending hospital as an out-patient?*
>   ... *Accident and Emergency departments?*

As Figures 2.3 and 2.4 show, there is a more mixed pattern of results for individual services than for satisfaction with the NHS overall. Of immediate note is that satisfaction with the NHS overall has been, for much of the period, somewhat lower than satisfaction with individual services. One – albeit speculative – reason for this difference may be that questions about individual services focus respondents' minds on clinical and care aspects of the NHS whereas a general question about the NHS as a whole may additionally encompass what the public may feel less sympathetic towards – politicians, managers and bureaucracy.[3] The fact that the gap between satisfaction with individual services and that for the NHS overall has narrowed in recent years may in part reflect a decline in such views and in part personal experience with some individual services.

GPs and dentists

For the record, Figure 2.3 shows that satisfaction with GP services – traditionally high – have been increasing from a dip around 2001 to three-quarters (76 per cent) now expressing satisfaction. This chapter focuses mainly on hospital services and satisfaction with the NHS as a whole, so we are not going to comment in depth on satisfaction with GPs. However, GP services are part of the NHS and multivariate analysis (reported in more detail in Table A.1 in the appendix to this chapter) shows that satisfaction with GPs is part of the group of attitudes that go into making up people's satisfaction levels with the NHS as a whole.

Figure 2.3 Satisfaction with GPs and NHS dentists, 1983–2007

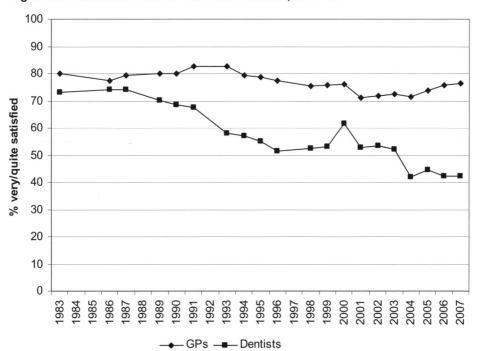

By contrast, views on dentists are largely unrelated to satisfaction with the NHS as a whole. This is probably just as well for the NHS, since satisfaction with dentistry has reached a low of around 40 per cent over the last four years – almost certainly due to continuing problems with access to NHS dentists in some parts of the country.

Hospital services

We turn now to the three hospital services covered by our question – inpatients, outpatients and accident and emergency. Here we see a very interesting picture (Figure 2.4). Until 1993, satisfaction with inpatient services was consistently higher than with outpatient services. But the long-term trend was a decline in satisfaction with inpatient services (from around 65 to 75 per cent satisfaction in the 1980s to around 50 per cent since the turn of the century). During the period 1994–2003, satisfaction levels with inpatient and outpatient services were almost identical. But since 2004, the pattern from the early years has been reversed. Satisfaction with outpatient services began to increase after 2001 and has increased in most years since. It is now at the highest level since the mid-1980s, at 60 per cent. In part this may reflect reductions in waiting times and increased choice over hospital (and appointment times).

Figure 2.4 Satisfaction with hospital services, 1983–2007

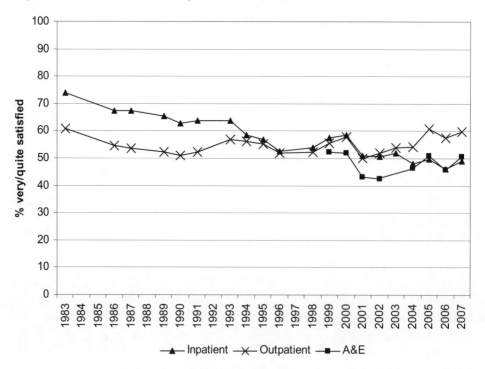

The decline in satisfaction with inpatient services has been arrested somewhat but it has nevertheless ended up 11 percentage points below outpatient services. In this chapter, we are going to use these two different trends in satisfaction with outpatient and inpatient services to try to delve a little deeper into the way satisfaction with NHS services is formed.

The survey question about satisfaction with A&E departments has a shorter time-series and has fluctuated substantially since it was first asked in 1999. In recent years, there have been modest improvements in satisfaction leaving it at a similar level to inpatient services (51 per cent).

The role of quality in satisfaction

With this largely improving picture of satisfaction, do the public still see any need for improvement in health services? We can look at this using the following question:

> *From what you know or have heard please tick a box for each of the items below to show whether you think the National Health Service in your area is, on the whole satisfactory or in need of improvement.*
>
> *Being able to choose which GP to see*
> *Quality of medical treatment by GPs*
> *Staffing level of nurses in hospitals*
> *Staffing level of doctors in hospitals*
> *Quality of medical treatment in hospitals*
> *Quality of nursing care in hospitals*
>
> *[In need of a lot of improvement, In need of some improvement, Satisfactory, Very good]*

Figure 2.5 shows the proportion identifying a need for improvements in each of these areas from 1989 to 2007. And, yes, when the question is put like that, there are a number of further improvements in quality that people would like to see. The worst perceptions are of staffing levels, where a substantial majority of respondents see the need for improvement, although the level of concern has fallen from a high of 79 per cent in 2001 to 62 per cent now (for staffing levels of doctors – shown in Figure 2.5; views on staffing levels of nurses follow an almost identical pattern and are therefore omitted from the figure).

The most noticeable feature of Figure 2.5 is the step change from 1999 to 2001. For all areas – from choosing a GP to staffing levels and quality of treatment and care – there was at that point a substantial increase in the proportion who felt there needed to be an improvement. This was particularly the case with some of the hospital-related issues: the quality of nursing care (+19 percentage points) and the quality of medical treatment in hospitals (+20 points).

This concern must have played a part in the government's decision to pump a lot more money into the NHS. But it is perhaps significant that, apart from concern about staffing levels, the various worries shown in Figure 2.5 have not returned to their pre-2001 levels.

When we conduct multivariate analysis, which considers these factors together with all the other issues covered in this chapter (see Table A.2 in the appendix to this chapter), we find that these concerns about quality are closely related to satisfaction with the NHS. In particular, concern about the quality of medical treatment and nursing care in hospitals is important, both in satisfaction with the NHS as a whole and in satisfaction with inpatient services. Views of staffing levels of doctors in hospitals also have an impact on satisfaction with the NHS as a whole. In part this may help explain why satisfaction with inpatient services is lagging behind satisfaction with outpatient services. The government would be well advised to pay careful attention to issues of quality of hospital care if it wants the voting public to be satisfied with the health service.

It is interesting to note that these declining trends in views on the need for extra staffing coincide with some of the largest increases in staffing – particularly in England – for many years. For example, total NHS staff in England increased by nearly 20 per cent between 2000 and 2006: consultants by 34 per cent, nurses by 19 per cent and GPs by 17 per cent (Information Centre, 2008).

Figure 2.5 Areas of NHS in need of improvement, 1989–2007

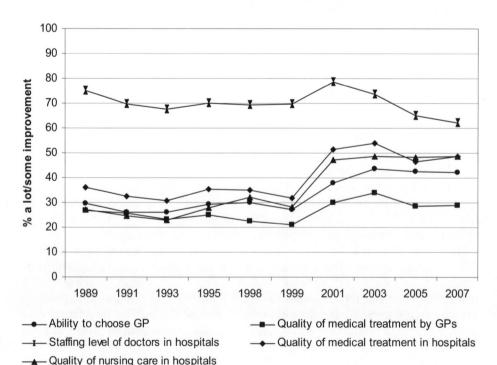

- ●— Ability to choose GP
- ━━ Quality of medical treatment by GPs
- ┼— Staffing level of doctors in hospitals
- ◆— Quality of medical treatment in hospitals
- ▲— Quality of nursing care in hospitals

Variation between different population groups

Experience of the NHS

Previous *British Social Attitudes* reports have highlighted the apparent gap in satisfaction between those with recent experience of the NHS and others (with the former reporting higher levels of satisfaction overall and with particular services) (Mulligan and Appleby, 2001; Appleby and Alvarez-Rosete, 2003, 2005). Here we shall report again on these differences and on trends over time. We ask to what extent changes in satisfaction overall have been driven by changes in satisfaction reported by those with recent contact.

An important reason for separating out those with and without recent contact is a presumption that the former will have a more informed opinion of the NHS, the quality of its services and particularly, over time, the possible impact of changes in the NHS on satisfaction; while for the latter there is a different underlying story largely concerning a second-hand portrayal of the NHS gleaned through the media and anecdote. For example, recent publicity concerning healthcare associated infection may suggest a high probability of actually acquiring an infection while an inpatient; in fact, the actual incidence of, for example, MRSA, is very low.[4] Similarly, the experience of actually getting an outpatient appointment quickly may well be different from reading (and possibly disbelieving) a newspaper report of a government announcement about reduced waiting times.

We are able to distinguish the level of recent contact with various parts of the health service through the following question:

> In the last *twelve* months, have you or a close family member or close friend…
> … visited an NHS GP?
> … been an *out-patient* in an NHS hospital
> … been an *in-patient* in an NHS hospital
> … had any *dental* treatment as an *NHS* patient?[5]
> … had any medical treatment at an NHS accident and emergency department?
>
> Yes, just me
> Yes, *not* me but close family member or friend
> Yes, *both* me *and* close family member or friend
> No, neither

Table 2.2 shows satisfaction with particular NHS services split up by those who had personal contact, 'second-hand' contact or no contact at all with that service. The results are really quite startling – those with personal experience are at least 18 percentage points more satisfied than those with no experience. The largest gap is for dentistry where 65 per cent of those with personal experience are satisfied compared with 26 per cent of those with no experience

– presumably because one source of dissatisfaction is the inability to find an NHS dentist. But GPs, outpatient services, inpatient services and accident and emergency services also show very substantial gaps. Moreover, the impact of contact with inpatient and outpatient services on satisfaction with those services remains when other factors (like age of respondent) are taken into account (see Table A.2 in the appendix to this chapter).[6]

Even having a friend or relative who has had contact with a particular health service improves satisfaction, although not by as much as personal contact. The NHS seems to be its own best advocate. This is very good news for GPs where only five per cent of respondents have had no contact (personal or through family or friends) in the last year, and this may in part account for the high levels of satisfaction with GP services that we saw in Figure 2.3. But the other services need to find ways of convincing non-patients that they really are improving – some 27 per cent have had no contact with outpatient services, while the figure is 52 per cent for inpatient services and 57 per cent for A&E departments.

Table 2.2 Satisfaction with NHS services, by recent contact with that service[7]

% satisfied with the specific NHS service	GP	Dentist	Out-patient	Inpatient	A&E
Personal contact	80	65	74	69	63
Close family member/friend *only*	67	33	54	48	55
No contact	60	26	47	43	45
Gap: Personal contact minus no contact	+20	+39	+27	+26	+18

Can the difference in satisfaction between patients and non-patients help explain the trends in satisfaction we saw in Figures 2.2 to 2.4? To answer this question we need to look at changes over time. Table 2.3 provides trend rates of satisfaction in two services – outpatients and inpatients – split between those with recent contact (either personal, or by a person close to the respondent) and those without contact.[8] The results are intriguing. First, for both outpatients and inpatient services the satisfaction gap has grown, from eight percentage points in 1987 to 19 and 13 points respectively by 2007. Could this be part of the reason why satisfaction has improved?

However, the reason for this growth is different between these services. For outpatients we see an increase in satisfaction among patients (or those whose friends or family have had contact) – mainly occurring between 2003 and 2007. We can conjecture that the additional resources have begun to do their job – waiting times are down, appointments more convenient, hospitals cleaner and more pleasant places to visit, and better staffed. But the public do not necessarily believe this until they see it with their own eyes (or hear it second hand), for the satisfaction levels of those with no contact have been static over the period. Not only is the NHS its own best advocate, but increasingly so as the promised reforms really do bring improvements.

But how is the story different for inpatient services? Here satisfaction among those with recent experience has fallen by 15 points over the period. However, the increased 'satisfaction gap' for inpatients is due to an even greater fall in satisfaction (20 points) among those with no recent contact. As we have seen, many people do not have any experience of inpatient services and this may make them more susceptible to high-profile media scares such as the MRSA issue. This underlines the fact that the NHS must not forget the importance of getting its message across to those who have been lucky enough not to have to use its services.

Table 2.3 Satisfaction with NHS outpatient and inpatient services, by recent contact with that service, 1987–2007[9]

% satisfied with …	1987	1990	1993	1996	1999	2003	2007
… outpatients							
Contact	55	53	60	56	61	57	66
No contact	47	44	47	42	47	46	47
Gap: contact minus no contact	+8	+9	+13	+14	+14	+11	+19
… inpatients							
Contact	71	69	72	60	64	58	56
No contact	63	58	56	46	56	47	43
Gap: contact minus no contact	+8	+11	+16	+14	+8	+11	+13

Contact = personal contact, or contact by a person close to the respondent

Age

In addition to recent contact with various health services, certain demographic factors have a bearing on how people view the NHS. In particular, as shown in Table 2.4, people of different ages have always expressed different levels of satisfaction with the NHS, with older people being much more satisfied than younger people. This is, no doubt, related to the fact that older people are more likely to come into contact with the NHS, though that is not the whole story, as the significance of age holds for inpatient and outpatient (though not overall) satisfaction even when we take recent contact into account (see Table A.2 in the appendix to this chapter). Nearly two-thirds of those aged 65 or over are satisfied with the NHS compared with 43 per cent of those aged 18–34. This may in part reflect a difference in experience of the NHS as people age, a so-called 'lifecycle effect'. As previous cohort analyses of changes in satisfaction have shown (Appleby and Alvarez-Rosete, 2003) 'period effects' – changes in attitudes affecting everyone – can be identified over time in changes in satisfaction, but these are attenuated in older age groups due, we assume, to these 'lifecycle effects'.

However, the gap between older and younger people has stayed fairly constant over time, so cannot really explain the substantial changes in satisfaction that we saw in Figures 2.2 to 2.4.

Table 2.4 Satisfaction with the NHS overall, by age, 1983–2007[10]

% satisfied	1983	1986	1989	1993	1996	2000	2003	2007
Age								
18–34	50	36	30	34	29	37	42	43
35–54	52	37	34	41	33	38	38	49
55–64	48	42	40	50	40	46	43	52
65+	70	54	50	61	51	54	58	64

Party identification

We can also track in our figures the extent to which views about the NHS are, and have been, associated with political party identification. Satisfaction with individual parts of the health service seem much less prone to this effect, but we probably have to live with the fact that the overall NHS satisfaction question is liable to be regarded by some respondents as a measure of their satisfaction with the government of the day. This is shown most clearly by the dip in satisfaction in the years leading up to the 1997 election (see Figure 2.2).

Table 2.5 Satisfaction with the NHS overall, by party identification, 1983–2007[11]

% satisfied	1983	1986	1989	1993	1996	2000	2003	2007
Party identification								
Conservative	57	46	44	55	49	44	38	46
Labour	56	37	29	37	28	44	50	57
Liberal Democrat[+]	44	33	30	33	33	37	45	55

[+] 'Alliance/SDP/Liberal' before 1989

Table 2.5 shows that this was particularly the case among Labour supporters, whereas satisfaction held up fairly well among Conservative supporters. Not surprisingly, the picture reversed after 1997, with Labour supporters now professing the greatest satisfaction with the NHS, the proportion of those stating they were satisfied more than doubling from 28 per cent to 57 per cent between 1996 and 2007. Meanwhile, those identifying with the Conservative Party have not become more satisfied over this period.

Patient choice

The ability to choose which hospital to go to has always been a feature of the NHS – at least for those patients with the knowledge, energy and assertiveness to persuade their GP to refer them and for the hospital consultant to then accept them as a patient. However, it was not until the publication of *The NHS Plan* in 2000 (Department of Health, 2000), and experiments in offering patients a choice of hospital in order to reduce waiting times (*cf.* the London Patient Choice Project; Burge *et al.*, 2005) and a return to ideas of an internal market that a more formal and deliberate policy on choice started to emerge in England. Choice was promoted not only on the grounds that it was a good thing in its own right, enabling patients better to match their needs with what was on offer, but also – combined with a money-follows-the-patient payment system for hospitals – as a new lever to exert pressure on hospitals to improve their services.

In England – where a policy on choice has been most explicitly pursued – a rolling programme to offer patients a choice of hospital for their first outpatient appointment (and subsequent inpatient care if required), as well as choices of appointment times, has culminated in April 2008 with the right of patients needing a referral to an outpatient department to have a choice of any hospital, NHS or private.

British Social Attitudes asks a series of questions about whether patients *should* have a say over various aspects of health care – hospital, outpatient appointment times and kind of treatment. We also ask respondents how much say patients *actually* have. The precise wording, shown here for the first of these areas (which hospital to go to), is as follows:

> *How much say do you think NHS patients **should have** over which hospital to go to if they need treatment?*

> *And how much say do you think NHS patients **actually have** over which hospital to go to if they need treatment?*

> *[A great deal, Quite a lot, A little, None at all]*

It is worth noting that these questions do not explicitly use the word 'choice', rather, the word 'say' which, as has been pointed out, could encompass not just the concept of choice but also 'voice', i.e. wider influence (Taylor-Gooby, 2008).

Table 2.6 presents the results. Because of the differences in policy context across England, Scotland and Wales, we limit this part of the analysis to England only. (Chapter 3 in this report looks specifically at attitudes to choice in England, Scotland, Wales and Northern Ireland across a range of policy areas.)

Having a say over aspects of NHS care is clearly popular: three-quarters (76 per cent) think patients should be able to choose which hospital to go to (while 71 per cent and 64 per cent feel the same about a say over treatments and outpatient appointment times). However, perceptions of whether patients *actually* have a say are far lower – only around two in ten think this is the case for the three areas we asked about.

These questions have been asked in two previous surveys since 2004, and so it is possible to identify some initial trends in the public's views. The first three columns in Table 2.6 show a distinct increase in the proportion saying patients should have "a great deal" or "quite a lot" of say – most notably in terms of which hospital to go to (+14 percentage points), followed by outpatient appointment time (+10 points) and then treatment (+five points). This seems a pretty clear cut case of increasing expectations, fuelled perhaps by the political rhetoric surrounding the reforms.

Table 2.6 Say over hospital, outpatient appointment time and treatment, 2004–2007: England only

	% who say patients should have a great deal/quite a lot of say			% who say patients actually have a great deal/quite a lot of say			Aggregate gap between expected and perceived say (should – actual)		
	2004	2005	2007	2004	2005	2007	2004	2005	2007
Which hospital to go to	62	68	76	9	12	19	53	56	57
Outpatient appointment time	54	57	64	14	17	20	40	40	44
Kind of treatment	66	70	71	17	21	21	49	49	50
Base	*2684*	*2721*	*2635*	*2684*	*2721*	*2635*			

Base: respondents in England

Alongside this increase in a desire for a say over aspects of NHS care, we also find that public perceptions of say have increased (columns 4–6): for all three areas, the proportion thinking that patients actually have a say has increased since 2004. However, expectations seem to be outstripping reality – or at least the public's perceptions of reality. Not only are the proportions thinking that there actually is say radically lower than the proportion thinking there should be say, but the gap has widened somewhat over the last three years (columns 7–9). For example, in 2004, 62 per cent thought that patients should have a say in which hospital to go to but only nine per cent thought that they actually did have this say. By 2007, the proportion thinking patients should have a say had grown to 76 per cent (an increase of 14 percentage points), while the proportion thinking they actually had a say had only grown to 19 per cent (an increase of 10 percentage points). This is a potentially dangerous situation for the NHS: reforms are having the effect of increasing the public's expectations but perceptions of actual improvements are not keeping pace. We say perceptions: it is almost irrelevant to this argument whether patients can actually choose their hospital – what matters here is whether the public think they can.

Our results on perceptions of *actual* say over which hospital to go to are somewhat at odds with figures collected by the Department of Health in England via their bi-monthly Patient Choice surveys. The Patient Choice survey for September 2007, for example, reports that 45 per cent of patients recall being offered a choice of hospital, an increase from 30 per cent in the first survey in May 2006 (Department of Health, 2008). However, in the 2007 *British Social Attitudes* survey only 19 per cent of respondents in England felt patients actually had a say over which hospital to go to. A small part of this difference is accounted for by the fact that the Department's survey asks people who have actually been referred by their GP, whereas our results are for the general public in England. When we look at those with recent personal contact with outpatients services, we find that 23 per cent believe that patients actually have a say over which hospital they go to for treatment, compared to 15 per cent of those with no such contact (figures for England only). Similar results are found for opinions about how much say patients actually have over outpatient appointment times.

As noted above, the wording of the questions did not explicitly use the word 'choice' and this may in part explain the difference in perceptions between our survey respondents and patients in the Department's survey. The word 'say' may not, for some people, immediately bring to mind the NHS choice agenda. In the most recent survey, we were able to test this theory by asking similar questions but this time referring explicitly to "choice":[12]

> *How much choice do you think NHS patients* **should** *have about which hospital to go to if they need treatment? Please choose a phrase from the card.*
>
> *And in your area, how much choice do you think NHS patients* **actually** *have about which hospital to go to if they need treatment? (Again please choose a phrase from the card.)*
>
> *[A great deal, Quite a lot, A little, None at all]*

In fact, the results to these questions are little different to those from the original "say" questions: 74 per cent think that NHS patients *should* have a choice of hospital, while 20 per cent think patients *actually* have a choice (compared to 75 and 18 per cent respectively for the "say" version of the questions; figures are for all respondents in Britain). A second pair of questions about choice of treatment had a similar result: both readings were just two percentage points different to the original questions. For the public it seems, having a say is as good or similar to having a choice – although whether views would remain similar in the context of full knowledge of what choice implies (in terms of the economic and new financial flows environment in the NHS) remains to be seen. This is explored further in the Curtice and Heath chapter in this report (Chapter 3).

Choice and satisfaction

If, as we have seen, for the public, a desirable attribute of the NHS is that it offers choice, but the desire for choice outstrips the perceived actual situation, what impact might this have on satisfaction with the NHS? To simplify the analysis, we concentrate on two key groups: those who think that patients already have a say and those who think patients *should* have a say, but do not yet do so.

The first two rows of data in Table 2.7 show (for England only – similar results were obtained for other parts of Great Britain), a notable gap in satisfaction between those who think patients do have a say and those who feel they should but do not. For example, 66 per cent of those who think patients have a say over choice of hospital are satisfied with the NHS overall, compared to 46 per cent of their counterparts who think patients should have a say but do not – a gap of 20 percentage points.

Similar, though smaller, gaps are found when we look at outpatient and inpatient satisfaction (remaining rows of Table 2.7). The gap for both outpatient and inpatient satisfaction, when it comes to a say over which hospital to go to, is 14 points. Virtually identical figures and patterns are found for the other two areas asked about: say over appointment time and say over treatment.

The role of say over which hospital to go to retains its importance for satisfaction with the NHS as a whole, even once all the other factors considered in this chapter are taken into account. Similarly, the role of say over treatment retains its importance for satisfaction with outpatient services. (See Table A.2 in the appendix to this chapter.)

This would appear to be a classic case of rising expectations threatening to undermine satisfaction. Bear in mind that the proportion thinking patients *should* have a say has been rising and it is easy to see the danger for the NHS. The improvements in satisfaction that we have seen in Figures 2.2 to 2.4 could be undone if the public become disillusioned about promised improvements in say. With apparently rising expectations about choice, the NHS needs to ensure not only that its policy on choice is being effectively implemented but that patients and the public come to see that choice is a reality.

Table 2.7 Satisfaction with NHS overall by perceived say, England only

	Say over hospital	Say over appointment	Say over treatment
% satisfied with NHS overall			
Has say	66	63	65
Should have say but *does not*	46	45	44
% satisfied with outpatient services			
Has say	71	72	71
Should have say but *does not*	57	55	55
% satisfied with inpatient services			
Has say	60	58	60
Should have say but *does not*	46	44	44
Base: Has say	*483*	*523*	*550*
Base: Should have say but does not	*1611*	*1255*	*1367*

Has say = great deal/quite a lot of say; does not have say = little say/no say/don't
know/not answered
Base: respondents living in England

Quality and responsiveness

But choice is not the only issue. Quality and responsiveness of care are also important. We asked respondents the following set of questions:

> *Now, suppose you had to go into a local NHS hospital for observation and maybe an operation. From what you know or have heard, please say whether you think ...*
>
> *... the hospital doctors would tell you all you feel you need to know?*
> *... the hospital doctors would take seriously any views you may have on the sorts of treatment available?*
> *... the operation would take place on the day it was booked for?*
> *... you would be allowed home only when you were really well enough to leave?*
> *... the nurses would take seriously any complaints you may have?*
> *.. .the hospital doctors would take seriously any complaints you may have?*
> *.. .there would be a particular nurse responsible for dealing with any problems you may have?*
>
> *[Definitely/Probably would, Probably/Definitely would not]*

The picture is largely a positive one (Table 2.8). Confidence is very high and rising in the two areas that relate directly to patient say over treatment – that hospital doctors would tell you what you need to know (76 per cent say they would) and take your views on treatment seriously (68 per cent). Confidence that complaints will be taken seriously is also high (above 70 per cent) but no longer rising. Even in the areas where confidence is weaker – that the operation would take place on the day it was booked for, that you would only be allowed home when well enough and that there would be a particular nurse for dealing with any problems – a majority actually think that this would happen.

Table 2.8 Perceived quality and responsiveness of hospital inpatient care, 1991–2007

	1991	1993	1995	1998	2001	2003	2005	2007
Hospital doctors would tell you all you need to know	%	%	%	%	%	%	%	%
Would	68	69	69	72	71	74	74	76
Would not	29	29	29	26	28	24	24	23
Hospital doctors would take views on treatment seriously	%	%	%	%	%	%	%	%
Would	57	58	59	64	61	67	66	68
Would not	36	36	37	33	35	30	31	29
Nurses would take complaints seriously	%	%	%	%	%	%	%	%
Would	78	80	84	77	77	77	73	71
Would not	17	16	14	20	21	21	25	26
Hospital doctors would take complaints seriously	%	%	%	%	%	%	%	%
Would	75	76	77	73	74	76	73	73
Would not	19	19	21	24	24	22	24	24
Operation would take place on the day it was booked for	%	%	%	%	%	%	%	%
Would	58	54	58	50	45	47	53	56
Would not	35	39	38	46	53	49	44	41
You would have a particular nurse responsible for dealing with any problems	%	%	%	%	%	%	%	%
Would	n/a	48	54	52	53	54	51	51
Would not	n/a	39	37	40	40	38	41	41
You would only be allowed home when well enough	%	%	%	%	%	%	%	%
Would	64	59	53	53	50	56	59	58
Would not	32	38	45	45	48	42	38	40
Base	*2918*	*2945*	*3633*	*3146*	*2188*	*2293*	*3193*	*3078*

n/a = not asked

This confidence is not a new thing: we have been asking most of these questions since 1991 and confidence in the quality and responsiveness of the NHS has always been pretty strong. Nevertheless, if anything, it is improving rather than weakening.

This confidence in the NHS is undoubtedly a factor in the improving satisfaction levels. Table 2.9 shows that in every single case, confidence in the responsiveness and quality of the service is related to satisfaction, both with the NHS overall and with inpatient and outpatient services.

Table 2.9 Satisfaction by perceived quality and responsiveness of hospital inpatient care

% satisfied with ...	... NHS Overall	... in-patients	... out-patients	Base
Hospital doctors would tell you all you need to know				
Would	57	55	64	2337
Would not	30	32	44	687
Hospital doctors would take views on treatment seriously				
Would	59	56	66	2082
Would not	32	34	46	891
Nurses would take complaints seriously				
Would	58	57	65	2211
Would not	31	30	47	764
Hospital doctors would take complaints seriously				
Would	58	56	65	2274
Would not	29	28	44	710
Operation would take place on the day it was booked for				
Would	60	58	67	1735
Would not	38	38	50	1228
You would have a particular nurse responsible for dealing with any problems				
Would	58	58	67	1573
Would not	41	40	51	1255
You would only be allowed home when well enough				
Would	60	59	69	1779
Would not	37	36	48	1229

For instance, whereas 55 per cent of those who think doctors would tell you all you need to know are satisfied with inpatient services, the equivalent figure for those who say doctors would not is 32 per cent. Moreover, much of the effect of this remains even when taking into account all the other factors considered in this chapter (see Table A.2 in the appendix to this chapter).

Conclusions

The proportion reporting they are either quite or very satisfied with the NHS overall has increased over the last six years and now stands at its highest – at 51 per cent – since 1984. It is hard to resist the conclusion that massively increased NHS spending over the last seven years, enabling the NHS to increase its staffing considerably and, through concerted effort, reduce waiting times to their lowest since the inception of the NHS, must have played a significant part in boosting satisfaction with the NHS overall by nine percentage points since the turn of the century (and by 17 points since 1997). Moreover, the question on taxation and spending suggests that the financial boost to the NHS has hit the mood just about right.

Nevertheless, the headline satisfaction results are not wholly mirrored throughout individual NHS services or all sections of the population; inpatient and dentistry satisfaction trends and satisfaction among those identifying with the Conservative Party buck the trend somewhat.

Moreover, with NHS funding increases now falling back to less than half the real increases per annum over the last seven years, coupled with waiting times now so short that further reductions look less likely (or indeed desirable), it is hard to see future increases in satisfaction driven by these factors.

As NHS experience shows, as one problem or public concern is dealt with another takes its place at the top of the list. Satisfaction amongst those with recent contact with outpatient services has grown over recent years – but the reverse is true for inpatients. The ability to choose a hospital (increasingly desired by the public), book appointments and shorter waiting times are likely to have driven the satisfaction trends in outpatient services. And looking ahead, if more people come to realise or appreciate that they do have choice (just one in five do so at the moment) and one that is effective and informed, satisfaction may well increase further. Conversely, a failure on the part of the NHS to convincingly demonstrate that choice is real may well have an adverse impact on satisfaction.

Inpatient waiting times have also reduced massively, while choice of hospital is related to choice of inpatient care as much as to choice of outpatients. So why such a fall in satisfaction amongst recent users of inpatient care? No doubt headlines over the last few years about health care associated infection rates have contributed to the fall in satisfaction amongst those without recent experience of inpatients. But for those with recent contact, other factors must have played a part. We have shown that the view that the quality of nursing care and medical treatment in hospital are in need of improvement is significantly associated with a tendency to be less satisfied with the NHS overall as well as with inpatient services. Perhaps it is this aspect of NHS care – quality, not, as the NHS has of necessity focused on for the last seven years, quantity – which in future is likely to be the route not only to a better health service, but to a public more satisfied with the care it receives.

Notes

1. Bases for Table 2.1 are as follows:

83	84	86	87	89	90	91	93	94	95	96
1761	1675	3100	2847	3029	2797	2918	2945	3469	3633	3620

97	98	99	00	01	02	03	04	05	06	07
1355	3146	3143	3426	2188	2287	2293	3199	3193	2143	3078

2. In fact, over the whole period since 1983, there is a clear association between higher satisfaction and with lower levels of support for higher taxes and spending. The correlation coefficient, r, between the proportion saying they are very or quite satisfied with the NHS overall and those supporting increased taxes and higher spending over the period 1983–2007 is -0.74.
3. We consider the link between attitudes to the NHS and party politics in more detail later in the chapter.
4. It is worth noting that the actual incidence of infections such as MRSA and *C. difficile* is really very low (0.116 and 1.18 per 1000 bed days respectively in England; total bed days, 36.6 million) Health Protection Agency (2008a, 2008b). The vast majority of NHS patients will not acquire an infectious disease while in hospital.
5. Before this statement there were three additional questions asking about visiting a patient and having medical/dental care as a private patient.
6. Having had experience of an NHS service also has an effect on overall satisfaction with the NHS but the picture is more muted. This is presumably because contact with one branch of the NHS does not necessarily improve views of other branches of the NHS. So, for example, respondents with recent personal experience of GP services are 13 percentage points more satisfied with the NHS as a whole than those with no recent personal contact with GPs; respondents with recent personal experience of outpatient services are seven percentage points more satisfied; and respondents with recent personal experience of inpatient services are five percentage points more satisfied. Oddly, respondents with experience of A&E are actually eight percentage points *less* satisfied with the NHS as a whole than those with no recent personal A&E experience, a finding that holds even when other factors are taken into account (see Table A.2 in the appendix to this chapter).

7. Bases for Table 2.2 are as follows:

Recent contact with specific services	GP	Out-patient	In-patient	Dentist	A&E
Personal contact	2080	1098	462	1062	456
Close family member/friend only	390	743	683	359	582
No contact	116	721	1364	1141	1524

8. The wording of the recent contact question has changed over time. In 2003 and 1999, not all of the follow-up questions were included, there was no reference to "friend" in either question stem or answer options, and the third answer option was simply "Yes, both". In 1996, 1993, 1990 and 1987 the reference period was two years rather than 12 months, with the question stem as follows "In the last two years, have you or a close family member …". Answer options were "Yes" or "No".

9. Bases for Table 2.3 are as follows:

% satisfied with …	1987	1990	1993	1996	1999	2003	2007
… outpatients							
Contact	848	1590	1673	2129	1501	1133	1841
No contact	409	789	777	899	854	629	721
… inpatients							
Contact	600	1110	1136	1425	863	662	1145
No contact	651	1254	1283	1586	1454	1078	1364

10. Bases for Table 2.4 are as follows:

	1983	1986	1989	1993	1996	2000	2003	2007
Age								
18–34	525	1003	933	862	1035	891	579	709
35–54	623	1121	1098	1040	1261	1236	842	1113
55–64	261	452	398	350	451	501	338	500
65+	346	521	590	679	858	791	533	753

11. Bases for Table 2.5 are as follows:

	1983	1986	1989	1993	1996	2000	2003	2007
Party ID								
Conservative	676	1054	1198	964	1012	937	568	786
Labour	584	1080	1017	1101	1528	1394	867	1083
Liberal Democrat	258	542	335	368	391	341	245	280

12. These questions were part of the Public Services module – see the Curtice and Heath chapter in this report (Chapter 3). Note there was an additional difference in wording: the second "choice" question asked respondents to answer for "your area", while the original "say" question did not specify any geographical reference.

References

Appleby, J. and Alvarez-Rosete, A. (2003), 'The NHS: keeping up with public expectations?' in Park, A., Curtice, J., Thomson, K., Jarvis, L. and Bromley, C. (eds.), *British Social Attitudes: the 20th Report – Continuity and change over two decades,* London: Sage

Appleby, J. and Alvarez-Rosete, A. (2005), 'Public responses to NHS reform' in Park, A., Curtice, J., Thomson, K., Bromley, C., Phillips, M. and Johnson, M. (eds.), *British Social Attitudes: the 22nd Report – Two terms of New Labour: the public's reaction,* London: Sage

Burge, P., Devlin, N., Appleby, J., Rohr, C. and Grant, J. (2005), *London Patient Choice Project Evaluation: A model of patients' choices of hospital from stated and revealed preference choice data,* Cambridge/London: RAND (Europe)/King's Fund/City University

Department of Health (2000), *The NHS Plan: A Plan for Investment, A Plan for Reform,* London: Department of Health

Department of Health (2008), *Report of the National Patient Choice Survey, England – September 2007,* Department of Health, available at http://www.dh.gov.uk/en/Publicationsandstatistics/Publications/PublicationsStatistics/DH_082508

Health Protection Agency (2008a), *Financial year annual counts and rates of MRSA bacteraemia,* Health Protection Agency, available at http://www.hpa.org.uk/web/HPAwebFile/HPAweb_C/1216193835014

Health Protection Agency (2008b), *Financial year counts and rates for c. Difficile for patients by age,* Health Protection Agency, available at http://www.hpa.org.uk/web/HPAwebFile/HPAweb_C/12161938348820

Information Centre (2008), *NHS Staff 1997-2007,* Information Centre, available at http://www.ic.nhs.uk/webfiles/publications/nhsstaff2007/NHS%20staff%20master%20table%201997-2007.xls

Mulligan, J.-A. and Appleby, J. (2001), 'The NHS and Labour's battle for public opinion' in Park, A., Curtice, J., Thomson, K., Jarvis, L. and Bromley, C. (eds.), *British Social Attitudes: the 18th Report – Public policy, Social ties,* London: Sage

Stevens, S. (2004), 'Reform strategies for the English NHS', in *Health Affairs,* **23(3)**: 37–44

Taylor-Gooby (2008), 'Choice and Values: individualized rational action and social goals', *Journal of Social Policy,* **37(2)**: 1–19

Wanless, D., Appleby, J., Harrison, A. and Patel, D. (2007), *Our Future Health Secured? A review of NHS funding and performance,* London: King's Fund

Acknowledgements

The *National Centre for Social Research* is grateful to the Department of Health for their financial support which enabled us to ask the questions reported in this chapter, although the views expressed are those of the authors alone.

Appendix

The multivariate analysis technique used is logistic regression, about which more details can be found in Appendix I of the report. The dependent variable for Table A.1 is satisfaction with the NHS overall (very/quite satisfied) and for Table A.2 satisfaction with the NHS overall, satisfaction with outpatient services and satisfaction with inpatient services. The tables present all the independent variables included in each regression model, giving the exponent of the coefficient statistic (the odds ratio), together with an indication of significance. A value of greater than one indicates that the group are more likely than the reference group (in brackets after the heading) to be satisfied. A value of less than one indicates that the group are less likely than the reference group to be satisfied.

Note that in some instances, a variable which *at an overall level* is not significant can have a significant individual category, and *vice versa*.

Table A.1 Satisfaction with NHS overall (very/quite satisfied): socio-demographic, tax and spend, and satisfaction with individual NHS services

Variable (reference category)	Categories	Exp (B)
Age (65+)	18–34	1.143
	35–54	0.976
	55–64	0.941
Sex (Female)	Male	1.020
Highest educational qual. (None)	Higher education	0.715
	A level	0.987
	O level/CSE	0.766
H'hold income quartiles (Highest £44k+)	Lowest quartile (<£12k)	0.637
	2nd lowest (£12k–<£26k)	0.782
	2nd highest (£26k–<£44k)	0.461**
Social class (Semi-routine & routine)	Managerial & professional	0.924
	Intermediate occupations	0.810
	Employers in small organisations	1.345
	Lower supervisory & technical	0.789
Party (None)	Conservative	0.801
	Labour	1.237
	Liberal Democrat	1.068
	Other	0.733
Taxation and spending (Increase taxes and spend more)	Reduce taxes and spend less	1.287
	Keep taxes and spending at same level	1.025
GP satisfaction (Dissatisfied)	Satisfied	2.910**
	Neither	1.134
Dentist satisfaction (Dissatisfied)	Satisfied	1.367
	Neither	1.424
Inpatient satisfaction (Dissatisfied)	Satisfied	4.477**
	Neither	2.428**
Outpatient satisfaction (Dissatisfied)	Satisfied	2.835**
	Neither	1.203
A&E satisfaction (Dissatisfied)	Satisfied	2.794**
	Neither	1.705*
Base:		*1153*

* = significant at 95% level; ** = significant at 99% level

Table A.2 Satisfaction with NHS, outpatient services, inpatient services (very/quite satisfied): full model

Variable (reference category)	Categories	NHS as a whole	Outpatient services	Inpatient services
		Exp (B)	Exp (B)	Exp (B)
Age (65+)	18–34	0.809	0.496**	0.412**
	35–54	0.990	0.751	0.478**
	55–64	0.921	0.689	0.524**
Sex (Female)	Male	1.090	0.745*	0.863
Highest educational qual. (None)	Higher education	0.879	0.818	0.959
	A level	1.043	0.684	0.957
	O Level/CSE	0.917	0.908	1.033
H'hold income quartiles (Highest £44k+)	Lowest quartile (<£12k)	0.917	0.890	1.781*
	2nd lowest (£12k– <£26k)	0.852	1.245	1.553*
	2nd highest (£26k– <£44k)	0.820	1.173	1.863**
Social class (Semi-routine & routine)	Managerial & professional	0.935	0.816	0.945
	Intermediate occupations	0.885	1.011	0.927
	Employers in small organisations	0.893	1.093	0.846
	Lower supervisory & technical	0.982	0.879	0.944
Party (None)	Conservative	0.972	1.097	1.157
	Labour	1.353	1.210	1.220
	Liberal Democrat	0.898	0.975	0.946
	Other	0.651	0.882	1.253
Recent contact with outpatients (No contact)	Respondent contact	1.210	2.560**	1.113
Recent contact with inpatients (No contact)	Respondent contact	1.278	1.216	2.891**
Recent NHS visit (No contact)	Respondent contact	0.947	1.087	1.096
Recent contact with A&E (No contact)	Respondent contact	0.564**	0.732	0.863
Staffing levels of nurses (Satisfactory/very good)	In need of a lot/some improvement	1.245	1.230	0.745

Table continued on next page

Variable (reference category)	Categories	NHS as a whole	Outpatient services	Inpatient services
		Exp (B)	Exp (B)	Exp (B)
Staffing levels of doctors (Satisfactory/very good)	In need of a lot/some improvement	0.623*	0.699	1.335
Quality of treatment in hospitals (Satisfactory/very good)	In need of a lot/some improvement	0.690*	0.669*	0.667*
Quality of nursing care in hospitals (Satisfactory/very good)	In need of a lot/some improvement	0.525**	0.777	0.563**
Hospital doctors tell you what you need to know (Would not)	Would	1.606**	1.326	1.499*
Hospital doctors take views on treatment seriously (Would not)	Would	1.371	1.045	1.187
Operation would take place on booked day (Would not)	Would	1.407*	1.032	1.459*
Would only go home when well enough (Would not)	Would	1.154	1.662**	1.180
Nurses would take complaint seriously (Would not)	Would	1.056	1.106	1.670**
Hospital doctors take complaint seriously (would not)	Would	1.303	1.127	1.460
Particular nurse for your problems (Would not)	Would	1.164	1.173	1.086
Say over hospital (None)	Great deal/quite a lot	2.695**	1.416	1.079
	Little	1.666**	1.118	1.244
Say over time of appointment (None)	Great deal/quite a lot	0.882	0.983	0.960
	Little	1.121	0.998	1.099
Say over treatment (None)	Great deal/quite a lot	1.298	1.681*	1.237
	Little	0.857	1.022	0.984

Base: 1457

* = significant at 95% level; ** = significant at 99% level

3 Do people want choice and diversity of provision in public services?

John Curtice and Oliver Heath[*]

'Reform' of the public services has been one of the key priorities of the current UK Labour government, and especially so since its second election victory in 2001 (Perri 6, 2003). In part, its approach to achieving improvement has been a centralised one; the government has set specific targets that particular public services are expected to achieve, rewarded those who were successful at meeting them and penalised those who failed. But increasingly the government has switched towards a very different approach. It has tried to empower citizens by enabling them to exercise 'choice' in their use of public services (Prime Minister's Strategy Unit, 2006; Cabinet Office, 2008). As a result, instead of meeting targets imposed by central government, public services are encouraged to meet the personal needs and preferences of individual users.

Two main arguments are commonly put forward in support of this latter approach (Dowding and John, forthcoming). The first emphasises the *intrinsic* benefits of choice. Service users derive psychological benefit from the sense of control and autonomy that comes from being able to say what kind of service they would like and how they would like to receive it. Indeed to a public that, as consumer in the marketplace, has become used to being able to exercise choice between a wide range of products and providers, it is no longer acceptable to be denied choice in accessing public services. In short, if they are to satisfy the public they are meant to serve, public services have to meet the increased expectations of a consumerist society.

The second main argument highlights the alleged *extrinsic* benefits of choice. If services are required to respond to the preferences of users, they will become more efficient and effective at meeting their needs. As a result, more people should be satisfied with the service they receive, while the costs of delivering public services are contained. Some proponents of choice argue, too, that promoting choice produces more equitable outcomes. Middle-class, well-

---

[*] John Curtice is Research Consultant at the *Scottish Centre for Social Research*, part of the *National Centre for Social Research*, and Professor of Politics at Strathclyde University. Oliver Heath is Lecturer in Politics, Royal Holloway, University of London and formerly Research Fellow in Politics, Strathclyde University.

educated people, they argue, have always been able to find ways of acquiring the service they want; if everyone has the explicit right to exercise choice then that advantage will be removed.[1]

The debate about choice is, however, not just about what users can do within the existing public services; it is also about who the providers are. Choice could simply mean being able to exercise a preference about how to access a service or what service is received (House of Commons, 2005). For example, a prospective patient might be able to choose when they attend hospital, or a pupil able to choose the subjects in which they specialise at school. Such choice could be provided without either the patient or the pupil being able to choose which hospital or school they attend. However, for most proponents of choice, including the UK Labour government, users should be able not only to choose how they access a service or the details of the service they receive, but also to specify who provides them with a service. Moreover, users' choice should not necessarily be confined to public sector providers, but should extend to private providers too. Thus, for example, since April 2008, NHS patients in England who are in need of elective surgery have been able to choose to attend a private hospital so long as that hospital is able to meet NHS standards and costs (Department of Health, 2004). Some have argued that this principle should be extended to schools too (Hockley and Nieto, 2004; Reform, 2005).

If users can choose who provides them with a service and providers (whether state or non-state) have to compete with each other for customers, then the delivery of public services in effect operates in a quasi-market environment. True, in contrast to a real market, users do not pay for the service they receive; instead the government does. But if providers are paid only for the patients they treat or the students they educate, their ability to remain in business depends on their success in attracting customers in much the same way as any company operating in the private market place has to do. It is this quasi-market mechanism, it is argued, that ensures providers have every incentive to meet users' preferences while keeping costs down, thereby delivering the extrinsic benefits of choice (Bartlett and Le Grand, 1993; Le Grand, 2003, 2007).

It thus perhaps should not come as a surprise that diversity of provision is often presented as a corollary of choice. In a report on choice in public services the Audit Commission argued that, "diversity of supply is a necessary condition of choice" (2004: 3). One of the key academic advocates of reform, Julian Le Grand, has stated that "it is necessary to have both user choice and provider competition" (2007: 44). In an important speech on public service reform in 2001, the then Prime Minister, Tony Blair, stated that one of the principles of the government's reform programme was, "the promotion of alternative providers and choice". Meanwhile, his eventual successor, Gordon Brown, argued in a speech to the King's Fund in 2008 that what he dubbed 'stage two' of the government's reform of the NHS, "was to widen diversity of supply to create new incentives for … more choice for patients".

The government is not alone in adopting this outlook. In claiming at the 2007 Conservative Party Conference that his party would "make the changes necessary to give parents reasonable choice", the party's education spokesperson, Michael Gove, went on to state that:

> we will ... remove the administrative obstacles which currently prevent charities, churches, voluntary groups and others from providing the new schools parents want and children need.

Not to be outdone, in his first major speech as Liberal Democrat leader in January 2008, Nick Clegg called for innovation in public services, claiming, "Freedom. Innovation. Diversity. Yes, choice too. These are liberal words. Let us take them back." So far as political elites are concerned it seems there is agreement that choice and diversity of provision are but two sides of the same coin.

The arguments in favour of introducing choice and diversity in public services are, however, far from uncontested (Perri 6, 2003; House of Commons, 2005; Audit Commission, 2006; Dowding and John, forthcoming). The psychological benefits of choice may be outweighed by the costs of exercising it, especially if users are faced with a myriad of possible choices (Schwarz, 2004) or have little information with which to assess the advantages and disadvantages of each option. Moreover, if users are poorly informed about different options they seem unlikely to choose one that will maximise their satisfaction. Meanwhile, far from making services more efficient, choice may be costly to implement and require services to be used at less than full capacity. At the same time, for critics of choice at least, its promotion simply seems designed to ensure that well-resourced and well-educated members of the public are better able to access better services, thereby increasing inequality (Farrington-Douglas and Allen, 2005).

Moreover, while these doubts may not currently be shared by any of the major political parties at Westminster, they are reflected in the policy positions adopted by the devolved administrations responsible for many public services outside England. The Welsh Assembly government, for example, has developed what it calls a 'citizen-centred' approach to the delivery of public services (Welsh Assembly Government, 2004; Beecham, 2006). This explicitly downplays the importance of competition between diverse providers and of choice in the delivery of public services, emphasising instead the importance of people being able to 'voice' their views about how public services should be delivered. In similar vein the Labour/Liberal Democrat administration that was in power in Scotland before 2007 struck a cautious note about choice between providers, and argued that 'voice' provided an alternative means of providing services that were more personal to the needs and wishes of the user (Scottish Executive, 2006: 10–11). Meanwhile the new SNP Scottish government elected in 2007 is even more clearly opposed to the use of quasi-market mechanisms that encourage competition between different public service providers. For example, in a speech in June 2007 the Health Secretary, Nicola Sturgeon, declared that "we reject the very idea that markets in health care are the route to improvement" (see also Scottish Government, 2007).

So despite the arguments put forward by the advocates of choice and quasi-markets it seems we cannot presume that there is widespread support for their use in the delivery of public services. Certainly politicians in Scotland and Wales have not felt impelled to adopt such reforms. Meanwhile, following an extensive investigation into 'Choice, Voice and Public Services' the Public Administration Select Committee of the House of Commons came to the equivocal conclusion that "while choice is regarded by the public as an important feature of good public services, it is not necessarily their highest priority" (House of Commons, 2005: 41). Moreover, we should certainly not presume that those who support choice necessarily favour the delivery of public services by non-state organisations such as private businesses or charities. Choice might be regarded as one thing, competitive quasi-markets quite another. People might, for example, consider it immoral for private organisations to make a profit out of treating people who are ill. They might believe that public sector professionals are ethically committed to putting the interests of users first (Le Grand, 2003; John and Johnson, 2008), whereas they fear private organisations will put profit before service. So while people might want to be able to choose when they go to hospital or even, perhaps, which NHS hospital they attend, they might draw the line at being able to choose a non-NHS hospital. Certainly the Public Administration Select Committee (House of Commons, 2005: 41) came to the view that:

> some of the most frequent users of public services appear to place greater emphasis on practical choices which have a direct and immediate impact on their quality of life than on the choice of service provider.

In view of these doubts this chapter undertakes an extensive examination of public attitudes towards choice and diversity in the provision of public services. In so doing we perform three tasks. First, we examine how important having choice appears to be to the public and whether they support measures that might make it possible for people to make effective and informed choices. Second, we consider public attitudes towards diversity of provision in the delivery of public services. Finally, we consider whether those who support choice necessarily also support diversity of provision and competition between providers, and thus, by implication, how far the public support the operation of quasi-markets in the delivery of public services.

In so doing we focus on three public services in particular: health, education and social care. We have two main reasons for doing so. First, we want to be able to consider the two most important and expensive public services: health and education, which have been the focus of much of the debate about public service reform. Second, we want to ensure we can take account of the possibility that people have different attitudes towards different services. Traditionally both health and education have been delivered with little or no use of the private sector (although general practitioners are self-employed and effectively run small businesses) and both are still (largely) free at the point of delivery. In contrast, much social care has always been provided privately, including by family members, and, outside Scotland at least, the level of funding provided by government depends on a person's means. Perhaps these different policy traditions are associated with different public attitudes, and thus that choice and diversity of provision are more acceptable for some services than others.

The demand for choice

We turn, then, to our first task, which is to assess how much support there is for choice in general in public services. The most straightforward way of doing this is to ask people "how much choice" they think users of public services should have.[2] Table 3.1 shows the answers we obtained to this question in response to a range of possible kinds of choice that people might be enabled to make.

Table 3.1 Attitudes towards exercising choice

How much choice should users of public services have about …		None	A little	Quite a lot	A great deal
… which state secondary school their children attend	%	2	16	50	31
… who provides them with personal care	%	3	16	51	29
… which hospital to go to if they need treatment	%	4	21	49	26
… what kinds of treatment they receive	%	3	22	52	21
… what their children learn at state secondary school	%	6	28	44	20

Base: 2022

Asked about in this way, choice seems to be popular. A substantial majority believe that users should be able to exercise "a great deal" or "quite a lot" of choice about which institution they attend. Around 80 per cent express this view in respect of who provides an older person in need of personal care, and which state secondary school a pupil attends, while three-quarters say the same about the hospital at which someone receives treatment. Indeed, contrary to what one might anticipate given the conclusion of the Public Administration Select Committee, the opportunity to choose a provider is rather more popular than the chance to choose the kind of service someone receives. A little under three-quarters say that NHS patients should have a great deal or quite a lot of choice about the kind of treatment they receive, while rather less than two-thirds say the same about the ability of parents of secondary school children to choose what their offspring learn at school. Even so, on these items, too, choice seems far more popular than not.[3]

Still, there is perhaps a hint here of the need for a little caution. Most people – in most cases around half – say that there should be "quite a lot" rather than "a great deal" of choice. This could be an indication that while choice is widely regarded as desirable it is not necessarily considered a high priority. This is certainly the impression that is gained when people are asked to consider how important choice is as opposed to a variety of other objectives that might be pursued by a public service.

For example, we asked our respondents to state which of a set of four possible priorities for the NHS was "most important for the NHS to achieve". No less than 78 per cent chose "make sure people who are ill get treatment quickly". In contrast, just six per cent say "make sure people have a lot of choice about their treatment and care", slightly less than the seven per cent who opt for "make sure that people on low incomes are as healthy as people on high incomes", though rather more than the two per cent who choose "get the number of people aged under 50 with heart disease down as low as possible". It would seem that the UK Labour government's attempts to reduce waiting times are valued more highly than its emphasis on the introduction of choice.

Much the same picture is obtained if we ask people what priority schools should pursue. No less than 70 per cent feel it is most important for them to "make sure all children, however able they are, do the best they can", while 12 per cent believe their primary obligation is to "make sure that children from poor backgrounds do as well as those from better off backgrounds" and eight per cent to "get the number of children who leave school with no qualifications down as low as possible". Only three per cent feel that what is most important is to "make sure parents have a lot of choice about the kind of school their child goes to". Evidently, while most people regard choice as desirable, few consider it a priority, at least for its own sake.

Facilitating choice

Most advocates of choice accept that the realisation of its benefits depends on the circumstances in which it is introduced. It is widely recognised, for example, that if people are to make an informed choice about what kind of medical treatment they should receive, they will need to be furnished with information about the possible benefits and risks associated with the possible alternatives. Similarly, parents need to be furnished with information about the performance of the possible schools that their child might attend. (House of Commons, 2005; Audit Commission, 2006, 2008; Le Grand, 2007; Cabinet Office, 2008). Thus, one of the initiatives commonly associated with the introduction of choice is the provision of information about the effectiveness of different institutions – and even individual public service professionals – as exemplified by the wide range of comparative information made available on the English NHS Choices website.[4]

We introduced this topic to our respondents as follows:

> *Some say certain kinds of information should be made available to people, to help them make informed choices about public services such as schools and hospitals. Others think this information is irrelevant or cannot be trusted.*

and then asked these two questions:

> *First of all, thinking about parents who are deciding which secondary school to send their children to, how useful do you think it would be for them to be given league tables that compare the exam results of different secondary schools in their area?*
>
> *And how useful do you think it would be for someone choosing which surgeon to see to be given league tables that show the number of patients who have died under the care of different surgeons?*

For the most part, providing such information appears to meet with public approval. As Table 3.2 shows, no less than 80 per cent say that league tables that compare the results of different secondary schools are "very" or "quite useful" to parents. On the other hand, attitudes towards the usefulness to prospective patients of the death rates of different surgeons are more equivocal; only just over half (53 per cent) think such information is "very" or "quite useful". Perhaps a surgeon's death rate is less likely to be regarded as a valid indicator of effectiveness than is the exam performance of a school. But perhaps the more circumspect attitude towards death rates also arises because the psychological costs involved in being asked to choose a surgeon are too burdensome for some people to bear.

Table 3.2 Support for league tables

Attitude towards users being given league tables of …		Very useful	Quite useful	Not very useful	Not at all useful
… the exam results of different secondary schools	%	33	47	14	4
… the death rates of different surgeons	%	25	28	29	17

Base: 2022

Still, providing league tables is not particularly expensive, and the potential benefit is equally available to all. However, it has been argued that if choice is to produce more equitable outcomes, members of disadvantaged groups will have to be given particular support (Department for Education and Skills, 2005; Prime Minister's Strategy Unit, 2006). For example, someone on a low income may feel unable to send their child to a school some distance away from home, even though they think it would be the best school for their child, because they cannot afford the travel costs involved. So perhaps the government should pay the cost? But if it does so, the cost of facilitating choice becomes immediately apparent, while the benefit of government help is available to some but not others. Such a practice seems far from guaranteed to secure public support.

Indeed, it seems to split public opinion down the middle. We presented respondents with this scenario:

> *Say a parent on a low income wanted to send a child of theirs to a school some distance from their home, because they thought that school was better than the local school. But they cannot afford to pay the bus fare every day. What do you think should happen?*

Just 49 per cent say that "the government should pay the [child's] bus fare", while almost exactly the same proportion, 47 per cent, reckon that "the child should go to a local school" instead. Opposition to government help with travel costs was even greater in the case of a hospital some distance away. We asked what should happen when:

> *... someone on a low income, who needed hospital treatment, decided they wanted to go to a hospital more than 100 miles from their home, because they thought they would get better treatment there.*

Just 38 per cent reckon that "the government should pay the train or bus fare", whereas 58 per cent feel "they should go to a local hospital". So it cannot be presumed that the public will necessarily support measures designed to ensure those with fewer resources are as equally capable of exercising their preferences as their fellow citizens.

Who wants choice?

In truth, if choice is to result in more equitable outcomes, there is perhaps an even more important condition that has to be satisfied than ensuring that those with fewer resources have the capacity to exercise choice. This is that those who are less well off should be just as keen as everyone else on exercising choice in the first place. Perhaps choice is only a middle-class obsession (Hattersley, 2003)? To establish whether or not this is the case, Table 3.3 shows how attitudes towards the provision of choice vary by social class, educational level and income group. This enables us to establish whether those in the working class, those with no educational qualifications and those with low incomes are more or less likely to be in favour of choice than those in other class, educational and income groups.

Table 3.3 Attitudes towards choice, by class, education and income

% say users should have a great deal of choice about ...	... which secondary school their children attend	... which hospital they go to	... who provides them with care	Base
Social class				
Managerial & professional	23	21	24	708
Intermediate	31	25	31	251
Small employers	35	34	34	185
Lower supervisory	30	28	31	248
Routine & semi-routine	32	27	31	576
Highest educational qualification				
Degree/other higher	23	16	25	567
A level or lower	32	26	28	753
None	36	35	34	519
Household income				
£50,000 or more	25	16	25	303
£26–49,999	30	23	26	468
£15–25,999	30	30	32	319
Less than £15,000	34	29	33	626

The table uncovers an important result. Those with fewer resources are, if anything, keenest on the provision of choice. Those most sceptical about choice are, in fact, those who might be thought to be most capable of exercising it, that is, those in receipt of some form of higher education, those in managerial and professional occupations and those on the highest incomes. There is certainly no reason to believe that those who are less well off are likely to be disadvantaged by the extension of choice simply because they would be unwilling to exercise it (see also Audit Commission, 2004; Appleby and Alvarez-Rosete, 2005).

Indeed, this is not the only pattern of note that we find. As seen in Table 3.4, women are keener on choice than men. For example, whereas 37 per cent of women believe parents should have a great deal of choice about which second school their child attends, just 24 per cent of men do. Similar, if somewhat smaller, differences are also evident in respect of choice of hospital and the provision of social care. Perhaps this reflects the greater likelihood that women will be involved in nurturing roles that involve interaction with public services.

Table 3.4 Attitudes towards choice, by sex and age group

% say users should have a great deal of choice about ...	... which secondary school their children attend	... which hospital they go to	... who provides them with care	Base
Sex				
Men	24	22	24	874
Women	37	29	34	1148
Age group				
18–29	31	21	25	298
30–44	33	25	30	569
45–59	31	27	30	502
60+	27	29	30	653

On the other hand, one pattern that we might have anticipated, given the claim that people have come to expect choice in public services because they are used to acting as consumers in the private marketplace, is not evident. This is the expectation that younger people, brought up in a time of relative affluence, would be keener on choice than older people, brought up in more austere times when choice in the private market was less abundant. But as Table 3.4 shows, this does not appear to be the case. Those aged under 30 are only slightly more likely than those aged 60 or over to say that parents should have a great deal of choice over which secondary school their children attend, while they are less likely to say that patients should have a great deal of choice about which hospital they attend or that older people should have much choice about who provides them care.

Of course, younger people are particularly likely to have children at school while being far less likely to have been a hospital inpatient or to be in receipt of personal care. In general, we might anticipate that choice matters more to those who use a service. They, after all, have most reason to appreciate its value. Indeed, of this there is some sign. No less than 40 per cent of those who currently have a child in a state school (primary or secondary) think parents should have a great deal of choice of secondary school, compared with 28 per cent of those without a child in a state school. Equally, whereas 33 per cent of those who themselves have been in need of regular personal care during the last 10 years feel that an older person should have a great deal of choice about who provides them with such care, only 25 per cent of those who have not needed such care (nor had someone close to them need such care) take that view.[5]

On the other hand, attitudes towards the provision of choice of hospital seems less clearly linked to recent experience of hospital care. Just 27 per cent of those who have been a hospital inpatient during the last year feel patients should have a great deal of choice over which hospital they attend, little different from the equivalent figure, 26 per cent, amongst those who have not recently been an inpatient.[6] Perhaps those who have recently been in need of treatment are aware of the difficulties involved in making what might be considered life or death decisions.

It has also been argued that choice is of much greater interest to those living in an urban environment than those living in more rural and more remote locations. Those living in a large city may well live within a few miles of more than one hospital or more than one school, and are thus easily able to travel to more than one institution. In contrast those living in a more remote rural location may well have to travel some distance to reach their nearest school or hospital, let alone any other, rendering choice effectively impossible. We see some of the expected difference on choice of schools: 33 per cent of those living in an urban environment say that parents should have a great deal of choice about which secondary school their child attends, compared with 26 per cent of those in more rural locations. But the two groups are almost equally likely to say there should be a great deal of choice in respect of hospitals and social care providers.[7]

Do we want diversity of provision?

Still, for the most part, our evidence so far has been supportive of the arguments put forward by the advocates of choice. There is broad public support for the idea, choice seems to be particularly valued by those who are less well off, and there is considerable support for some of the measures at least that might be taken to make choice informed and equitable. True, choice might not be a high priority for many, but we have produced little evidence so far to suggest that a policy maker who wishes to introduce choice should stay their hand.

This picture is indeed largely in tune with previous findings that have eagerly been seized upon by the advocates of choice (Audit Commission, 2004; Le Grand, 2007). But we should not necessarily assume, as those advocates have been inclined to do, that because people say they are in favour of choice they are necessarily in favour of the diversity of providers and competition that are also regarded as an integral part of a quasi-market. The link between choice and diversity may be clear in the minds of politicians and policy makers, but we should not assume that public opinion is structured in the same way. Certainly, if we are to argue that there is public support for the operation of a quasi-market we need to demonstrate that there is public support not only for choice, but also for diversity of provision.

An initial warning that diversity of provision may not necessarily be appreciated by the public comes from the responses we received to two very general questions about the priorities that should be pursued by secondary schools and by the NHS. In the case of secondary schools we asked respondents which of the following two statements came "closest" to their view:

> They should all provide much the **same kind** of education so that every child gets the same chance in life
> OR
> They should **vary** in what they provide so that parents can **choose** the kind of education that's best for their child

While so far as the NHS is concerned we asked which of the following it was "more important" for it to do:

Meet the wishes of individual patients about how and when they are treated
OR
Ensure that every patient receives the same standard of service regardless of whether they have particular wishes or not

Thus in both cases, respondents were being asked to assess the relative merits of a more varied and potentially more personalised service as opposed to ensuring that every pupil or patient is treated equally. The latter seems to matter more to most people. No less than 72 per cent say that secondary schools should provide much the same kind of education for every child, while 65 per cent believe that it is more important for the NHS to ensure every patient receives the same standard of service. Only 19 per cent and 23 per cent respectively back the alternative view. It is, perhaps, little wonder in the light of these figures that claims that access to good quality public services can be a 'postcode lottery' have such resonance. Certainly, such public attitudes are hardly conducive to the provision of a more diverse range of services that might make choice meaningful.

Still, we should not presume from these responses towards general propositions that particular concrete instances of diverse provision within the state sector are necessarily unpopular. We asked respondents:

Some people say that all schools should offer much the same kind of education. Others say that parents should be able to choose between schools of different kinds. How much do you support or oppose having some schools that ...

... specialise in a particular subject, such as maths or music?

... are linked to a particular religious denomination, such as Roman Catholic?

No less than 58 per cent support the idea of schools that specialise in maths or music. Such 'specialist schools' were initially introduced in England by the previous Conservative government, and then expanded considerably by the current Labour government. On the other hand, a much older form of diverse provision, schools that are "linked to a particular religious denomination, such as Roman Catholic", is far less popular. Only 30 per cent support the existence of such schools, rather less than the 34 per cent who are opposed. Evidently, some forms of diversity are more acceptable than others.

Specialist schools and faith schools linked to a particular religion or denomination are, of course, forms of diversity within the state sector. But many advocates of quasi-markets in the delivery of public services argue that it should also be open to non-state providers to offer such services. Indeed, as we have already noted, patients in England now have the right to choose to be treated at a private rather than an NHS hospital. The government's programme of 'city academy' secondary schools in England involves such schools being established by and securing some funding from non-state organisations. Some users of personal care services receive a 'direct payment' that they can use to employ whom they wish to provide them with personal care.

To establish how much public support there is for such arrangements we first of all reminded our respondents that some people say that a public service "should be run by organisations other than government as they can do a better job", while others say "these organisations cannot be trusted" to run a public service "properly". Then we asked them whether they supported or opposed "private companies or businesses", running state schools, running NHS hospitals or providing government-funded personal care for older people. In each case, we asked also for their view of "charities or other 'not for profit' organisations" doing so.

As Table 3.5 shows, the public are clearly suspicious of private organisations running or providing public services. Even in the case of social care, where private provision has long been common, only 31 per cent are in favour of private companies being involved, while 43 per cent are opposed. Meanwhile, so far as both NHS hospitals and state schools are concerned, over half say they are opposed. True, the public are less hostile to charities being involved in the delivery of public services. So far as schools and hospitals are concerned, roughly a third are in favour and a third opposed, while just over half are supportive of charities providing government-funded personal care for older people. But even so, it is very clear that the public's support for choice is not necessarily accompanied by enthusiasm for a diversity of providers.

Table 3.5 Attitudes towards non-state provision of public services

		Support	Neither	Oppose
Attitude towards charities …				
… providing personal care for older people	%	53	24	21
… running state schools	%	36	29	33
… running NHS hospitals	%	36	26	37
Attitude towards private companies …				
… providing personal care for older people	%	31	24	43
… running NHS hospitals	%	22	20	57
… running state schools	%	19	24	55
Base: 2022				

Meanwhile, there are severe doubts indeed about implementing the full rigours of a competitive market as implied by systems of funding that are designed to ensure that money follows the patient or pupil. Such mechanisms imply that where a school fails to attract sufficient pupils or a hospital sufficient patients to be able to cover its costs it should close – just as a private company is forced to close and make its employees redundant if it proves to be persistently unprofitable. Yet only eight per cent agree with the proposition that "schools that fail to attract enough pupils should be closed and the teachers lose their jobs", while 67 per cent disagree. Equally, only 11 per cent agree that "hospitals that fail to attract enough patients should be closed and the doctors lose their jobs", while 59 per cent disagree.

Even rather less stark suggestions that public services might be delivered through a competitive market seem to engender wariness. Respondents were advised that:

> It has been suggested that the government gives all parents a 'voucher', which they can use to 'buy' their children's education at whatever state school they want to send them to. Schools would only get paid for the number of pupils they teach.

They were then asked whether they supported or opposed this idea. Just 26 per cent say that they support it, whereas 45 per cent indicate they are opposed. Of course, we cannot be sure whether people are unhappy with the idea of vouchers, with schools only being paid for the number of pupils they teach, or both. But their wariness hardly signifies acceptance of the idea that public services should be delivered via quasi-markets.

Who supports diversity of provision?

So it seems that having a diverse range of public service providers and quasi-market competition between different providers is far less popular than the idea of choice. But perhaps it is still the case that those most in favour of having different kinds of providers are the less well off, the group whom the advocates of choice claim are most likely to benefit?

Table 3.6 repeats for attitudes towards having private companies run and provide public services, the same analysis by social class, education and income group that we previously undertook for attitudes to choice in Table 3.3. Here, however, in contrast to Table 3.3, there is no sign that those in a working-class occupation, those with no educational qualifications or those on the lowest household incomes are particularly in favour of allowing private companies to run public services. Indeed, if anything, the opposite is true. Thus, for example, amongst those on household incomes of £50,000 p.a. or more, 30 per cent support private companies running NHS hospitals, almost twice the proportion amongst those with incomes of less than £15,000 p.a.[8] Here the argument that the introduction of choice and competition is particularly attuned to the wishes of the less well-off sections of society seems more dubious.

Table 3.6 Attitudes towards private companies delivering public services, by class, education and income

% support private companies …	… running state schools	… running NHS hospitals	… providing personal care	Base
Social class				
Managerial & professional	21	23	32	708
Intermediate	15	23	33	251
Small employers	25	26	36	185
Lower supervisory	17	19	32	248
Routine & semi-routine	18	21	28	576
Highest educational qualification				
Degree/other higher	20	23	35	567
A level or lower	21	24	35	753
None	18	18	23	519
Household income				
£50,000 or more	26	30	39	303
£26–49,999	22	23	33	468
£15–25,999	17	22	32	319
Less than £15,000	16	17	25	626

Equally, and again in contrast to what was true of attitudes towards choice, women are not particularly keen on private companies delivering public services. If anything, the opposite seems to be true. For example, 25 per cent of men favour private companies running NHS hospitals compared with 19 per cent of women. There is no sign either that those who have recently used a service are more likely to favour private provision.[9]

So, not only is having diversity of provision less popular than choice, but it seems to be supported by different kinds of people. It is beginning to look as though choice and diversity of provision do not necessarily go together in the public mind, and that it is dangerous to assume that expressions of support for one necessarily translate into a demand for the other. But what happens when we look directly at the relationship between the two sets of attitudes?

Do choice and diversity go together?

There certainly seems to be only a limited link between favouring choice and supporting the principle that public services should provide a varied, personalised service. Thus, for example, amongst those who believe that parents should have a great deal of choice about which secondary school their children attend, just 19 per cent say it is more important for secondary schools to vary the kind of education they provide so that parents can choose the best kind of education for their child. The equivalent figure amongst those who say parents should have little or no choice is, at 13 per cent, only a little lower. Even amongst those who think that parents should have a great deal of choice about what their children are taught at secondary school, only 20 per cent prioritise schools varying the education they provide, only somewhat higher than the equivalent figure, 10 per cent, amongst those who favour little or no choice.

In the case of attitudes towards the NHS the link is, admittedly, a little stronger. Amongst those who say that patients should have a great deal of choice about the hospital they attend, 29 per cent say that it is more important that hospitals meet the wishes of individual patients, compared with just 15 per cent of those who say that patients should have little or no choice of hospital. Much the same difference, 28 per cent as opposed to 13 per cent, is found between those who believe that patients should have a great deal of choice about the kind of treatment they receive and those who think they should have little or no choice. Nevertheless, equality of service provision still emerges as the stronger impulse amongst those who apparently favour choice in the NHS.

In any event, the link between choice and attitudes towards diversity proves to be very weak indeed when we look at attitudes towards private companies and charities providing public services. As Table 3.7 shows, those who say that they favour people having a great deal of choice in respect of schools or hospitals are only a little more likely than those who feel people should have little or no choice to support either private companies or charities running schools and hospitals. For example, just 24 per cent of those who favour parents having a great deal of choice of secondary school support private companies running state schools, only a little higher than the equivalent figure, 18 per cent, amongst those who say that parents should have little or no choice. The equivalent comparisons in the remainder of the table exhibit similarly small differences. It clearly cannot be presumed that because people say they want choice that this means they believe people should be able to choose to receive a public service from a private provider.

Equally, those who say they support choice are no more likely to believe that the competitive logic of the market should prevail when public service organisations fail to attract sufficient 'customers'. For example, just 11 per cent of those who say that parents should have a great deal of choice about which secondary school their children attend also say that schools that fail to attract enough teachers should close; this is almost the same as the equivalent figure, 12 per cent, amongst those who feel parents should only have a little or no choice. Similarly, just nine per cent of those in favour of patients having a great deal of choice of hospital believe that hospitals that fail to attract enough patients should be closed, little more than the equivalent figure of seven per cent amongst those who believe in little or no choice of hospital. Only when it comes to the idea of funding schools via vouchers given to parents do we uncover some link between attitudes towards choice and the use of a market-style mechanism. As many as 33 per cent of those who say parents should have a great deal of choice of secondary school support the idea, compared with 17 per cent of those who think that parents should have little or no choice.

Table 3.7 Attitudes towards non-state providers, by attitudes towards choice

	Attitude towards choice of secondary school		Attitude towards choice of hospital	
	A great deal	A little/none	A great deal	A little/none
Attitude towards private companies running state schools/NHS hospitals	%	%	%	%
Support	24	18	25	19
Neither	23	23	21	17
Oppose	51	58	54	62
Attitude towards charities running state schools/NHS hospitals	%	%	%	%
Support	37	30	39	33
Neither	25	31	22	27
Oppose	36	38	37	38
Base	*622*	*363*	*528*	*508*

The first two columns show attitudes towards private companies/charities running state schools, while the second two columns display the equivalent information for running NHS hospitals

Indeed, there is also some link between attitudes towards choice and the provision of different kinds of schools. Amongst those who support a great deal of choice of secondary school, 62 per cent support having schools that specialise in a particular subject, compared with 48 per cent of those who believe in little or no choice. There is also a slight difference of view between these two groups in their attitude towards faith schools; 35 per cent of those who prefer a great deal of choice support such schools compared with 24 per cent of those who believe in little or no choice. But, of course, specialist and (for the most part) faith schools together with vouchers can be and are provided within the framework of state provision; they do not necessarily imply non-state organisations running public services.

So support for choice and support for diversity of provision do not necessarily go together. In particular, support for choice does not necessarily imply a significantly greater wish to see public services delivered by non-state providers or a belief in the power and discipline of the competitive quasi-market. At most, it implies a somewhat greater likelihood of supporting some diversity of provision amongst services run by the state, although even then apparently subject to the constraint that doing so does not undermine equality of service. Perhaps in saying they support choice, some people may simply be indicating they feel they should have the ability to avoid a poor service where it exists – or even to secure the best possible service for themselves – but that their interest in choice does not extend beyond this instrumental consideration. Such expressions of support certainly do not necessarily imply a belief in the merits of competitive market-style provision.

The politics of choice and diversity

We can, in fact, cast some light on why those who favour choice do not necessarily back non-state provision of public services, by looking at the relationship between, on the one hand, people's attitudes towards choice and diversity and, on the other, their broader political preferences. We might anticipate that, for the most part, support for the idea of non-state organisations providing public services would be greater amongst those who are broadly on the right of the political spectrum together with Conservative voters. These, after all, are groups that are inclined to prefer a smaller state and to believe in the merits of market mechanisms. But what is less clear is who might be more inclined to favour choice in the provision of public services. On the one hand, such an attitude might be regarded as the preserve of those on the right, in so far as it implies a wish that users of public services should be able to act like consumers in the marketplace. But on the other hand, perhaps choice matters more to those who believe in the value and importance of public services, and have less wish and opportunity to opt for private alternatives, a sentiment that we would associate more with those on the left of the political spectrum.

In Table 3.8 we show how attitudes towards choice and private companies running services vary according to where people stand on the left–right spectrum and the political party that they support. (Position on the left–right spectrum is measured using the left–right attitude scale, about which further details are given in Appendix I of the report.) As we anticipated, those on the right of the political spectrum together with Conservative identifiers are somewhat more inclined to support private companies running or providing public services. But it is, in fact, those on the left who are somewhat more inclined to back choice, while there is no consistent relationship with party identification at all.

In short, it seems that far from being two sides of the same coin, choice and diversity of provision are two different coins that appeal to rather different political constituencies amongst the wider public. Diversity is rather more of a right-wing impulse, while choice in public services matters more to those on the left. It is, then, little wonder that we find so little coherent support for using competitive quasi-market mechanisms for delivering public services.

Table 3.8 Attitudes towards choice and private provision, by political attitudes

	% say users should have great deal of choice about …			% support private companies running/providing …			
	… which secondary school	… which hospital	… who provides care	… state schools	… NHS hospitals	… pers- onal care	*Base*
Left–right scale							
Left	33	27	33	17	19	26	*725*
Centre	30	26	28	20	21	33	*768*
Right	22	22	26	25	29	37	*214*
Party ID							
Conser- vative	30	26	30	26	30	35	*519*
Labour	34	27	31	17	17	29	*703*
Liberal	25	25	33	13	19	32	*186*
None	37	30	32	22	21	33	*329*

Right: those with an average score of between 1 and 2.5 on the left–right scale (see Appendix I of the report); centre: score of between 2.5 and 3.5; left: score of 3.5 or more

Devolution differences

So far we have confined our attention to looking at public opinion across Great Britain as a whole, an entity in which England predominates and of which Northern Ireland does not form part. But as we noted at the beginning of this chapter, while an emphasis on choice and diversity of provision has been a key characteristic of recent UK government policy towards the 'reform' of public services in England, this approach has largely been rejected by the devolved administrations in Scotland and Wales. Equally, although Northern Ireland was administered by UK government ministers before the restoration of devolved rule in May 2007, the debate about choice and diversity has received relatively little attention there (Greer, 2004; Knox and Carmichael, 2005, 2006; Northern Ireland Office, 2006). This inevitably leads one to wonder whether these differences of policy are a reflection of differences in public attitudes.

The data we have used so far have come from the 2007 *British Social Attitudes* survey. However, in recognition of the different situation outside England, the same questions were also asked as part of the 2007 *Scottish Social Attitudes* survey, the same year's Northern Ireland Life and Times survey and a specially commissioned survey in Wales. This means that we have sufficient sample sizes to examine whether the conclusions we reach for Britain as a whole – and thus primarily England – are also valid for the smaller territories of the UK.

If the differences of policy between the UK government and the devolved administrations are a reflection of differences in public attitudes, we might perhaps anticipate three differences in particular. First, we would expect that choice matters less for those living outside England. Presumably, too, they should also be even less interested in diversity of provision than are people in England. And, perhaps, in opposing both choice and diversity the attitudes of people in Scotland, Wales and Northern Ireland should actually be more consistent with each other than they are in England.

Table 3.9 examines the first of these expectations by showing the proportion of people in each of the four parts of the UK who feel that it should be possible to have a great deal of choice about who provides a service. The pattern it reveals is the very opposite of what we have anticipated. Fewer people in England than in any other part of the UK say that there should be a great deal of choice about which hospital a patient attends or who provides someone with personal care. Meanwhile, so far as attitudes towards choice of secondary school are concerned, the proportion favouring a great deal of choice in England is little different from that in the rest of the UK.

Table 3.9 Comparison of attitudes across the UK towards choice

% say users should have great deal of choice of ...	... secondary school	... hospital	... who provides care	Base
England	32	26	30	1735
Scotland	27	33	36	1508
Wales	36	41	43	884
N. Ireland	29	36	39	1179

Sources: Scotland: *Scottish Social Attitudes* survey, 2007; Wales: Wales Life and Times survey, 2007; N. Ireland: Northern Ireland Life and Times survey, 2007

On the other hand, although less than a third of people in England favour private companies providing public services, support is still for the most part higher than it is elsewhere in the rest of the UK (Table 3.10).[10] Meanwhile, explicit opposition to private companies having a role in running state schools and NHS hospitals is particularly high in both Scotland and Wales. The greater reluctance outside England to use private companies to provide public services does reflect a difference in public attitudes, but that does not imply that the policy is particularly popular in England either.

So diversity of provision is less popular outside England, but choice is at least as popular. Once again it seems the two sets of attitudes do not necessarily go together. It should thus come as little surprise that if we look at the relationship between the two sets of attitudes within each of the four parts of the UK, we tend to uncover a pattern much like that in Table 3.7 above. For example, in

Scotland, there is only a six-point difference in the proportion that support private companies running NHS hospitals between those in favour of a great deal of choice of hospital and those who only back little or no choice. In Wales and Northern Ireland the equivalent differences are just four and five points respectively. It seems that consistent supporters of competitive quasi-markets are thin on the ground throughout the UK.

Table 3.10 Comparison of attitudes across the UK towards private companies providing public services

		Private companies running state schools			Private companies running NHS hospitals			Private companies providing personal care		
		Support	Oppose		Support	Oppose		Support	Oppose	Base
England	%	20	53	%	23	56	%	31	43	1735
Scotland	%	11	66	%	17	65	%	28	51	1508
Wales	%	14	64	%	18	64	%	29	50	884
N. Ireland	%	14	55	%	17	58	%	27	49	1179

Sources: Scotland: *Scottish Social Attitudes* survey, 2007; Wales: Wales Life and Times survey, 2007; N. Ireland: Northern Ireland Life and Times survey, 2007

Conclusions

For advocates of public service reform the ability to make effective choices in accessing public services goes hand in hand with a diversity of alternative providers that compete with each other for business in a quasi-market. As evidence of public support for such a policy they have pointed to previous survey evidence – which our research affirms – that most people say they want choice in accessing and using public services. But the more detailed questions in our survey show that the fact that people say they want choice does not necessarily mean that they want public services to be provided by a variety of competing providers, including providers from the private and charitable sectors. They may simply fail to see the supposed intimate connection between the two ideas. Or what they mean by choice may be more limited – perhaps an ability to exercise some discretion in what state-provided services are accessed and how – than is the case for the advocates of reform. Either way, our research indicates that the public do not necessarily accept the link between choice and competitive quasi-markets populated by private providers. Rather, the two ideas seem to appeal to somewhat different publics. As a result, the UK Labour government's promotion of choice and competition in England – a policy largely ignored or opposed in the rest of the UK – can be expected to remain contentious.

Notes

1. Tony Blair, for example, argued in a speech in 2003 that:

   The over-riding principle is clear. We should give poorer patients … the
   same range of choices the rich have always enjoyed. In a heterogeneous
   society where there is enormous variation in needs and preferences, public
   services must be equipped to respond.

2. 'Users' of public services were defined in the question text according to the public
   service asked about: "NHS patients" (for questions about hospitals and treatments);
   "parents" (in the case of questions about schools); "older people in need of personal
   care funded by the government" (for personal care questions).
3. As discussed in Chapter 2, the 74 per cent of people who favour patients having a
   great deal or quite a lot of choice about the NHS hospital they attend is almost the
   same as the 75 per cent who say that patients should have a great deal or quite a lot
   of "say" in the hospital they attend. Taylor-Gooby (2008) has argued that as 'say'
   could be achieved through affording more opportunities for 'voice' rather than
   'choice', a question that refers to "say" rather than "choice" cannot be regarded as
   an adequate measure of support for 'choice'. It seems that in practice this concern is
   not valid.
4. See www.nhs.uk.
5. We defined personal care as follows in the question text:

   *At some point in their lives people can need regular help looking after
   themselves because of illness, disability or old age. This can include help
   with things like getting washed and dressed, and getting a meal ready. Have
   either you, or someone you are close to, been in need of any regular help like
   this at any time during the last ten years?*

   *[Answer options: Yes, respondent only; Yes, someone else only; Yes,
   respondent and someone else; No]*

6. However, those who have been an outpatient are six percentage points more likely to
   favour a great deal of choice of hospital, though neither recent inpatients nor
   outpatients are more likely to favour a great deal of choice about the treatment they
   receive.
7. Those living in an urban environment are defined as those resident in postcode
   sectors where there are more than 37.3 persons in private households per hectare.
   More rural locations are those postcode sectors where the population density is less
   than 3.96 persons per hectare.
8. The pattern of attitudes towards charities providing public services is also very
   similar to that in Table 3.6. Similarly, there is little evidence that those who are less
   well resourced are particularly in favour of school vouchers or the closure of
   hospitals and schools that fail to attract enough patients or pupils.

9. There is no consistent evidence either that younger people are in favour of non-state provision.

10. The same is true also of attitudes towards charities providing public services.

References

Appleby, J. and Alvarez-Rosete, A. (2005), 'Public responses to NHS reform', in Park, A., Curtice, J., Thomson, K., Bromley, C., Phillips, M. and Johnson, M. (eds.), *British Social Attitudes: the 22nd Report – Two terms of New Labour: the public's reaction*, London: Sage

Audit Commission (2004), *Choice in Public Services*, London: Audit Commission

Audit Commission (2006), *Choice and Competition in Local Public Services*, London: Audit Commission

Audit Commission (2008), *Is the Treatment Working? Progress with the NHS system reform programme*, London: Audit Commission

Bartlett, W. and Le Grand, J. (1993), 'The theory of quasi-markets', in Le Grand, J. and Bartlett, W. (eds.), *Quasi-markets and Social Policy*, Basingstoke: Macmillan

Beecham, J. (chm.) (2006), *Beyond boundaries: Report of the Review of Local Service Delivery*, Cardiff: Welsh Assembly Government

Blair, T. (2001), speech on public service reform, available at http://www.number10.gov.uk/Page1632

Blair, T. (2003), speech at South Camden Community College, quoted in Le Grand, J. 'Equality and Choice in Public Services', *Social Research*, **73**: 695–710

Brown, G. (2008), speech on the National Health Service, available at http://www.number10.gov.uk/Page14171

Cabinet Office (2008), *Excellence and fairness: achieving world class public services*, London: Cabinet Office

Clegg, N. (2008), 'Clegg Calls for Grassroots Innovation in Public Service Provision', speech given at Manifesto Conference, available at http://www.libdems.org.uk/news/clegg-calls-for-radical-grassroots-innovation-in-public-services-9782

Department for Education and Skills (2005), *Higher standards: better schools for all*, White Paper Cm 6677, London: The Stationery Office

Department of Health (2004), *The NHS Improvement Plan: putting people at the heart of public services*, White Paper Cm 6268, London: The Stationery Office

Dowding, K. and John, P. (forthcoming), 'The Value of Choice in Public Policy', *Public Administration*

Farrington-Douglas, J. and Allen, J. (2005), *Equitable Choices for Health*, London: Institute for Public Policy Research

Gove, M. (2007), 'It's time for modern compassionate Conservative education policy', speech given at Conservative Party Conference, available at http://www.conservatives.com/News/Speeches/2007/10/Michael_Gove_Its_time_for_m odern_compassionate_Conservative_education_policy.aspx

Greer, S. (2004), *Territorial politics and health policy: UK health policy in comparative perspective*, Manchester: Manchester University Press

Hattersley, R. (2003), 'Agitators will inherit the earth', *Guardian,* 17 November

Hockley, T. and Nieto, D. (2004), *Hands up for school choice!,* London: Policy Exchange

House of Commons (2005), *Choice, voice and public services: fourth report of the Public Administration Committee, Session 2004–5,* HC 49–I, London: The Stationery Office

John, P. and Johnson, M. (2008), 'Is there a public service ethos?', in Park, A., Curtice, J., Thomson, K., Phillips, M., Johnson, M. and Clery, E. (eds.), *British Social Attitudes: the 24th Report,* London: Sage

Knox, C. and Carmichael, P. (2005), 'Improving public services: public administration reform in Northern Ireland, *Journal of Social Policy,* **35**: 97–120

Knox, C. and Carmichael, P. (2006), 'Bureau shuffling? The review of public administration in Northern Ireland', *Public Administration,* **84**: 941–965

Le Grand, J. (2003), *Motivation, agency and public policy: of knights and knaves, pawns and queens,* Oxford: Oxford University Press

Le Grand, J. (2007), *The other invisible hand: delivering public services through choice and competition,* Princeton: Princeton University Press

Northern Ireland Office (2006), *Better government for Northern Ireland: final decision of the Review of Public Administration,* Belfast: Northern Ireland Office

Perri 6 (2003), 'Giving consumers of British public services more choice: what can be learned from recent history?', *Journal of Social Policy,* **32**: 239–270

Prime Minister's Strategy Unit (2006), *The UK Government's approach to public service reform,* London: Cabinet Office

Reform (2005), *The potential benefits of real education reform in England,* London: Reform, available at http://www.reform.co.uk/website/education.aspx

Schwarz, B. (2004), *The paradox of choice: why more is less,* New York: Harper Collins

Scottish Executive (2006), *Transforming public services: the next phase of reform,* Edinburgh: Scottish Executive

Scottish Government (2007), *Better health, better care: action plan,* Edinburgh: Scottish Government

Sturgeon, N. (2007), 'A different path to reform', speech at NHS Confederation Annual Conference, reported at
http://www.scotland.gov.uk/News/Releases/2007/06/21083635

Taylor-Gooby, P. (2008), 'Choice and values: individualised rational action and social goals', *Journal of Social Policy,* **37**: 167–185

Welsh Assembly Government (2004), *Making the connections: delivering better services for Wales,* Cardiff: Welsh Assembly Government

Acknowledgements

The *National Centre for Social Research* is grateful to the Economic and Social Research Council (RES-166-25-0043) for their financial support which enabled us to ask the questions reported in this chapter, although the views expressed are those of the authors alone.

4 Has welfare made us lazy? Employment commitment in different welfare states

Ingrid Esser[*]

Most modern industrialised countries have sought to provide at least some social protection for their citizens. Arrangements typically include income during periods of illness, unemployment and family formation, as well as support for those on low incomes and help with childcare for working parents. Benefits may often be based on citizenship or social insurance principles (whereby people 'earn' benefits by paying contributions) but are often supplemented by social assistance policies that act as a 'safety net'. However, there the similarities end. Over time, different countries have followed diverse paths in the arrangements of such social protection, resulting in very different entitlements and levels of generosity.

The question of how far social protection should go has been politically controversial in many countries. A central and critical aspect of these debates has been the contention by some politicians, economists and commentators that there is a trade-off between, on the one hand, the adequacy and equity of social protection and, on the other, the promotion of dependency and the distortion of work incentives. A common argument – not only on the political right – is that a more generous welfare state will eventually undermine people's commitment to paid work.

Given this, it is unsurprising that the provision of strong and positive incentives for work has been important to policy makers in this area. Some countries, such as the United Kingdom and the United States, have followed the path of providing fairly basic levels of benefits in order to minimise any unintended consequences in the form of distorted work incentives. Also, the more generous welfare states of the Nordic countries were intentionally designed to encourage labour market participation and were, in fact, strongly dependent on its attainment (Esping-Andersen, 1990). Often these latter countries combine a broad social policy agenda with expansive macro-economic policies and extensive active labour market policies aimed at guaranteeing full employment (Benner, 2003; Kvist and Ploug, 2003). On the whole, all welfare states seek to provide work incentives and opportunities to

---

[*] Ingrid Esser is Assistant Professor of Sociology, Swedish Institute for Social Research (SOFI), Stockholm University

make it both economically and normatively rational for individuals to take part in paid work and foster a commitment to it which we shall refer to as "employment commitment".

But to what extent does welfare provision create disincentives to work? Is it true that too much safety makes people lazy? These are the basic questions we examine in this chapter. We do this by using survey data from 13 countries to examine how employment commitment has developed in different types of welfare states, and how this has changed since the late 1980s.[1] Together these countries span a wide range of welfare state types and offer us an ideal opportunity to examine how employment commitment might be affected by welfare provision.

Why might social benefits affect employment commitment?

We begin by considering *why* social benefits might act as a disincentive to work. From a strict economic perspective, there is a basic assumption that leisure time is valued more highly than work time and, if given a free choice, individuals will opt for leisure. The straightforward expectation from this perspective is that welfare states providing more generous social insurances and social assistance will experience weaker and/or weakening employment commitment. This has led many commentators to argue that a generous welfare state will make citizens lazy and work-shy and that benefits and social assistance should be cut back to encourage more employment commitment. Our new comparative data on employment commitment will certainly allow us to assess the extent to which this assertion is correct.

A contrary view is given by a broader institutional perspective which recognises that higher benefits are usually provided according to earnings-related principles. The argument from this perspective draws mainly on an understanding of how work and welfare are tightly tied together through the reciprocity of requirements of reference and qualification periods. In other words, in order to qualify for benefits, a person has to have done a required amount of work (qualification period) within a specified span of time (reference period). Benefits are, of course, also conditional on the recipient fulfilling a specific condition of need (for example needing to be incapable of work before being able to claim sickness benefits). Individuals' 'choices' between work and leisure cannot therefore be regarded as unrestrained or free. Furthermore, benefits are higher with higher levels of pay and participation. For example, in the case of unemployment benefits, it can be argued that more generous benefits allow a better 'match' between individuals' skills, preferences and work positions (Burdett, 1979; Åberg, 2003; Pollmann-Schult and Büchel, 2005), thereby providing better opportunities for taking part in the labour market on more favourable terms, which will in turn serve to strengthen the positive experiences of employment. This positive matching effect can be seen as in addition to any significant positive intrinsic values of work, as well as any strong negative psycho-social effects of being out of work.

The picture is more complex in the case of family benefits. It has been shown that higher earnings-related family benefits provide incentives (especially for women) to participate in paid work, although the effect varies according to design of the benefits (Daly, 2000; Ferrarini, 2006). Different benefit structures can also help explain variations in gender-role attitudes across countries (Sjöberg, 2004). When combined with the provision of extensive public childcare services for younger children, higher earnings-related parental leave benefits facilitate an earlier return to the labour market than is the case in countries where services are more limited (and which instead create incentives for the parent with lower earnings to stay at home and care for the children, often resulting in a more traditional division of labour during prolonged periods of parental leave).

Lastly, previous research has found that earnings-related social insurance schemes and social assistance safety nets are best understood as mutually reinforcing parts of the welfare system (Nelson, 2003). In countries where the two systems are closely interdependent and earnings-related schemes are strong, the institutional disincentive effects of social assistance may be expected to be less pronounced, as strong overall institutionalised work incentives and work orientation permeate also to domains covered by social assistance.

In summary, then, we can contrast two views of the welfare state. On the one hand, those who argue that it promotes dependency and undermines work morale in the form of weakened commitment to employment and, on the other, proponents of the view that more generous earnings-related benefits will relate closely to participation in paid work and as such imply strong and/or strengthened employment commitment.

Research context

A number of studies have already found interesting differences between levels of employment commitment in different countries. Research on employment commitment conducted before the mid-1990s tended to focus on within-workplace, within-organisation or within-country comparisons, or was limited to two or a few country comparisons (see, for example, the classic work by Lincoln and Kalleberg, 1985; Lincoln and Kalleberg, 1990). Typically, most attention was paid to individual characteristics or the organisation of work at the workplace and less to the importance of cross-national institutional differences. The few broader comparative studies that have taken place have either found no clear relationship between employment commitment and welfare provision, or have found *stronger* employment commitment in countries known to have more generous welfare states. Conclusions drawn from two studies comparing six countries tell us that employment commitment is stronger in the coordinated market economies of Sweden, Norway and Germany (and especially in the Scandinavian countries) while weaker commitment exists in the liberal market economies of New Zealand, the United Kingdom and the United States (Berglund, 2001; Hult and Svallfors, 2002).

With data from the Employment in Europe Survey of 1996 for 15 European Union member states, Gallie and Alm (2000) focused on differences between employees and the unemployed, but found no evidence that employment commitment in general was related to the generosity of unemployment benefits. However, an association did appear between unemployment benefits and lower commitment in the specific case of married/cohabiting unemployed women (as compared to employed women) in societies with a more traditional gender culture such as Austria, Germany, Britain, Ireland and Italy (Gallie and Alm, 2000).

Although these previous studies have uncovered some interesting differences between levels of employment commitment in different countries, these differences have not previously been related to specific measures of welfare state institutional "generosity".[2] In this chapter we seek to overcome this by including more elaborate measures of social protection while also taking into account international differences in the composition of the workforce and other relevant contextual factors. This is made possible by new survey data and a more thorough collection of welfare state institutional data. Moreover, we are able to look at how attitudes in certain countries have changed over the last two decades, meaning that we can evaluate more clearly how current levels of employment commitment reflect the institutional structures within different welfare states. This is, after all, the contention in much of the current policy debate.

Before we look closer at different welfare state arrangements, a few important reflections are warranted. Firstly, though we focus on the role of welfare state institutions, we should recognise that other factors, for example religious or political beliefs or traditions, may also shape individuals' attitudes to work. However, it could be argued that such factors are, in fact, partly captured by welfare state institutional design. After all, the emergence and development of welfare arrangements have been closely related to national traditions in partisan politics and religion, especially where social democratic or Christian democratic parties have championed the development of the welfare state (Korpi, 2001).

Secondly, although often overlapping, attitudes clearly differ from behaviour; what people think and what people do are not always the same. This has caused policy makers, as well as researchers, to question the worth of studying attitudes in the first place. However, attitudes do matter. After all, behavioural measures of labour force participation tell us very little about a person's attitude towards his or her work. Equally, it is very difficult to implement policy changes in opposition to widespread public attitudes or preferences. Policies that are generally aligned with individuals' preferences quite simply stand a better chance of attaining real and intended effects.

Thirdly, it is important to consider how a range of contextual factors, primarily unemployment and female labour force participation, might influence a country's overall levels of employment commitment. For example, it has been argued that rising and/or high unemployment rates shift norms away from materialist concerns towards an increased emphasis on freedom, self-expression and quality of life. By this logic, the importance of non-financial work values will be more extensively emphasized (Clark and Lipset, 1991). Hence we would expect strengthened employment commitment during periods of higher unemployment. But the opposite relationship may also be predicted; as the number of unemployment benefit recipients increases, it becomes easier to deviate from the social norm of working (Lindbeck, 1997). We might also expect to find that overall levels of commitment will be related to whether women are encouraged to participate in paid work since family policies provide qualitatively different opportunities in different countries (Daly, 2000; Ferrarini, 2006). These issues mean it is important to take account of factors such as unemployment and female labour market participation in our analysis of how countries differ in their levels of work commitment.

Fourthly, we need to comment on the central issue of causality and how welfare state institutions may have *caused* normative changes. Our inquiry starts from the basic assumption that institutions can, to some degree, affect norms. By providing incentives through the organisation of social protection, institutions generate motivations for actions that may otherwise not take place, and from there go on to change attitudes. In this way, institutions provide a link between individuals' actions and the structure within which they live, to some extent affecting strategic actions and rational calculation, as well as preferences and beliefs within normative orders (March and Olsen, 1984). However, with repeated cross-sectional survey data (that is, data collected by interviewing different samples of people at different points in time), there is limited scope for demonstrating strictly causal explanations. So our general aim, therefore, needs to be less ambitious and restricted to testing the proposition that work morale over time has been influenced by the generosity of the welfare states within which people live. This would be indicated by a reasonable correspondence between, on the one hand, observable attitude patterns today and attitude change over the past two decades and, on the other, welfare state generosity. There is less scope here for uncovering causal factors that may truly explain the formation of norms around work. For example, historical (pre-modern welfare state) levels of employment commitment may have differed greatly across the countries we compare, possibly in close correspondence to the spread of the 'Protestant work ethic'.

What may be evaluated here is the accumulated normative impact of modern institutional welfare state structures which, in all the countries compared, have been present in their current forms for several decades (and in some instances much longer). Consequently, we might expect them to have had an impact on people's attitudes by the early 2000s.

Welfare state generosity

This chapter examines employment commitment in 13 mature welfare states. In addition to Britain, the countries included in the study are Australia, Belgium, Canada, Denmark, Germany,[3] Ireland, Japan, New Zealand, Norway, Sweden, Switzerland and the United States. We begin by considering how welfare states within these countries differ in terms of their generosity. By generosity we mean the level of state-legislated social insurance benefits across the most common areas of social protection available to non-retired citizens who are temporarily unable to support themselves and their families adequately: sickness cash benefits, unemployment benefits, family benefits and social assistance.

In his seminal work, Esping-Andersen (1990) distinguished three types of capitalism: social democratic, conservative and liberal welfare states. However, in this context, it is more relevant to use definitions based directly on institutional characteristics, such as the principles they use to govern benefit replacements. Consequently, we follow the categorisation of welfare states proposed by Korpi and Palme (1998) below: [4]

- *Encompassing welfare states* generally provide earnings-related benefits with high replacement rates (that is, generous benefit levels that replace a high percentage of what an individual might earn in the labour market). They tend also to have generous family benefits which, together with extensive day-care services for young children, promote dual earner families and thus encourage higher levels of female labour force participation (Ferrarini, 2006). The Nordic countries are typical encompassing welfare states.

- *Corporatist welfare states* also provide high replacement rates for sickness cash benefits and unemployment benefits, but benefits are usually provided to the active labour force within occupational programmes, and so exclude groups who are more loosely attached to, or outside, the labour force (Korpi and Palme, 1998). Family benefits and social assistance benefits are less generous than those found in encompassing welfare states, and day-care services are more limited (for example, they might be restricted to part-time care centres for somewhat older children). For women in particular, this encourages a more traditional division between paid and unpaid work (Korpi, 2000; Ferrarini, 2006). Most western continental European countries have developed this type of welfare state, as has Japan.

- In *basic security welfare states*, benefits are generally low and are usually provided as flat-rate benefits or involve means-testing (as in Australia and New Zealand). Where earnings-related benefits exist, they tend to have low benefit ceilings. Family policy programmes provide relatively low benefits and there is only limited provision of public day-care services, encouraging reliance on market resources or informal help for the supply of caring services (Korpi, 2000). This type of welfare state includes a number of English-speaking countries such as Australia, Canada, Ireland, New Zealand, the United Kingdom and the United States.

Figure 4.1 shows how levels of welfare state benefits varied across the 13 countries in 2000. The overall height of the bars shows the average 'replacement rate' across the four social protection areas considered – that is, the average net rate at which the earnings of an average production worker are replaced by state-legislated benefits. For example, in the British case the overall benefit replacement rate of 28 per cent is the average of the following: sickness cash benefits that replace 19 per cent of the earnings of an average production worker's wage; unemployment benefits that replace 17 per cent; family benefits that replace 31 per cent; and social assistance benefits that replace 44 per cent. A more detailed description of these data can be found in the appendix to the chapter. Although other aspects of these benefits (such as who the insurance covers, what qualifying conditions exist and what membership requirements apply) are also important, the overall indicator gives a reasonable measure of welfare state generosity.

Clear regime differences are discernable. Total generosity is, as expected, highest in encompassing welfare states (69 per cent on average) and lowest in basic security welfare states (33 per cent on average), with the corporatist welfare states falling somewhere in between (59 per cent) Nevertheless, there are exceptions in each group. Generosity is decidedly lower in Denmark than in the two other Scandinavian encompassing welfare states,[5] and higher in Germany than in the other corporatist welfare states. Canada also stands out as being more generous than other basic security welfare states.[6] Along with the United States, New Zealand and Australia, the United Kingdom has one of the least generous welfare regimes of the 13 countries considered.[7]

Figure 4.1 Welfare regime generosity in 13 countries, 2000

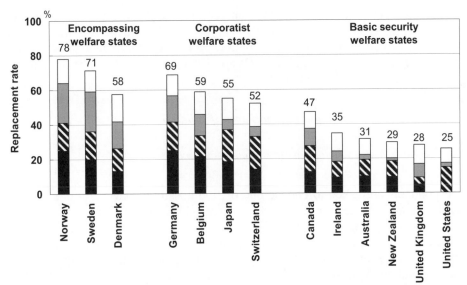

■ Sickness cash benefits ◨ Unemployment benefits ▨ Family benefits (total) □ Social assistance

Sources: SCIP, SaMip (see appendix to this chapter)

The subdivisions within the bars show the relative proportions of each type of social benefit within each country. In the corporatist countries, for example, sickness and unemployment benefits play a bigger role than do family benefits or social assistance. This is especially true in Germany and Belgium, although Germany's distinctive character is also related to its noticeably high levels of family benefits. By contrast, in basic security countries, social insurance schemes tend to be less generous and social assistance therefore stands out, in relative terms, as a more significant component of social protection. Notably, in the British case, family benefits, which replace 31 per cent of an average worker's wage (of which half comprise low flat-rate benefits and the other half earnings-related benefits payable at a high rate but for a shorter duration), stand out as rather generous as compared to the low flat-rate benefits of both sickness cash benefits (statutory sick pay) and unemployment benefits (job seekers allowance). Each of these replace less than 20 per cent of average earnings. Worth noting is also the absence of any national legislated health insurance programme in the United States.

Measuring employment commitment across 13 countries

We turn now to evaluate employment commitment across 13 countries in 2005. This is made possible by the high-quality survey data provided by the *International Social Survey Programme* and a series of questions about work orientation included in the 2005 survey. Two questions in particular relate closely to the concept of employment commitment used in earlier studies; commitment as an indication of the degree to which a person *wants* to be engaged in paid employment and, more specifically, the extent to which this applies regardless of financial need (Warr, 1982; Jackson *et al.*, 1983). The two questions are phrased as statements:

> *I would enjoy having a paid job even if I did not need the money*

> *A job is just a way of earning money – no more*

Respondents are asked to choose one of five possible answers: strongly agree, agree, neither agree nor disagree, disagree and strongly disagree. Following previous comparative research, we calculated an employment commitment index as the summed average measure of these two questions.[8] Each respondent's score on the index varies from one to five, with higher values corresponding to stronger employment commitment and lower values to weaker employment commitment. Those at the high end of this continuum can be seen as having strong non-financial commitment. Low scores can be seen as indicating a commitment to employment which is more contingent on financial rewards – and is thus more instrumental. For these people, the difference between wage levels and the available welfare state benefits is more likely to become a crucial 'deciding factor' in their 'decision' to participate in paid work.

Table 4.1 shows how levels of employment commitment vary across the 13 countries of interest. For each country, we present the findings for men and women separately, for reasons we shall explore shortly. Firstly, however, we note that that there are indeed clear differences between people in different types of welfare states. Among both men and women, the strongest commitment is found in the encompassing welfare states. For example, the first line in the table shows that men in encompassing welfare states have an average employment commitment score of 3.72 (out of a maximum score of 5), and women a score of 3.87. This is significantly higher than average commitment scores in corporatist welfare states (3.45 for men and 3.53 for women) or basic security welfare states (3.36 and 3.49).

There are wide variations in the levels of commitment across corporatist and basic security welfare states. Out of the corporatist welfare states, the strongest commitment is found among the Swiss (3.66 and 3.77), at levels similar to those found in the Nordic encompassing welfare states. This is significantly stronger than the commitment found in the other corporatist states. The relatively high levels of commitment found among Japanese men is also noteworthy, as is the quite low commitment among Belgian men.

Among the basic security welfare states, Britain stands out as the country with the weakest employment commitment of all, among men as well as women. Consequently, British employment commitment is the lowest among the 13 countries we examined.

The obvious question is, of course, whether these differences relate in any systematic way to welfare state generosity; we shall turn to this in the next section.

A second finding in the table is the clear difference between employment commitment among men and women, with women's commitment overall being stronger than men's, rather than weaker. However, these gendered differences are actually only significant in half of the countries: Norway, Sweden, Belgium, Australia, New Zealand and Britain.

Why might commitment to work vary between men and women? One obvious reason relates to their different opportunities to participate in paid labour. Commitment may relate to the prospects women have to take part fully in paid labour, or, alternatively, to how opportunities (or the lack of opportunities) instead support an alternative self-identity, either primarily as a homemaker, or an 'adaptive' identity, seeking a combination of responsibilities in both spheres (Hakim, 2002). Such circumstances appear to be manifested through larger numbers of women than men in part-time work, in less career-oriented (but often service-oriented) occupations often found in the public sector, usually also receiving lower pay (Daly, 2000; Hakim, 2002). At the same time, many women working in service-oriented occupations may be highly motivated, but by different factors to those that motivate others (for example, Waerness's notion of 'care-rationality', 1984, 2003).

Since gender-role attitudes differ widely across countries (Sjöberg, 2004), and women's work orientations have been found to be quite heterogeneous (Hakim, 2002; Doorewaard et al., 2004), it is not always clear how employment commitment will differ between men and women. Participation may promote stronger commitment, but the conditions under which women participate can be expected to matter as well. If women participate in paid work more reluctantly, either on a part-time basis or in occupations that mainly accommodate traditional familial roles (short hours of work, less demanding tasks), this may *weaken* commitment (Hansen, 1997; Mandel and Semyonov, 2003). On the other hand, women who intentionally 'choose' such employment may be equally (or more strongly) committed to it, as this accommodates their preference for combined responsibilities (Hakim, 2002). Although several recent studies have found quite small or non-existent differences between men's and women's employment commitment (Halvorsen, 1997; Gallie *et al.*, 1998; Gallie and Alm, 2000), other research has found women to be overall more committed to paid work than men (Svallfors *et al.*, 2001; Gallie and Paugam, 2002; Hult and Svallfors, 2002). This also coincides with the picture in Britain reported in *The 23rd Report*: although women's non-financial commitment to work might once have been lower than that of men, women are now at least as 'committed' to employment as men are, if not more so (Crompton and Lyonette, 2007). And, as Table 4.1 shows, this picture is not just confined to Britain.

Table 4.1 Employment commitment in 13 countries, 2005

	Men		Women	
	Average	*Base*	Average	*Base*
Encompassing welfare states	3.72	*1358*	3.87	*1422*
Norway	3.82	*412*	3.95	*446*
Sweden	3.53	*418*	3.77	*429*
Denmark	3.82	*528*	3.90	*547*
Corporatist welfare states	3.45	*1326*	3.53	*1378*
Germany	3.37	*326*	3.44	*337*
Belgium	3.28	*445*	3.48	*439*
Switzerland	3.66	*336*	3.77	*344*
Japan	3.51	*219*	3.44	*258*
Basic security welfare states	3.36	*2193*	3.49	*2706*
Canada	3.48	*256*	3.54	*283*
Ireland	3.47	*245*	3.51	*400*
Australia	3.32	*567*	3.48	*674*
New Zealand	3.48	*396*	3.63	*486*
Britain	3.18	*219*	3.37	*307*
United States	3.48	*510*	3.48	*556*
Total average	3.51	*5368*	3.61	*6220*

Base: all aged 18–59 in paid work, unemployed, or looking after the home
The employment commitment index is measured on a scale 1–5 (higher values = stronger work commitment; lower values = weaker work commitment)

Employment commitment and welfare state generosity

Earlier we saw that employment commitment appears to be greatest in the encompassing welfare states which offer their citizens the most generous benefits. The scatterplots in Figure 4.2 demonstrate this relationship in more detail, by plotting the relationship between employment commitment and welfare regime generosity (using the measures described in Figure 4.1). The trend line for both men and women shows that there are clear positive and significant correlations between welfare generosity and employment commitment (although the correlation is of medium strength). In other words, employment commitment tends to be greater in countries with a more generous welfare regime than it is in less generous countries. At the highest end of the spectrum, among both men and women, we find Norway and Denmark, as well as Swedish women. These countries appear towards the top right corners in Figure 4.2. In these countries, high welfare state generosity clearly coexists with high levels of employment commitment. Clustering at the low end of the continuum, towards the bottom left sides in the figure, we find the United Kingdom and Australia, as well as American women. A weaker relationship is found in Germany and Belgium, as well as among Japanese women. Here, somewhat weaker commitment is found than we might expect among reasonably generous welfare states. The Swiss, on the other hand, seem to have slightly higher levels of commitment than would be expected.

Figure 4.2 Employment commitment and welfare regime generosity, 2005

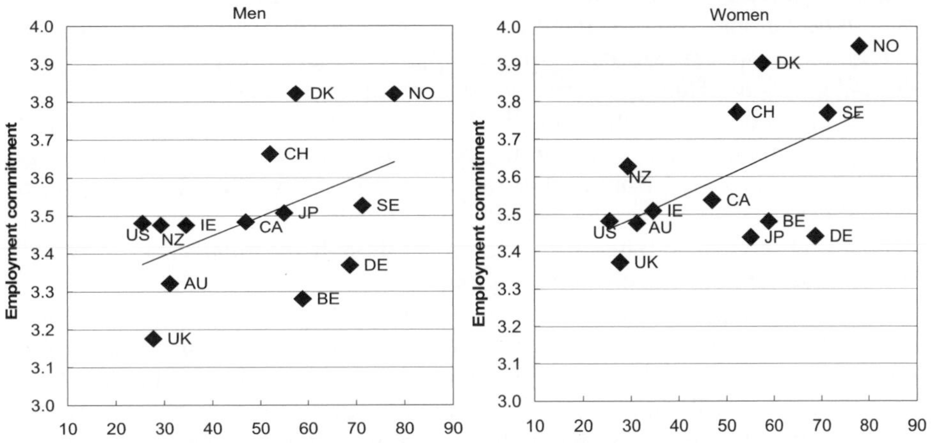

These simple bivariate evaluations offer some initial support for the propositions that the design of generous welfare state benefits is congruent with high levels of commitment to paid work – possibly upholding or even strengthening them – and certainly *not* indicative of undermined employment commitment. Yet to be sure that this is really the case, we need to examine other differences between countries, as well as how employment commitment and welfare policy have changed over time.

Diversity across countries

Previous research has shown that employment commitment is strongly related to a number of individual characteristics. Although both theoretical claims and empirical findings have often been contradictory, the most recent comparative research leads us to expect socio-economic characteristics such as a person's occupation and education to be more important predictors of their commitment than their age or household composition (Hult and Svallfors, 2002). For example, we might expect to find that graduates have higher commitment than those with few qualifications and that workers in professional occupations are more strongly committed than unskilled workers. We might also expect to find workers in the public sector have greater employment commitment than workers in the private sector – as found for Britain in *The 24th Report* (John and Johnson, 2008). Of course, different countries have very different proportions of graduates or employees working in the public sector. So, might international diversity in these sorts of socio-economic characteristics explain the different levels of employment commitment we have found, rather than variations in welfare state generosity?

Table 4.2 shows the levels of employment commitment found among a range of demographic and socio-economic groups for the three types of welfare states, using Norway, Germany and Britain as examples. The findings largely confirm our expectations. Within none of the three countries does employment commitment appear to relate to age, marital status or the presence of a dependent child. However, stronger commitment is found among the more highly educated and higher social classes in all countries. Expectations of stronger commitment in the public sector do hold true, but this group only differs significantly from other workers in Germany. Lastly, weaker commitment is found among people outside paid work – here, unemployed people and women looking after the home, though the small bases mean the results must be treated with some caution.

If we now compare the different countries in the table, we see that the country distinctiveness noted in the previous section remains in almost every aspect considered. For almost every category considered, the employment commitment of Norwegians is the strongest. Only commitment among Norwegian women looking after the home, the unemployed and the highest social class does not differ significantly from the levels found in Germany or Britain (though this may, in part, be due to small base sizes). As before, the employment commitment of the Germans tends to be stronger than that of the British – significantly so across educational categories, most social classes, part-time working women and people working in the public sector.

Table 4.2 Employment commitment and demographic/socio-economic status in three countries, 2005

	Employment commitment			Bases		
	Norway	**Germany**	**Britain**	*NO*	*DE*	*GB*
Economic status						
Men: working full-time	3.85	3.37	3.18	*378*	*283*	*184*
Women: working full-time	4.00	3.53	3.45	*334*	*120*	*137*
Women: working part-time	4.04	3.63	3.35	*75*	*91*	*106*
All: unemployed	3.27	3.19	3.18	*34*	*60*	*24*
Women: looking after home	3.27	3.28	3.20	*25*	*101*	*55*
Age						
18–34	3.87	3.39	3.31	*238*	*192*	*176*
35–49	3.91	3.38	3.29	*397*	*315*	*225*
50–59	3.86	3.48	3.21	*223*	*156*	*125*
Household type						
Single person household	3.87	3.33	3.23	*208*	*128*	*187*
Married/cohabiting	3.89	3.42	3.30	*650*	*535*	*338*
Children						
No child in household	3.90	3.38	3.29	*402*	*352*	*306*
Child in household	3.88	3.42	3.28	*455*	*299*	*220*
Education						
University level	4.12	3.79	3.52	*418*	*99*	*194*
Not university level	3.66	3.34	3.13	*438*	*560*	*332*
Social class[9]						
Unskilled worker	3.51	3.14	2.79	*133*	*144*	*105*
Routine non-manual	3.93	3.43	3.40	*198*	*208*	*175*
Lower-grade professions	3.98	3.67	3.48	*197*	*122*	*98*
Higher-grade professions	4.18	4.08	3.65	*175*	*36*	*89*
Sector						
Private	3.85	3.35	3.24	*423*	*452*	*316*
Public	3.97	3.73	3.40	*324*	*112*	*145*
Total	3.89	3.40	3.28	*858*	*663*	*526*

Base: all aged 18–59 in paid work, unemployed, or looking after the home
The employment commitment index is measured on a scale 1–5 (higher values = stronger work commitment; lower values = weaker work commitment)

The fact that, among almost every group in Table 4.2, Norwegians have higher levels of employment commitment than either Germans or the British (while, in turn, Germans have higher levels than the British), suggests that national differences in employment commitment cannot only be explained by differences between these countries in education, employment status or occupational sector. However, it is possible that some of the differences we see between employment commitment in these countries reflect their varying social constituencies. Table 4.3 summarises some of the key differences. It shows, for example, that in Norway around a half of the 'active' population (that is, those in work, unemployed or women looking after the home) are graduates, compared with only 37 per cent of people in Britain or 15 per cent of people in Germany.[10]

Table 4.3 Demographic and socio-economic status in three countries, 2005

	% of active population aged 18–59			Bases		
	Norway	**Germany**	**Britain**	*NO*	*DE*	*GB*
Economic status						
Men: working full-time	94	89	90	*412*	*326*	*219*
Women: working full-time	75	36	44	*446*	*337*	*307*
Women: working part-time	15	27	32	*446*	*337*	*307*
All: unemployed	4	9	4	*858*	*663*	*526*
Women: looking after home	6	30	19	*446*	*337*	*307*
Age	%	%	%	*858*	*663*	*526*
18–34	28	29	39			
35–49	46	48	39			
50–59	24	24	22			
Household type	%	%	%	*858*	*663*	*525*
Single person household	24	19	29			
Married/cohabiting	76	81	71			
Children	%	%	%	*857*	*651*	*526*
No child in household	47	54	58			
Child in household	53	46	42			
Education	%	%	%	*856*	*659*	*526*
University level	49	15	37			
Not university level	51	85	63			
Social class	%	%	%	*834*	*627*	*522*
Unskilled worker	16	23	21			
Routine non-manual	24	33	32			
Lower-grade professions	24	20	20			
Higher-grade professions	21	6	17			
Sector	%	%	%	*838*	*617*	*522*
Private	51	73	61			
Public	39	18	27			
Total	100	100	100	*858*	*663*	*526*

The active population refers to everyone aged 18–59 who is in paid work, unemployed or looking after the home

The employment commitment index is measured on a scale 1–5 (higher values = stronger work commitment; lower values = weaker work commitment)

Other very notable disparities relate to women. In Norway, the proportion of women working full-time by far outnumbers their part-time working counterparts (75 and 15 per cent respectively), which is certainly not the case in Germany and Britain. Note, however, that if Germany and Britain were to find themselves with a similar employment profile among women to Norway, their overall levels of employment commitment would *fall*, as in both countries women working part-time have *higher* levels of work commitment than women working full-time (a situation that is not the case in Norway).

Only six per cent of the active female population in Norway are women looking after the home, compared with three in ten in Germany and two in ten in Britain. Germany also has a decidedly larger proportion of less committed unemployed people compared with the other countries. As the unemployed and women looking after the home have lower levels of employment commitment than those in work, this might partly explain some of the overall differences in commitment levels we find between these three countries. Lastly, the proportions of highly educated Norwegians as well as Norwegians belonging to the 'highest' social class (which includes those in higher-grade professional occupations, as well as administrators, officials and managers in large establishments) is decidedly large, especially compared with Germany. On these measures, if the socio-economic profile of Germany and Britain were more like that of Norway, overall levels of commitment in those two countries would have been higher.

To expand our analyses to all 13 countries, we performed multivariate analysis, the results of which are shown in detail in the appendix to this chapter. In summary, the effects of individual level factors (such as age or social class) on employment commitment are very similar to what is shown in Table 4.2; commitment increases with higher education and social class, and employment status also matters. Women working part-time are more committed than full-timers, and unemployed women and those looking after the home are less committed than working persons. Age is a less important factor, although commitment does seem to weaken somewhat with age among men. Household composition is of no relevance among women or men.

After we have taken account of all these individual characteristics, there remains a clear positive and significant relationship between commitment and welfare state generosity – employment commitment is stronger in countries with higher levels of welfare state generosity. This relationship remains when we take account of the negative effects of countries' unemployment rates (shown) as well as the positive effects of female labour force participation (not shown).

So far we have found no support for the proposition that employment commitment is weaker in more generous welfare states. But perhaps there has been weakened employment commitment in more generous welfare states *over time*. So, although employment commitment is stronger in the Nordic countries now, commitment might have been *even stronger* in an earlier phase, and then declined due to the serious disincentive effects of the welfare state. It is to this proposition that we now turn.

Employment commitment over time

We can examine how employment commitment has changed over time by making use of two earlier rounds of the *International Social Survey Programme*'s work orientation module, carried out in 1989 and 1997. We do not have data for the full set of 13 countries, but we can look at Norway, Germany, Britain and the United States, which gives us a range of examples from all three types of welfare states.

Before we look closer at commitment levels over time, it is worth reflecting on what developments in welfare state generosity have taken place over the last two decades. We have already argued that welfare states in all the countries compared here have been present in their current form for several decades (and in some instances more than several decades). None have, however, remained entirely static over time. This is shown in Figure 4.3, which illustrates developments in these four countries since 1985. It confirms that, throughout the period, generosity has been highest in Norway, and substantially lower in the two basic security countries, the United Kingdom and the United States. In the United Kingdom, generosity has declined somewhat, whereas it has increased slightly in the United States in more recent years. Changes in Norway and Germany are primarily related to increases in family benefits, introduced earlier in Norway than in Germany.

Figure 4.3 Welfare regime generosity across four countries, 1985, 1995 and 2000

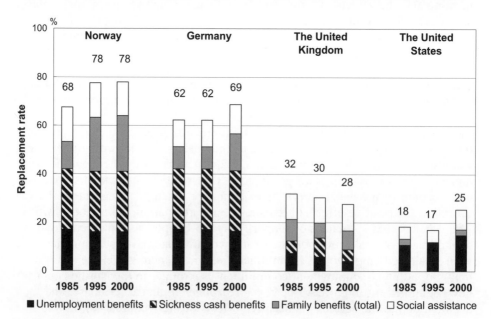

Sources: SCIP, SaMip (see appendix to this chapter)

Data for social assistance was not available for 1985; data from 1992 is used instead

Tables 4.4 and 4.5 show the average employment commitment among men and women in the four countries for three points in time: 1989, 1997 and 2005. Looking first at the initial levels in 1989, the employment commitment of Norwegians was the highest (both for women and for men), and the lowest commitment for men and women was found in Germany. Of the two middle positions, the Americans' commitment (both men's and women's) is decidedly higher than that of the British. Again, we note how women in general are more strongly committed than men.

Looking at the changes over the entire period from 1989, the average trend across all four countries (shown in the 'total' row at the bottom of each table) is stable among men, while there is a slight and significant overall increase of employment commitment among women. However, the level of commitment appears to be diverging between the four countries. Among men in the encompassing welfare state of Norway and those in the corporatist Germany, commitment *increased* between 1989 and 1997, while it *decreased* in both the basic security welfare states (the United Kingdom and the United States). By 2005, the lowest commitment is found among British working men.

Table 4.4 Employment commitment among men in four countries, 1989, 1997 and 2005

	Men						Bases		
	1989	**1997**	**2005**	**89–97**	**97–05**	**89–05**	*1989*	*1997*	*2005*
Norway	3.64	3.80	3.82	+	0	+	*741*	*725*	*412*
Germany	3.19	3.40	3.37	+	0	+	*397*	*418*	*326*
Britain	3.32	3.14	3.18	–	0	–	*401*	*289*	*219*
United States	3.54	3.44	3.48	–	0	0	*467*	*383*	*510*
Total	3.46	3.52	3.50	+	0	0	*2006*	*1815*	*1467*

The employment commitment index is measured on a scale 1–5 (higher values = stronger work commitment; lower values = weaker work commitment)
+/– = a significant in-/decrease at the 95% level
0 = no significant change
Base: men aged 18–59 in paid work, unemployed and looking after home

The trend among women is somewhat similar. The Norwegians' commitment increases over the entire period, while in Germany it increases between 1989 and 1997, but declines slightly afterwards. In contrast, the employment commitment of working women in Britain declines significantly between 1989 and 1997 (although a small but non-significant increase after 1989 means that there is no significant change overall between 1989 and 2005). American women's commitment remains fairly stable over the entire time period. Consequently, the overall increase in employment commitment among women shown in the bottom line of Table 4.5 reflects strengthened commitment in

Norway and Germany. Separate evaluations of the commitment among the unemployed and women looking after the home (not shown) reveal significant changes over time only in Germany, where commitment among these groups increased somewhat in the earlier time period (1989–1997).[11]

Table 4.5 Employment commitment among women in four countries, 1989, 1997 and 2005

	Women						*Bases*		
	1989	**1997**	**2005**	**89–97**	**97–05**	**89–05**	*1989*	*1997*	*2005*
Norway	3.74	3.86	3.95	+	+	+	*708*	*728*	*446*
Germany	3.21	3.60	3.44	+	–	+	*527*	*363*	*337*
Britain	3.44	3.33	3.37	–	0	0	*487*	*401*	*307*
United States	3.55	3.48	3.48	0	0	0	*551*	*525*	*556*
Total	3.51	3.61	3.57	+	0	+	*2273*	*2017*	*1646*

The employment commitment index is measured on a scale 1–5 (higher values = stronger work commitment; lower values = weaker work commitment)
+/– = a significant in-/decrease at the 95% level
0 = no significant change
Base: women aged 18–59 in paid work, unemployed and looking after home

The evidence so far does not support expectations of finding weakened employment commitment over time in more generous welfare states – rather the contrary. However, we have only looked at four countries over the 1989–2005 period and there is always a risk that these countries do not illustrate trends that would be present in a larger sample. We can address this by examining changes across 10 welfare states for the period 1997 to 2005. In Figure 4.4 the average commitment for men and women in paid work across countries in 1997 is plotted against the average level in 2005. So countries found *above* the diagonal line have experienced increased commitment, whereas commitment in countries *below* the line has decreased. Statistically significant differences are marked by filled-in symbols.

Clearly the overall pattern is one of stability. In no country is there a significant change over time in working men's commitment. When working women's commitment is considered, changes over time are significant in half of the countries, but in diverging directions. Commitment increased in Norway and Canada, while it decreased in Germany, Japan and Denmark. So there are no clear trends within countries with similar welfare states (as Norway and Denmark are both encompassing welfare states, while Japan and Germany are both corporatist). The clustering of countries further up the diagonal line in the right-hand graph again indicates women's stronger commitment than men's to paid work.[12]

Figure 4.4 Employment commitment of men and women in paid work, 1997 and 2005

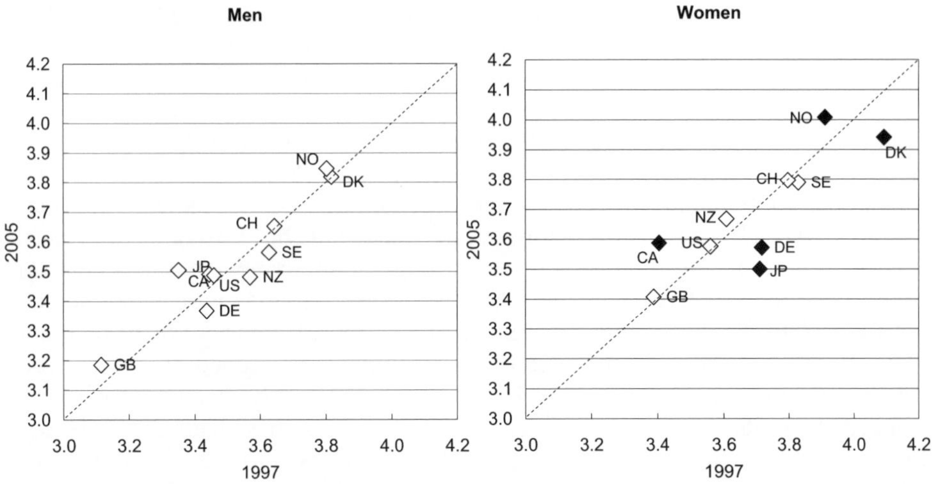

◇ Non-significant change 1997–2005 ◆ Significant change 1997–2005 at the 95% level

These findings suggest that trends in employment commitment are characterised more by stability than by change. In countries where changes have occurred, they do not confirm the expectations of those who would argue that generous welfare states experience weaker employment commitment than less generous ones. On the contrary, between 1989 and 1997, employment commitment weakened in the two basic security welfare states and it became stronger in the encompassing welfare state of Norway. And the pattern of changes across 10 countries from 1997 onwards primarily indicates stability.

Conclusions

In this chapter we have evaluated the role of welfare state institutions in explaining differences in employment commitment across 13 mature welfare states. The findings show that employment commitment is decidedly stronger within the more generous ('encompassing') welfare states, even when important individual characteristics and variations in these across countries are taken into account.

Neither does it seem that today's levels of employment commitment are the outcomes of trends towards lower employment commitment in more generous welfare states. The general impression is rather one of stability over time. In the period 1989–1997 there is instead evidence of increased commitment in the encompassing welfare state of Norway but decreased commitment in two of the basic security countries – the United Kingdom and the United States. There were rather few changes in the latter period of 1997–2005 when a larger number of countries were compared. These findings do not lend support to the expectations of the narrow economic perspective that employment commitment has declined from initially higher levels through serious disincentive effects of generous welfare state benefits. Rather, they lend some support to the opposite expectations from a broader institutional perspective that high and/or increasing levels of employment commitment are linked to a generous welfare state.

In sum, work morale cannot be described as being undermined by generous welfare states today. Social benefits do not appear to have made people lazy. Given the political controversy that has raged on this point, this is an important finding. At the same time, correlation must not be mistaken for causal explanation. The correlation between stronger employment commitment and more generous welfare states necessitates further research into which societal and social mechanisms may, in fact, explain the differences we have found. This is an important point, because it is sometimes argued that the strong reciprocity between work and welfare encouraged by the design of earnings-related benefits in more generous welfare states has had the effect of maintaining or possibly even encouraging strong work norms and high levels of employment commitment. So our findings should not be read as a call for increased benefit levels in order to strengthen employment commitment. The proper conclusion from the work presented here is, rather, that it appears to be quite possible to maintain strong work morale within a generous welfare state.

The focus on welfare state generosity in this chapter is obvious. Yet, welfare states also tend to be highly interconnected with labour market organisation. Encompassing welfare states in particular have combined a broad social policy agenda with expansive macro-economic policies and extensive active labour market policies. For a deeper explanation of the formative processes of employment commitment, it seems reasonable to expand the analysis to the organisation of work and the quality of the jobs available. There is now increasing attention paid to comparing job quality across countries (in terms of extrinsic and intrinsic rewards, work conditions, work control, autonomy and work relations with colleagues and managers). Introducing such essential aspects of everyday work life into the analysis would certainly bring further nuance to the explanation of what motivates people to take part in paid work.

Notes

1. Throughout this chapter, we limit the analysis to those aged 18–59 who are in work, unemployed or looking after the home.
2. Typically these studies have used country-dummy variables or simple country-level measures as a sum-measure of all country-specific effects.
3. To make over-time comparison possible, we restrict 'Germany' to respondents residing in the geographical area of the former West Germany.

4. Strictly speaking this categorisation was developed with reference only to sickness cash and pension benefits. For reasons of simplicity we are applying the same institutional concepts to all four social protection dimensions, even though this notably alters the grouping of Denmark and Switzerland.

5. Denmark is generally recognised as a mixed model but is still grouped with the Scandinavian countries because its overall institutional configuration is more similar to these countries in important ways, especially with respect to active labour market and dual-earner policies and high levels of social spending on social services encouraging full employment and high female labour force participation (Greve, 2004) and extensive day-care services for young children, thus promoting dual earner families (Ferrarini, 2006). All social insurance benefits are also designed according to the income security principle – as a percentage of previous earnings – although a low benefit ceiling lowers the actual replacement rate relative to the average production worker's wage.

6. Canadian sickness cash benefits and unemployment benefits are in fact earnings related, replacing 55 per cent of previous gross earnings. Sickness cash benefits are, however, limited to a maximum of 15-week duration, which lowers the overall replacement rate for Canada in relation to a 26-week spell of sickness or unemployment period (for further details please see the chapter appendix).

7. The UK welfare system places particular emphasis on *in-work* benefits (which can be thought of as comparatively generous); however, that is not the focus of this chapter (see the appendix to this chapter for more detail on the benefits included in the analysis).

8. We used principal component analysis (a statistical method similar to factor analysis) to establish that these two questions measure individual employment commitment accurately and with acceptable robustness in the same way across all 13 countries. We found that responses to these questions were clearly distinct from other questions about commitment to the employees' specific firm or organisation, the pride a person takes in his or her working profession or working for his/her employer, or his/her willingness to work harder in order for the firm to succeed.

9. Social class is measured by a six-category Erikson Goldthorpe Portocarero (EGP) classification scheme (for example, see Erikson and Goldthorpe, 1992), by recoding international occupational class (ISCO) codes aided by syntax provided by Ganzeboom and Treiman (1996); also available online (Ganzeboom, 2007).

10. The low proportion of graduates in Germany is indicative of the strong vocational track within Germany's educational system, which by international comparison is not regarded as tertiary education, although some of these occupations would require tertiary degrees in other countries (e.g. medical nurses). Also, the German educational system is quite selective already at the secondary level, which implies that a relatively small proportion of the general population are in fact eligible for tertiary education.

11. The few statistically significant changes for these groups may, of course, in part be a consequence of the smaller sub-samples.

12. Using a similar comparison, very few changes were again seen among unemployed persons or women looking after the home. Only the commitment among the Swiss unemployed and women looking after the home increased substantially, while it decreased among Japanese women at home.

References

Åberg, R. (2003), 'Unemployment persistency, over-education and the employment chances of the less educated', *European Sociological Review*, **19(2)**: 199–216

Benner, M. (2003), 'The Scandinavian challenge. The future of advanced welfare states in the knowledge economy', *Acta Sociologica*, **46(2)**: 132–149

Berglund, T. (2001), *Attityder till arbete i Västeuropa och USA (Attitudes to work in Western Europe and the USA)*, Göteborg: Department of Sociology, Göteborg University

Burdett, K. (1979), 'Unemployment insurance payments as a search subsidy: a theoretical analysis', *Economic Inquiry*, **17(3)**: 333–343

Clark, T. and Lipset, S. (1991), 'Are social classes dying?', *International Sociology* **6(4)**: 397–410

Crompton, R. And Lyonette, C. (2007), 'Are we all working too hard? Women, men and changing attitudes to employment', in Park, A., Curtice, J., Thomson, K., Phillips, M. and Johnson, M. (eds.), *British Social Attitudes: the 23rd Report – Perspectives on a changing society*, London: Sage

Daly, M. (2000), 'A fine balance: women's labor market participation in international comparison', in Scharpf, F.W. and Schmidt, V.A. (eds.), *Welfare and work in the open economy: diverse responses to common challenges*, Oxford: Oxford University Press

Doorewaard, H., Hendrickx, J. and Verschuren, P. (2004), 'Work orientations of female returners', *Work, Employment and Society* **18(1)**: 7–27

Erikson, R. and Goldthorpe, J. (1992), *The constant flux: a study of class mobility in industrial societies*, Oxford: Clarendon Press

Esping-Andersen, G. (1990), *The three worlds of welfare capitalism*, Cambridge: Polity Press

Ferrarini, T. (2006), *Families, states and labour markets*, Cheltenham: Edward Elgar

Gallie, D. and Alm, S. (2000), 'Unemployment, gender and attitudes to work', in Gallie, D. and Paugam, S. (eds.), *Welfare regimes and the experience of unemployment in Europe*, Oxford: Oxford University Press

Gallie, D. and Paugam, S. (2002), *Social precarity and social integration*, Report written for the European Commission Directorate – General Employment, Brussels: European Opinion Research Group

Gallie, D., White, M., Cheng, Y. and Tomlinson, M. (eds.) (1998), *Restructuring the employment relationship*, Oxford: Clarendon Press

Ganzeboom, H. (2007), *Tools for deriving status measures from ISCO-88 and ISCO-68*, available at:
   http://home.fsw.vu.nl/~ganzeboom/PISA/INDE4.HTM (Accessed September 2007)
   Vrije Universiteit Amsterdam, Faculteit der Sociale Wetenschappen

Ganzeboom, H. and Treiman, D. (1996), 'Internationally comparable measures of occupational status for the 1988 International Standard Classification', *Social Science Research*, **25(3)**: 201–239

Greve, B. (2004), 'Denmark: universal or not so universal welfare state', *Social Policy and Administration*, **38(2)**: 156–169

Hakim, C. (2002), 'Lifestyle preferences as determinants of women's differentiated labor market careers', *Work and Occupations*, **29(4)**: 428–459

Halvorsen, K. (1997), 'The work ethic under challenge?', in Holmer, J. and Karlsson, J. (eds.), *Work - quo vadis?*, Aldershot: Ashgate

Hansen, M. (1997), 'The Scandinavian welfare state model. The impact of the public sector on segregations and gender equality', *Work, Employment and Society*, **11(1)**: 83–99

Hult, C. and Svallfors, S. (2002), 'Production regimes and work orientations: a comparison of six western countries', *European Sociological Review*, **18(3)**: 315–331

Jackson, P., Stafford, E., Banks, M. and Warr, P. (1983), 'Unemployment and psychological distress in young people: the moderating role of employment commitment', *Journal of Applied Psychology*, **68(3)**: 525–535

John, P. and Johnson, M. (2008), 'Is there still a public service ethos?', in Park, A., Curtice, J., Thomson, K., Phillips, M., Johnson, M. and Clery, E. (eds.), *British Social Attitudes: the 24th Report*, London: Sage

Jones, K. and Duncan, C. (1998), 'Modelling context and heterogeneity: applying multilevel models', in Scarbrough, E. and Tanenbaum, E. (eds.), *Research strategies in the social sciences: a guide to new approaches*, Oxford: Oxford University Press

Korpi, W. (2000), 'Faces of inequality: gender, class, and patterns of inequalities in different types of welfare states', *Social Politics*, **7(2)**: 127–191

Korpi, W. (2001), 'Contentious institutions: an augmented rational-actor analysis of the origins and path dependency of welfare state institutions in the western countries', *Rationality and Society*, **13(2)**: 235–283

Korpi, W. and Palme, J. (1998), 'The paradox of redistribution and the strategy of equality: welfare state institutions, inequality and poverty in the western countries', *American Sociological Review*, **63(5)**: 661–687

Kvist, J. and Ploug, N. (2003), *Active labour market policies. When do they work - and where do they fail?*, paper presented at New Challenges for Welfare State Research, The RC 19 Annual Conference, University of Toronto, 21–24 August 2003

Lincoln, J. and Kalleberg, A. (1985), 'Work organization and workforce commitment: a study of plants and employees in the U.S. and Japan', *American Sociological Review*, **50**: 738–760

Lincoln, J. and Kalleberg, A. (1990), *Culture, control, and commitment: a study of work organization and work attitudes in the United States and Japan*, Cambridge: Cambridge University Press

Lindbeck, A. (1997), 'Incentives and Social Norms in Household Behavior', *The American Economic Review*, **87(2)**: 370–377

Mandel, H. and Semyonov, M. (2003), *The prevalence of welfare state policies and gender socioeconomic inequality: a comparative analysis*, paper presented at ISA Research Committee on Social Stratification and Mobility RC28, Tokyo, Japan, March 2003

March, J. and Olsen, J. (1984), 'The new institutionalism: organizational factors in political life', *American Political Science Review*, **78(3)**: 734–749

Nelson, K. (2003), *Fighting poverty. Comparative studies on social insurance, means-tested benefits and income redistribution*, Doctoral Dissertation Series, No. 60 Thesis, Stockholm: Swedish Institute for Social Research, Stockholm University

Nelson, K. (2007), 'Universalism versus targeting: the vulnerability of social insurance and means-tested minimum income protection in 18 countries, 1990–2002', *International Social Security Review*, **60(1)**: 33–58

OECD (2004), *OECD employment outlook 2004*, Paris: Organisation for Economic Co-operation and Development

OECD (2007), *OECD employment outlook 2007*, Paris: Organisation for Economic Co-operation and Development

Pollmann-Schult, M. and Büchel, F. (2005), 'Unemployment benefits, unemployment duration and subsequent job quality', *Acta Sociologica,* **48(1)**: 21–39

Sjöberg, O. (2004), 'The role of family policy institutions in explaining gender-role attitudes: a comparative multilevel analysis of thirteen industrialized countries', *Journal of European Social Policy*, **14(2)**: 107–123

Svallfors, S., Halvorsen, K. and Andersen, G. (2001), 'Work orientations in Scandinavia: employment commitment and organisational commitment in Denmark, Norway and Sweden', *Acta Sociologica*, **44(2)**: 139–156

Waerness, K. (1984), 'The rationality of caring', *Economic and Industrial Democracy*, **5(2)**: 185–211

Waerness, K. (2003), 'Some reflections on the healthy individual, feminist care ethics, and the sociological tradition', *Sosiologisk tidsskrift*, **11(1)**: 12–22

Warr, P. (1982), 'A national study of non-financial employment commitment', *Journal of Occupational Psychology*, **55(4)**: 297–312

Acknowledgements

The *National Centre for Social Research* is grateful to the Economic and Social Research Council (ESRC) (grant number RES-501-25-5001) for their financial support which enabled us to ask the *International Social Survey Programme* (ISSP) questions reported in this chapter in Britain. Further details about ISSP can be found at www.issp.org. The views expressed are those of the author alone.

Appendix

Welfare state categorisation

The social insurance data presented in Figures 4.1 and 4.3 are from the Social Citizenship Indicator Program (SCIP), which was constructed at the Swedish Institute for Social Research, Stockholm University and is available at: https://dspace.it.su.se/dspace/handle/10102/7.

The database contains information on social rights accruing through old-age pensions, sickness, unemployment, work-accident insurance, child benefits as well as marriage subsidies in 18 countries from 1930 to 2000. The data are being extended with information on parental leave benefits and also to cover six new welfare democracies.

The welfare state "generosity" measure refers to the average benefit replacement rate across four social protection areas. The measure is made comparable by representing the benefit percentage rate of the average production worker's wage in each respective country. The data for **unemployment and sickness cash benefits** used here refer to the average net replacement rate across two types of households (a single person household and a two-person household) and for two cases of unemployment and sickness spells (one week and twenty-six weeks).

For **family benefits**, data refer to the average net replacement rate of total family benefits (including childcare leave and maternity grants, marriage subsidies, child benefits, as well as all types of earnings-related parental insurance benefits, paid to the mother, the father or both) available to a two-earner household with two children 0 and 5 years of age in relation to 52 weeks of reliance on family benefits or social assistance.

Data on **social assistance** are from the Social Assistance and Minimum Income Protection Interim Data-Set (SaMip), also based at the Swedish Institute for Social Research, Stockholm University. It contains data on social assistance and related policy programmes of last-resort regarding the level of means-tested benefits in 22 industrialised welfare democracies year-by-year for the period 1990–2005 (see also further documentation in Nelson, 2007). Data used in this study refer to the average replacement rate of social assistance as a mean of benefits available to three types of households net of taxes and excluding housing costs.

Multivariate analysis of employment commitment

The multivariate analysis technique used in this chapter was a random intercept multi-level model, using the MLwiN 2.02 statistical package. This technique is appropriate for hierarchically structured data, here individuals are clustered within countries. By this method, effects of predicting variables are correctly referred to their specific levels and the variance is separated between levels (see, for example, Jones and Duncan, 1998). All estimated models are random intercepts models, allowing average commitment to vary across countries.

Data on female labour force participation rates in 2002 (persons aged 25–54) are from OECD (2004: 303–306) and standardised unemployment rates (as an average for 2004–2005) are from OECD (2007).

Table A.1 Predictors of employment commitment across 13 countries

Variables	Men		Women	
	coefficient	s.e.	coefficient	s.e.
Intercept	3.184***	0.083	3.200***	0.062
Individual level variables (reference category in brackets)				
Age (18–34)				
35–49	-0.060	0.032	-0.045	0.036
50–59	-0.100*	0.042	-0.043	0.042
Civil status (single)				
Married/cohabiting	0.076	0.042	-0.021	0.043
Child (no child)				
Child in household	-0.067	0.036	0.008	0.049
Education (non-graduate)				
Graduate	0.204***	0.026	0.245***	0.040
Social class (unskilled worker)				
Skilled manual	0.046	0.036	-0.058	0.071
Routine non-manual	0.228***	0.052	0.248***	0.051
Lower-grade professions	0.315***	0.042	0.366***	0.046
Higher-grade professions	0.487***	0.047	0.478***	0.070
Self-employed	0.456***	0.054	0.597***	0.077
Employment status (full-time)				
Part-time worker			0.083*	0.040
Unemployed	-0.192	0.147	-0.351***	0.089
Women looking after home	n.a.	n.a.	-0.250***	0.055
Sector (private)				
Public	-0.018	0.042	0.051	0.035
Macro-level variables				
Welfare state generosity	0.930***	0.205	0.984***	0.140
Unemployment rate	-0.076***	0.014	-0.061***	0.014
Variance excluding macro variables				
Country level	0.034	0.012	0.031	0.009
Individual level	0.831	0.049	0.708	0.051
Variance including macro variables				
Country level	0.011	0.005	0.006	0.003
Individual level	0.831	0.049	0.708	0.051
Intraclass correlation coefficient: micro variables only	3.93		4.19	
Intraclass correlation coefficient: including macro variables	1.30		0.84	
Number of observations	*4182*		*4067*	

* = significant at 95% level; ** = significant at 99% level; *** = significant at 99.9% level
Estimates for unemployed people and women looking after the home relate to models excluding social class. n.a. = not applicable

5 Exploring parents' views

*Geoff Dench**

Since the middle of the last century, attitudes in Britain towards parents and parenthood have changed a great deal. Parents used to be regarded as central to society. Becoming a good citizen was seen as assisted by parenthood and by the experience of taking responsibility for others that this entailed. Indeed, civil society itself was often constructed as an extension of shared parenthood (see, for example, Young and Halsey, 1995). But it is different now. The British government still appears to regard parents as important, as affirmed in its recent Children's Plan (Department for Children, Schools and Families, 2007). However, some feel that, in practice, state policies have become increasingly interventionist towards parents and consequently "marginalise them and exclude them from their children's lives" (Family and Youth Concern, 2008: 1).

This shift in policy can be traced back to the 1960s and early 1970s, as a corollary of the radical model of meritocracy adopted to modernise British society (Dench, 2007). The Labour Party modernisers driving this process saw families as an obstacle to social mobility in the public realm, and even to good citizenship. There is a long line of left-wing authors who rail against parents, and blame them for many social ills, running from Laing (1971) to James (2002). A key assumption behind British meritocracy at the time was that the public domain of work is more fulfilling, for men and women alike, than the 'private' realm of family life.[1] Accordingly, great attention was paid to state promotion of individual freedom. Much of Harold Wilson's reworking of opportunity structures and welfare support systems consisted of measures to liberate individuals from the limiting and unwelcome demands of families – through movement away from educational selection, easier divorce and abortion, and the provision of personal rather than family or community-based entitlements to income and housing supports.

Young meritocrats rising in the public realm protected themselves from possible family interference by generating a new set of public conventions which denied that family relationships had a positive effect on values, or even

---

* Geoff Dench is a Fellow of the Young Foundation and Visiting Professor at Greenwich University.

any influence at all (for example, Barrett and McIntosh, 1982). As commentators in this generation like Joan Smith have put it, "the world of ideas exists independently of personal experience" (Smith, 1999). A 'child-free' person herself, Smith often argues that if she were a mother it would not change her views in any respects. It follows that, if the views of parents do not differ from those of non-parents, there is no compelling reason to pay attention to the values of 'parents' as such. Similar discussions have taken place in the US. But parents there have retained a more independent lobby and voice than in Britain, and so a market exists for commentaries which question these new ideas (for example, Maushart, 1999). We do not have this in Britain; and we may have a less robust understanding of our society as a result.

One danger of this shift away from the family and towards a focus on the public realm of work and formal citizenship is that we become less able to appreciate the part that parents play in contemporary society. A particular cause of anxiety is that in recent decades social surveys have adopted strict definitions of parenthood which make it hard to establish the views that parents do actually hold. This may inadvertently reinforce the idea that parents do not have any distinctive views worth knowing. A key problem arises from the now almost universal practice of defining parents as being those who live with (and have legal responsibility for) legal minors. This definition may suit administrators of state services reasonably well, but for broader analysis of the place of parents in society it has some unfortunate consequences.

Firstly, it ignores the obvious fact that, within the private realm of personal relationships, parenting does not end when children become 16 or 18. A most important stage of parenthood, which hardly figures at all in official reports, occurs as children make the difficult transition to adulthood. After this, parenthood transmutes more or less imperceptibly into *grand*parenthood, which is as much about helping one's children learn to become parents themselves as it is about doing a bit of childcare for working mothers (see Dench *et al.*, 1999, for a discussion about the main stages in grandparenting). This is the only family activity later in life which many social modernisers seem to notice – presumably as it serves public realm purposes. Secondly, this practice obscures the possibility that parental solicitude towards offspring, and any changes in values and attitudes which accompany this, may continue after the main period of parenting activities is over – in principle even for the rest of one's life (see, for example, Hrdy, 1999). This would include the effects of being a grandparent (Dench and Ogg, 2002). Such long-term effects are not detectable in surveys which define parents solely through co-residence. In the analysis of such survey data, parents of grown-up children tend to get put back into a general category of 'non-parent' respondents. As a result, any attitudes they retain as a result of being parents become mixed up with those of childless respondents, producing a blend very close to the population average. The narrow definition of parenthood may also blunt subsequent analysis and exploration. For example, as older people are more likely than younger ones to have children, the consequences of parenting experience are most likely to show up in relation to age. There is then a high probability that analysts will conclude that it is simply age, or generation, which is important, and not parenthood. In this way, parenthood as such is rendered invisible. There are also minor difficulties arising from current definitions of parenthood – such as the exclusion of those parents who do not live with their children or bear legal responsibility for them. This is not a large category. Nor does it appear to be growing just at the moment. But the experiences of parenting it provides to some people may well be valuable to them, and we need concepts that encompass this.

To avoid these pitfalls, a parent needs really to be defined as *anyone* who has or has had children. But after decades of surveys adopting more limited concepts, we no longer have much current data which is constructed on this basis. This chapter aims to begin the process of rectifying this situation, by examining whether there are any signs that contemporary parenthood has any of the effects that used to be attributed to it. Traditionally, the experience of having children, with direct responsibility for their well-being, was assumed to foster solicitous attitudes towards them and others – and indeed to have a profound effect on people's views of the world generally (see, for instance, Becker, 1981; Willets, 1993). So we will explore how far this may (still) be the case, and also how far, in a society which is now explicitly organised around the public domain and regards the private realm as having little influence on it, relationships in private life may (still) generate useful public values and attitudes. The chapter will do this by examining the views of parents and non-parents on a range of issues to do with family relationships, work and family life. What we are particularly interested to see is how parenthood interacts with other key characteristics such as age and class, and may in some situations be masked by them. We will also examine how views about family relationships and work vary between two very different groups of parents; those in couples and lone parents.[2]

Parenthood and age

Before we begin, it is worth considering how parenthood varies by age. This provides a general context for the following discussion, while also highlighting some of the limitations of what is possible in this chapter. For the purposes of Table 5.1 and subsequent tabulations, a parent is defined as someone who reports having a living child or grandchild. A lone parent is defined as a parent who is not currently living with a partner of the opposite sex (excluding widows and widowers).[3] For illustrative purposes, the table also indicates the proportions of 'parents with dependent children', the group normally identified as 'parents' in contemporary research.

The key point made by the first two rows of our table is not surprising; parenthood varies hugely by age. The childless are heavily concentrated in the youngest age group, in which just over one third are parents. By contrast, among older age groups well over four-fifths are parents. A significant minority of people are lone parents, as shown in the third row. Among the two middle age groups (35–49 and 50–64), around one seventh are lone parents (accounting for around one fifth of all parents in those age ranges). But not everyone is a parent; one fifth of 35–49 year olds are childless, as are one seventh of those aged 50 and above. Finally, as shown in the penultimate line, the people most likely to be classified as 'parents' in contemporary research are clearly those in the 35–49 age group, 61 per cent of whom have dependent children. Not surprisingly, this proportion is far lower among older age groups.

Table 5.1 Parental status, by age, 2007

	18–34	35–49	50–64	65+
% childless	67	21	15	14
% parent	33	80	85	86
% lone parents	8	16	14	7
% parents with partner	25	64	71	80
% parents with dependent child	32	61	12	1
% parents with no dependent child	1	19	73	85
Base	*929*	*1192*	*978*	*1022*

These findings reflect well-documented changing trends in parenthood. According to the latest *Social Trends* (Office for National Statistics, 2008), over the last few decades there has been a notable increase in the proportion of people who live alone (up from six per cent of the population in 1971 to 12 per cent now), or who live with their children but no partner (up from four to 12 per cent over the same period). At the same time, the average age of mothers at the birth of their first child has increased, from 24 in 1971 to 28 now (or 30 among married mothers).

Taking account of age

When comparing the views of parents and non-parents we will clearly need to take account of the close relationship between parenthood and age shown in Table 5.1. Otherwise any differences we find between parents and non-parents may simply reflect their different age profiles. Unfortunately, this limits the level of detail and complexity attainable in any analysis undertaken, because it multiplies the number of cases needed for reliable readings.

Of course, when it comes to it, 'age' itself is not a single, simple factor but a shorthand for a variety of possible influences on behaviour and values, each of which may interact with parenthood in complex ways. Two main examples are normally distinguished. On the one hand we have lifecycle factors, which constitute individual experiences encountered at different points in life – and among which becoming or being a parent is likely to figure strongly itself, perhaps in a number of different ways. Then there are cohort influences, which relate to formative, collective experiences shared by people of the same age, and which usually arise out of public rather than private situations. People socialised in the same historical period are likely as a result to share similar approaches to family life, and attitudes to parents and children.

Classifying generations

To clarify what effect parenthood might have on a person's attitudes and values, we need to try to unscramble the different contributions of lifecycle and cohort influences, and see how these may interact with parenthood. Because 'age' is commonly cited as a key determinant (or, at least, correlate) of family values and attitudes, it is something which needs to be central to our own analysis here. We cannot expect to unravel things very far with the data at present available to us. But we can do some tentative unscrambling, to help identify useful lines of enquiry.

With this in mind, we have selected four age-groupings for this analysis which should be pertinent to consideration of both lifecycle and cohort effects:

- The oldest age-category used here consists of people aged 65 or over in 2006. In lifecycle terms, this group can be seen as containing people who are (overwhelmingly) retired from work. They are entitled to wide-ranging access to state supports, and have (long since, in some cases) raised any offspring they may have produced – though many now may be involved in grandparenting. They now have some leisure and security. As a cohort we are labelling them the 'traditional' generation. This is because they were born at a time when conventional families were still treated in British social policy as the main source of personal security – with any welfare benefits channelled through such families. So these respondents share the experience of growing up at a time when the private realm was seen publicly as important.

- The next group, aged 50–64 in 2006, contains people at the peak and towards the ends of their careers, many with children moving through their teenage years and into early adulthood. Many will be 'sandwiched' between such demands and those of aged parents – and possibly resentful of this. So there may be stress in their lives. But in terms of cohort identity we are designating them as the 'choice' generation (Attias-Donfut and

Segalen, 1998). They are united historically by the fact that, whatever path they may have trodden since, traditional family life was still strong during their childhood and adolescence in the early 1940s to mid-1950s. But new welfare state supports were also opening up, boosting their opportunities as individuals. So they enjoyed maximum choice, across both the private and the public realms. This cohort corresponds with many commentators' definition of the core 'baby boomer' generation. The personal characteristics (such as revolutionary inclinations, and absorption with self) which are often attributed to 'boomers' could plausibly be an outcome of the youthful security and choice mentioned here.

- Next we have those aged 35–49. By this age, most people who are going to become parents have done so; and many will already be starting to experience the pressures of middle age mentioned for the 50–64 grouping above. But unlike the 'choice' generation, this cohort (born between the late 1950s and early 1970s) will have grown up in a period when traditional family life was being replaced as the centre of a child's universe. The family itself had become a contentious issue in British politics, and a range of legal and public welfare supports to help people escape from it was multiplying. So we see them as a 'transitional' generation.

- Finally there is the 18–34 age group. This is quite a diverse category in terms of current experience, embracing some who are still effectively living as dependent children as well as others who are well established in their careers and have growing families of their own. The minority who are parents are mainly in the early stages of that role, and are also probably the keenest within their generation to take on parenthood. So we should expect them to be quite enthusiastic about it. What they have in common publicly, though, is that they have grown up in a period (from the mid-1970s to the late 1980s) when relatively few wholly traditional families remained in Britain. Even if their own parents were married, and together, and practising a traditional sexual division of labour, many would have friends in different circumstances. They may therefore have shared a sense that conventional family life was a thing of the past, no longer to be relied on. On top of this the welfare state was finding it hard during that period to cope with all the new expectations placed on it. So they were children in a world of uncertainty, and we are calling this group the 'risk' generation.

New family values?

Traditional family life in Britain used to be geared to a world in which there was relatively limited provision of personal security by public institutions. So it revolved around conventions about how to balance self-reliance and reciprocity in the private realm. To be good citizens, people living as household units were expected to be as self-sufficient as possible. This was achieved through a sexual division of labour, whereby women were in charge of domestic matters and men served families mainly by bringing in material resources through their work in the public domain. Stability in domestic arrangements was sought through marriage, and wider security was maximised through reciprocal supports within extended families and larger kinship groups – which often overlapped with and blended into local community ties. Within this context, parenthood gave people a valued place in society which may not exist today.

From the 'traditional' to the 'risk' generation

The post-war development of the welfare state has introduced an alternative source of personal security, located in the public realm, and which has been increasingly honed to enable citizens to make their own way as free individuals, in particular as workers. New family conventions which have emerged as part of the modernisation process emphasise the centrality of personal choice, rendering marriage and prescribed sex roles out of favour.

Tables 5.2 and 5.3 present the responses to two sets of attitudinal questions relating to these matters, tabulated according to age. One set deals with the tension between domestic roles and paid work which now confronts mothers; the other compares levels of support for new, and for traditional, conventions regarding domestic relationships.

One pattern in Table 5.2 is very clear; the youngest group places more value on work and less on domesticity than the oldest, those aged 65 and over. So agreement with the 'pro-work' sentiment in the first statement, that mothers should work full-time once their youngest child goes to school, is only 15 per cent among the over 65s, half the proportion found among the youngest generation (34 per cent of whom agree). But it is not the case that support for more traditional beliefs incrementally increases as we move from each group to the next oldest. Indeed, in most cases the 'fault-line' lies between our two oldest groups; the 'choice' and 'traditional' generations. The most extreme example relates to the view that what women really want is "a home and children". While 43 per cent of the 'traditional' generation agree with this, only 26 per cent of the 'choice' generation do so, little different to the proportion of the 'risk' generation who take the same view (28 per cent). In fact, on most of the statements shown in the table, the difference in responses between the 'traditional' and 'choice' generations is greater than the difference between the 'choice' and 'risk' generations, the youngest in our analysis. This finding perhaps demonstrates the radical character of the 'choice' generation, who (still) manifestly take a different line from the 'traditional' generation, after nearly half a century, even though only a few years stand between many of them.

BRITISH SOCIAL ATTITUDES

Table 5.2 Attitudes towards work and domestic life, by generation, 2006

	Risk (18–34)	Transitional (35–49)	Choice (50–64)	Traditional (65+)
% agree with pro-work value				
Women should work outside the home full-time after the youngest child starts school	34	24	15	15
% agree with pro-domestic values				
A pre-school child is likely to suffer if his or her mother works	33	30	38	43
All in all, family life suffers when the woman has a full-time job	27	36	36	45
If a couple with children divorce, the children should normally live with the mother for most of the time	16	19	26	37
Being a housewife is just as fulfilling as working for pay	41	40	41	55
A job is all right, but what most woman really want is a home and children	28	24	26	43
% agree strongly with pro-domestic value				
Watching children grow up is life's greatest joy	31	28	32	36
Base range	*430–777*	*543–910*	*443–772*	*427–734*

Table 5.3 reveals a broadly similar pattern when it comes to attitudes relating to marriage and domestic partnerships. Support for traditional views is highest among the 'traditional' generation. For example, approval for the proposition that "marriage is still the best kind of relationship" stands at 84 per cent among this generation, then falls to 62 per cent among the 'choice' generation (and continues right down to 38 per cent for the 'risk' generation). However, this pattern is unusual; as in Table 5.2, on all other questions the difference between the 'traditional' and 'choice' generations is the largest, and in some cases quite considerable. Thus 52 per cent of the oldest group agree that "married couples make better parents", compared to just 26 per cent of the 'choice' generation.

These two tables confirm that age does seem to explain a lot of variation in how people think about these issues. But the picture changes somewhat, and becomes quite complex, when we bring in the factor of parenthood, too.

Table 5.3 Attitudes towards new and traditional family life, by generation, 2006

	Risk (18–34)	Transitional (35–49)	Choice (50–64)	Traditional (65+)
% agree with pro-choice/new family values				
If a couple with children divorce, the children should normally live with the parent best able to look after them	62	60	59	43
Children could be brought up just as well by their mother and her new partner as they could by their mother and father	48	40	34	17
With so many marriages ending in divorce these days, couples who get married take a big risk	34	29	34	40
% agree with pro-marriage/ traditional family values				
Even though it might not work out for some people, marriage is still the best kind of relationship	38	43	62	84
Marriage gives couples more financial security than living together	51	55	64	81
Married couples make better parents than unmarried ones	22	17	26	52
It should be harder than it is now for couples with children under 18 to get divorced	26	25	29	46
Base range	*665–777*	*793–910*	*689–772*	*623–734*

Does parenthood make a difference?

Table 5.4 shows what happens when the data for Table 5.2 are divided between parents (shown on the right-hand side of the table) and the childless (shown to the left of the parents' column). The main consequence of this split is that it reveals that parents' attitudes tend to favour domesticity more than those of non-parents. But this is not a uniform effect across all generations, principally because of interaction between parenthood and cohort factors. The resulting pattern can, we think, be summarised in terms of a few general principles.

The first is that when parents and childless respondents are split, the gap between responses of the 'traditional' and 'choice' generations increases among the childless, but decreases among parents. For example, the gap between the 'traditional' and 'choice' generations in agreement with the proposition that being a housewife is fulfilling stands at 21 percentage points, compared with just 12 percentage points among parents. This is a consistent effect, which is quite strong for some variables.[4]

Our second general observation is that the spread of responses between generations is generally greater among the childless than among parents. To take a particularly strong example of this, the difference in support for the idea that family life suffers if women work among parents is only eight percentage points (43 per cent agree among the 'traditional' generation, to 35 per cent among the 'risk' generation). But the equivalent gap is some 37 percentage points among those who are childless (59 per cent down to 22 per cent). The resulting overall impression is therefore of greater stability and uniformity of attitudes among parents. Significantly, 'traditional' parents emerge as being more modern in their views than childless 'traditional' respondents; for no age differences of attitudes among parents here are very great. This suggests that parents may be united by their similar personal experiences, and concern for children's well-being; while the childless for their part may be more divided, perhaps because they remain more influenced by different public ideologies dominant at formative stages in their lives. The gulf between the 'traditional' and 'choice' generations, that is, between people growing up before and after the burgeoning of the post-war welfare state, appears as a major fault-line among childless respondents, on almost all variables. True, there is also a gap between parents in these generations; but this seems to be moderated by common personal experience. To sum this up, perhaps lifecycle effects related to parenthood over ride cohort differences among parents, but for childless people cohort influences remain strong.

The findings in this table also prompt questions about how far we can treat parenthood as an independent variable, rooted in personal experience, and how far we need to take into consideration other influences that might drive parenthood itself. In the last row in Table 5.4, about the joys of watching children grow up, the enthusiasm shown by young parents far exceeds that expressed even by 'traditional' parents. (The support shown for "being a housewife", a little higher in the table, is almost as great.) To start with, it is obvious that there must be a strong lifecycle effect operating here, presumably linked to having young children in the household.[5] But this is surely compounded by the probability that people who become parents when young will include many of those in their generation who are most strongly drawn to parenthood.[6] In this respect it is useful to remember Catherine Hakim's thesis that in all societies there will be people who are unlikely to respond to pressures to give priority to public realm activities like 'work', over the private domain of family (Hakim, 2000, 2004). It would be impossible from the data now available to unscramble how much of the response given by parents can be attributed to the experience of being a parent, and how much may arise out of deeper predispositions which create a desire to become a parent. But in the longer run these are certainly important questions to consider.

Table 5.4 Attitudes towards work and domestic life, by age/generation and parenthood

	Childless				Parents			
	Risk	Trans.	Choice	Trad.	Risk	Trans.	Choice	Trad.
	18–34	35–49	50–64	65+	18–34	35–49	50–64	65+
% agree								
Mother should work full time after child at school	38	27	19	15	26	23	14	14
Family life suffers when woman has full-time job	22	38	35	59	35	35	36	43
After divorce kids should live with mother	11	16	20	45	23	20	27	36
Pre-school child suffers if mother works	32	29	35	49	33	31	39	42
Being housewife as fulfilling as paid work	37	36	35	56	49	42	42	54
Job okay, but woman wants home and children	26	21	25	42	32	25	27	43
% agree strongly								
Watching children grow is life's greatest joy	18	21	18	35	55	30	34	37
Base range	*248–441*	*124–200*	*76–142*	*59–101*	*182–335*	*419–710*	*367–629*	*368–633*

When a similar break-down to that in Table 5.4 is carried out for the data presented in Table 5.3, regarding family values, the resulting pattern is similar but less clear. This is probably due in part to a stronger rooting of these values in cohort ideology, so that parenting experience has less purchase.

Class values

We turn now to examine the interaction of parenthood with class. Occupation is significant because work now provides a citizen's best chance to make a valuable contribution to society, and be valued by it. The type of work that people do strongly influences their social standing and the level of economic security they live with. However, the notion of class embraces a range of factors or influences, and we need to unpick some of these before we begin.

The most important dimension of class for present purposes concerns the relative satisfaction available to people in the public and private realms. People in high-status jobs, seen as important to society and often more interesting, are likely to value the public realm more highly than the private. People in lower-status jobs, on the other hand, are more likely to find their satisfaction in family life. This should not been seen as just a matter of 'class determination' of family values. It operates both ways, with some interaction between the two in the form of self-selection. For in a society with a reasonable amount of social mobility, those most keen on the world of work will try to move into higher-status jobs, while those less keen, and with higher opinions of ordinary family life, will be more likely to settle for a humbler occupation. The lifestyles of working-class people in Britain have often been described as family-centred – in particular as involving frequent contact with relatives. Park and Roberts note that "respondents in working-class occupations who had non-resident adult children were significantly more likely to see them at least once a week than were those in middle-class occupations" (Park and Roberts, 2002: 193). It may well be that such behaviour and values are to some extent a direct and specific consequence of the greater enthusiasm with which they have embraced parenthood.

Table 5.5 examines this interaction by looking at attitudes to the family and work, and seeing how parents and non-parents in different classes vary in their views. We have grouped people into three broad classes based upon their current or most recent occupation: 'professionals', 'intermediate workers' and 'routine workers'.[7] The results indicate a broad class pattern, whereby professional and managerial workers do indeed appear more likely than manual workers to attach more importance to work, and less to domestic roles. But there are, of course, variations within this. Taking the explicitly pro-work proposition that mothers should work full-time when children start school, we can see that there is very little difference in class terms among childless workers. However, while all parents register clearly lower levels of agreement with this view than do childless respondents, parents in routine manual occupations are the least likely to agree.

There are equivalent differences for 'pro-domestic' values. Thus, with the statement that being a housewife is fulfilling, there are no significant class differences at all among the childless, around two-fifths of whom agree. But among parents, those in professional occupations are substantially less likely than either those in intermediate non-manual occupations or those in manual jobs to agree (35, 47 and 53 per cent respectively). In fact, parents in professional jobs are less likely to agree with the view that being a housewife is fulfilling than non-parents in the same sorts of jobs. This contrasts with the other occupational groups included in the table, among whom parents are more likely to agree than non-parents. But for professional parents there is actually a slight drop in agreement, reflecting in part the stress and conflicting feelings experienced by many high-status workers when faced with demands on their time (and challenges to their interesting careers) from family life. All the other variables here share a simpler pattern. Its two defining features are less support for domestic values the higher the job status of the respondent, coupled with higher levels of support among parents than among the childless.[8]

Table 5.5 Attitudes towards work and domestic life, by class and parenting status

	Childless			Parents		
	Prof.	Inter.	Routine	Prof.	Inter.	Routine
% agree with pro-work value						
A mother should work full-time after the youngest child starts school	35	29	31	27	18	14
% agree with pro-domestic values						
Being a housewife is just as fulfilling as working for pay	40	39	38	35	47	53
A job is okay, but a woman wants home and children	17	26	32	18	35	37
After divorce kids should live with the mother	8	18	21	16	28	31
% agree strongly with pro-domestic value						
Watching children grow up is life's greatest joy	16	22	22	31	38	38
Base range	*164–270*	*189–325*	*131–241*	*345–552*	*539–946*	*429–757*

Another important dimension of class, less easy to assess or measure than social status, is that of economic security. The issue here has become complicated, however, by the current welfare system. Basically, high-status jobs tend to be more secure as well as more highly rewarded. This is why traditional working-class culture was more attached to marriage, and the security it provided, than middle-class culture (Dench *et al.*, 2006). This would also lead us to expect that contemporary professional workers would be the happiest to adopt new family conventions which value personal choice more than marriage conventions.

But it no longer follows that people at the bottom of the scale are the least secure. The state now provides security, because the welfare system operates to redistribute resources from the most secure to those whom it defines as least well off. However, those receiving support may do so at the cost of some social status. For better-off people, who give to others through the state, redistribution is a source of additional social esteem and satisfaction. In all cultures, supporting and giving to others imparts superior moral status, and gives people the feeling of making a valuable contribution to society. And in this respect the welfare state may now operate as a form of charitable 'giving' between classes. (see, for example, chapter 5 in Dench *et al.*, 2006). This is probably why the professional classes are the most enthusiastic upholders of welfarist values. For the *recipients* of benefits, however, it may confer or confirm social inferiority. So, lower down the social scale, feelings about welfare become more mixed, and those people who are willing to derive their income and security from public welfare may be those already at or near the bottom. People in the middle may be more inclined to 'hang on to self-respect' by struggling to manage without public help, and to rely instead on private ties of family. So the least secure (and most sceptical about the welfare state, from which they derive neither enhanced status *nor* much material help) are probably now those in 'intervening' occupational categories.

Table 5.6 explores this by looking at the effects of class and parenthood on attitudes relating to family values and relationships.

Table 5.6 Attitudes towards new and traditional family life, by class and parenting status

	Childless			Parents		
	Prof.	Inter.	Routine	Prof.	Inter.	Routine
% agree with new family values						
One parent can bring up a child as well as two	48	51	51	28	37	49
A mother and new partner can raise a child just as well as parents	51	43	35	30	36	33
% sympathetic to welfare values*	46	26	33	43	30	34
% agree with traditional values						
Marriage is still the best kind of relationship	40	44	41	60	61	58
Married couples make better parents	23	34	27	25	30	28
Divorce should be harder where children are under 16	23	30	27	26	30	39
Base range	*243–270*	*294–325*	*200–241*	*495–552*	*829–946*	*633–757*

*This is derived from the welfarism scale, which has been used to group respondents into one of three equally sized categories: sympathetic, average and hostile

Here we find a weaker relationship with class than that found in Table 5.5, reflecting the greater complexity of possible connections. Firstly, as hinted earlier, the responses of different groups of workers do not necessarily fall along a simple class 'gradient'; this reflects the dual nature of economic security these days. Thus professional workers show the greatest attachment to welfarism, and intermediate workers the least. But there is little difference here, in parent status terms, between parents and childless respondents. On some issues, though, notably whether "one parent can bring up a child as well as two" and "marriage is still the best kind of relationship", all parents stand out as more traditional, while all non-parents are neo-conventional. On a few issues the effect of parenthood is class-specific. Being (and this may mean 'becoming') a parent appears, for example, to have a dampening effect on professional workers' ideas that a mother and new partner can raise a child just as well as parents. On some other issues, however, neither class factors nor parenthood seem to have much effect.

Couples and lone parents

So far we have seen that both age and class provide a useful way of examining differences between parents and non-parents. But this ignores the fact that in Britain we now have effectively two overlapping but nevertheless divergent parenting (sub-)cultures – that of parents living in couples, and that of lone parents. Where these groups are lumped together the differences between them confuse the analysis of family culture issues. So in this next section we will attempt to separate out these two groups.

Changes to the welfare regime in the late 1960s and early 1970s made it easier for mothers to manage without the support of a co-resident partner; and during the final quarter of the 20th century the number of children being raised in lone parent households – almost entirely by lone mothers – grew steadily. So alongside the traditional model of support for mothers through private realm relationships – that is, from conjugal partners and other family members – we also have a system of public funding. As might be expected, lone parents and those living with partners do not see eye-to-eye on the viability and desirability of this development – nor indeed on the modernisation of family life generally. Table 5.7 contains responses to a selection of questions which have a bearing on such issues. Respondents are divided here into three categories – those with no children, lone parents, who may or may not be living with their children, and parents with partners. In addition to looking at responses to some of the questions already considered in earlier tables, the table also shows the extent to which the different groups have views that are particularly sympathetic or hostile when it comes to welfare. These are measured by a welfarism scale, more details of which can be found in Appendix I of this report.

As Table 5.7 shows, lone parents and parents with partners do indeed have very different views on these issues. In spite of the relative youth of childless respondents, it is lone parents, and not the childless, who occupy the more radical, anti-traditional end of the spectrum. Thus, although a greater proportion of childless respondents than parents with partners (50 and 35 per cent respectively) argue that one parent can bring up a child as well as two, this view is held by almost six in ten (57 per cent) lone parents. Similarly, lone parents are the most likely to agree that getting married is "a big risk", that one parent can bring up a child as well as two, or that the parent–child bond is stronger than that between couples. They are also the most likely to *disagree* with the view that marriage gives couples more financial security, and (perhaps as a measure of their agreement with the shift of personal supports into the public realm) have the most sympathetic view of the welfare state – on which, of course, a significant proportion of them depend.

Table 5.7 Attitudes towards new and traditional family life, by parenting status

	Parenting status		
	Childless	**Lone parent**	**Parent with partner**
% agree with traditional family values			
Married couples make better parents	27	21	30
Marriage gives couples more financial security	60	49	64
% agree with new family values			
One parent can bring up a child as well as two	50	57	35
Getting married is a big risk these days	35	47	30
Parent-child relationship is stronger than between any couples	42	60	39
% hostile to welfare values*	23	19	23
% sympathetic to welfare values*	34	42	33
Base range	*779–886*	*454–542*	*1521–1768*

*This is derived from the welfarism scale, which has been used to group respondents into one of three equally sized categories: sympathetic, average and hostile

It should be noted at this point that not all of the variables used here do have an unambiguously radical dimension. The statements referring to financial security (getting married is a big risk, and "marriage gives couples more financial security") do not necessarily mean the same thing to participants in the two different parenting cultures. In the 1980s, questions like this about marriage and security were basically addressing the fact that *un*married (or 'common-law') mothers then were still concerned that they could find themselves in hardship if their partners walked out on them (see, for example, Witherspoon, 1985). Marriage was still seen as giving women some protection, and still is today by some women. But 20 years later, for many women from poorer backgrounds, the issue is about access to welfare benefits. If you get married, you may find yourself tied to a man who does not or cannot provide for you (de Waal, 2008). So it may be better – less risky – to be dependent on the state.

Perhaps the most significant measure in this table is the one summarising attitudes on welfare issues. This matters because responses to it mirror political tensions over lone parenting. Parents in couples are clearly less attached to the current welfare regime than lone parents. This could reflect the fact that some poorer working parents, themselves struggling to make ends meet, feel resentment towards people they see as choosing to live off state handouts.[10] Certainly, previous *British Social Attitudes* surveys have found that there is concern about the perceived 'unfairness' of people benefiting from services that they have not contributed towards (Sefton, 2005). Of course, parents with partners fall into a number of different categories. Perhaps the most important are those who are married to their partner and those who are cohabiting, with the former tending to be considerably older than the latter (Barlow *et al.*, 2007). If we examine the views of these groups separately, there are only two issues, that of married couples making better parents, and marriage offering financial security, where their views differ more than we would expect given their age differences. This is not, perhaps, surprising, in that cohabiting respondents are almost by definition those who do not (yet) regard marriage as better.

There is a possible dilemma here for policy makers. The ultimate justification for a system of centralised, personalised social welfare, not operating through local communities and family groups, is that it increases the mobility and efficiency of labour, both occupationally and geographically – hence the pressures placed on lone parents to work, and on taxpayers to accept that the overall system is efficient and cost-effective. However, current government strategies may be too optimistic. They assume implicitly that lone parents who rely on public benefits to survive must be equally committed to participating in the public realm as workers. But when we look at their responses to the set of issues summarised in Table 5.8, it quickly becomes clear that they are not.

The key finding in this table, which if replicated in other studies would have important implications for social policy and our understanding of parenthood, is that being a parent seems extremely important for lone parents – and especially for lone mothers. This group records a low level of support for women working full-time when children start school, and the highest levels of approval for many of the propositions valuing domestic life. All these effects are even stronger than they appear here, as the tabulation does not control for age. For while lone parents are generally younger than parents with partners, their attitudes are more traditional and so in many respects 'older'.

Perhaps not surprisingly, the table also shows that the views of fathers and mothers living in couples are generally more similar than the views of parents living apart. (Men's responses can be deduced roughly from the figures given here, assuming that they will lie about as far on one side of the total figure as women's lie to the other.) So among lone parents there are manifest disparities between the views of men and women. To take responses to the first question, the view that mothers should work full-time when children start school, 17 per cent of lone mothers agree, around half the rate found among lone fathers (32 per cent of whom agreed). Frequent divergence of opinion might be part of the reason why lone parents are living separately in the first place. But what is likely to be of equal importance is that living separately allows differences of opinion to survive and flourish. Perhaps sharing the experience of parenting is linked with shared attitudes towards it. Living together encourages (mutual) accommodation.

Table 5.8 Attitudes towards work and domestic life, by parenting status

	Parenting status					
	Childless		Lone parents		Parents with partners	
	All	Women	All	Women	All	Women
% agree with pro-work value						
A mother should work full-time after the youngest child starts school	31	33	23	17	18	18
% agree with pro-domestic values						
A pre-school child suffers if his/her mother works	30	28	34	32	35	29
Family life suffers when a woman has a full-time job	30	26	33	33	38	39
After divorce kids should live with the mother	16	16	29	33	26	27
Being a housewife is just as fulfilling as working for pay	39	41	44	48	47	53
A job is okay, but a woman wants home and children	26	23	33	34	31	32
% agree strongly						
Watching children grow up is life's greatest joy	20	21	39	42	36	36
Base range	*508–886*	*237– 413*	*301–542*	*203–368*	*1036– 1768*	*571–985*

Parents with partners and lone parents also differ in the extent to which they feel happy with their lives, and their family life in particular. This may, of course, reflect the trials and tribulations of bringing up children on one's own, as well as the difficulties of negotiating arrangements with a child's other parent. It might also partly reflect the contradiction we have found between lone parents' sentiments that strongly value home and private life, and their close attachment to the state – on which quite a number are materially dependent – with its attendant pressures on them to prioritise work. But whatever the cause, while nearly seven in ten (68 per cent) parents with partners say they are "very" or "completely" happy with their family life, the same applies to only 43 per cent of lone parents (and 55 per cent of the childless). The same is true in relation to happiness in general; while 56 per cent of parents with partners say they are very or completely happy in general, only 35 per cent of lone parents feel the same way (as do 48 per cent of those without children). So there are clearly issues here, which impinge on the quality of life of a large number of parents and children, which require further analysis in their own right.

Conclusions

Much of the discussion here is inevitably tentative, and in some ways we are ending up with more questions than answers. But there does seem enough data to indicate in general terms that parenthood *does* appear to have some effects on people's attitudes and values that are not just attributable to other factors such as age and class. In fact, it is arguable that the real question is not whether being a parent influences people's attitudes. It should be, rather, in view of the way that social analysis has neglected consideration of parenting influences, how much of the lifecycle dimension of ageing, and the lifestyle aspect of class is produced by the direct or indirect influences of parenthood itself.

This point may appear as rather academic. But it does have serious political and policy implications. As the data presented here suggest, many parents are out of step with recent social modernisation. They do, however, still have legitimacy within the political system, in that no government would be happy to visibly disregard their opinions. So if inconvenient sentiments can be attributed to age or class, rather than parenthood, perhaps life is made easier for governments. In recent years, senior politicians have made quite hostile comments about old, working-class people. In April 2000, Clive Soley, then chairman of the Parliamentary Labour Party, told a party strategy meeting that old age pensioners were "predominantly Conservative", leading to a number of condemnations of them by other MPs as being "like Alf Garnett" (see Furedi, 2001). This may help to draw attention away from discontented or dissident parents.

There may be a lack of representation of parents' views in Britain that needs to be addressed – although Conservative politicians have already started to rectify this (see Report of the Social Justice Policy Group, 2007). But no party, even the Conservatives, can do this successfully without explicitly acknowledging the importance of parenthood. And perhaps a factor behind the weakness of parents' voices at the moment could paradoxically be the *increase* of opportunities brought by social modernisation for women to participate directly in the public realm. For the women best placed and most inclined to benefit from this have been disproportionately young and childless, and thus do not necessarily speak for mothers. In more traditional times, mothers could be confident of representation in public discussions because husbands were primed to listen to them and act on what they heard. And childless women, too, took their cues from mothers. But we now have many commentators who believe that they know all they need to, and may refuse to listen. Joan Smith has an answer ready for those who ask her whether, as a childfree person, she can understand children and their needs. "Personally, whenever anyone starts suggesting I know nothing about children, I point out that I was a child for quite a long time" (Smith, 2005). But our findings suggest that we *do* need to pay more attention to the views of parents and we cannot assume they are the same as those held by non-parents. Of course, it is also clear that not all parents are the same. In particular, we need to look in more detail at the different attitudes and values held by the two main parenting groups in contemporary Britain; parents with partners and lone parents.

Notes

1. For a discussion of some of the issues, see Brown, 2007.
2. This chapter is the beginning of our investigation of these issues, as we have only collected a limited amount of data so far. The findings are mainly drawn from the 2006 *British Social Attitudes* survey (unless otherwise indicated, this is where the most pertinent questions were asked most recently).
3. On most measures, widows and widowers have similar views to elderly parents with partners. This is perhaps not surprising, as most widowed people maintain strong relations with the kin of their children's other parent – and this may be different from the behaviour of parents who no longer, or never did, live with a surviving other parent.
4. The childless 'traditional' generation has a relatively small base; so care is needed in drawing inferences from some of these figures. But the effect is strong and consistent enough to merit attention.
5. And this is very similar to the burst of enthusiasm shown for their role by grandparents in the first years following the birth of a grandchild. See Dench and Ogg, 2002.
6. There are other possibilities. Such figures might indicate some longer-term 'cohort' bounce-back towards more positive evaluations of domestic life, with young parents in the vanguard.
7. The 'professionals' category includes those in higher managerial and professional occupations, as well as in lower professional and higher technical occupations. 'Intermediate workers' includes lower managerial jobs, supervisors, small

employers and the self-employed. 'Routine' includes lower technical occupations, semi-routine and routine jobs. Further information about NS-SEC, the classification schema upon which this is based, can be found in Appendix I of this report.

8. Note that responses to the question of where children should live after a divorce are being used here as indicative of traditional feelings about sex roles.
9. For a critical commentary on this, see Phillips, 1999.
10. See Dench *et al.*, 2006: 208. A number of couples in this study argued that lone parents were undermining the implicit reciprocity informing the welfare state, by taking out much more than they put in. It may be growth in such attitudes as these that is causing the loss of support for welfarist values in recent years.

References

Attias-Donfut, C. and Segalen, M. (1998), *Grands-Parents: La famille a travers les generations*, Paris: Odile Jacob

Barlow, A., Burgoyne, C., Clery, E. and Smithson, J. (2007), 'Cohabitation and the law; myths, money and the media', in Park, A., Curtice, J., Thomson, K., Phillips, M., Johnson, M. and Clery, E., (eds.), *British Social Attitudes: the 24th Report*, London: Sage

Barrett, M. and McIntosh, M. (1982), *The Anti-Social Family*, London: Verso/New Left Books

Becker, G. S. (1981), *Treatise on the Family*, Boston: Harvard University Press

Brown, B. (2007), Resolving the conflict between family and meritocracy, in Dench, G. (ed.), *The Rise and Rise of Meritocracy*, Oxford: Blackwell

de Waal, A. (2008), *Second Thoughts on the Family*, London: Civitas

Dench, G. (ed.) (2007), *The Rise and Rise of Meritocracy*, Oxford: Blackwell

Dench, G., Gavron, K. and Young, M. (2006), *The New East End*, London: Profile

Dench, G., Ogg, J. and Thomson, K. (1999), 'The role of grandparents', in Jowell, R., Curtice, J., Park, A. and Thomson, K. (eds.), *British Social Attitudes: the 16th Report*, Aldershot: Ashgate

Dench, G. and Ogg, J. (2002), *Grandparenting in Britain*, London: Institute of Community Studies

Department for Children, Schools and Families (2007), *The Children's Plan: Building brighter futures*, London: Department for Children, Schools and Families

Family and Youth Concern (2008), *Family Bulletin*, **130**, Winter 2007/2008

Furedi, F. (2001), 'British racism; a new original sin.' Spiked-online, available at www.spiked-online.com/Articles/00000002D092.htm

Hakim, C. (2000), *Work-Lifestyle Choices in the 21st Century: Preference theory*, Oxford: OUP

Hakim, C. (2004), *Models of the Family in Modern Societies*, Aldershot: Ashgate

Hrdy, S. (1999), *Mother Nature*, London: Chatto & Windus

James, O. (2002), *They F*** You Up: How to survive family life*, London: Bloomsbury

Laing, R.D. (1971), *The Politics of the Family and other essays*, New York: Pantheon

Maushart, S. (1999), *The Mask of Motherhood: How becoming a mother changes everything and why we pretend it doesn't*, New York: The New Press

Office for National Statistics (2008), *Social Trends 38*, Basingstoke: Palgrave Macmillan

Park, A. and Roberts, C. (2002), 'The ties that bind', in Park, A., Curtice, J., Thomson, K., Jarvis, L. and Bromley, C. (eds.), *British Social Attitudes: the 19th Report*, London: Sage

Phillips, M. (1999), *The Sex-Change Society*, London: Social Market Foundation

Sefton, T. (2005), 'Give and take: public attitudes to redistribution', in Park, A., Curtice, J., Thomson, K., Bromley, C., Phillips, M. and Johnson, M. (eds.), *British Social Attitudes: the 22nd Report*, London: Sage

Smith, J. (1999), 'Women v. Real Women', *Guardian*, 2 March, available at http://www.guardian.co.uk/world/1999/mar/02/gender.uk

Smith, J. (2005), 'I am over 40 and childless. Sorry, Doris', *The Independent on Sunday*, 18th September, available at http://www.independent.co.uk/opinion/commentators/joan-smith/joan-smith-i-am-over-40-and-childless-sorry-doris-507304.html

Social Justice Policy Group, Chair S. Callan (2007), *Breakthrough Britain: Ending the costs of social breakdown, Volume 1: Family Breakdown - Policy Recommendations to the Conservative Party*, available at http://www.centreforsocialjustice.org.uk/default.asp?pageRef=226

Willetts, D. (1993), *The Family*, London: WHSmith

Witherspoon, S. (1985), 'Sex roles and gender issues', in Jowell, R. and Witherspoon, S. (eds.), *British Social Attitudes: the 1985 Report*, Aldershot: Gower

Young, M. and Halsey, A. H. (1995), *Family and Community Socialism*, London: IPPR

Zaretski, E. (1988), 'The place of the family in the origin of the welfare state', in Held, D., *States and Societies*, Cambridge: Polity

Acknowledgements

The author would like to thank the Hera Trust and the Robert Gavron Charitable Trust for their generous support of the programme of research on which this chapter is based, although the views expressed are those of the author alone.

6 Pay more, fly less?
Changing attitudes to air travel

*Sarah Butt and Andrew Shaw**

The future for flying is under intense scrutiny. Fuelled by rising prosperity and lower fares, travel by air has increased substantially in recent decades. The number of passengers travelling through UK airports is 10 times greater than 40 years ago. Until recently, the increase appeared inexorable: passenger numbers more than doubled in the last 15 years. In 2007, as many as 216 million passengers departed from or arrived at UK civilian airports (Department for Transport, 2008a).

As recently as 2003, the British government projected continuing rapid growth in demand and, in the light of this, set out a strategic framework for the long-term development of airport capacity in the UK (Department for Transport, 2003). This policy framework was presented as a "measured and balanced approach" to facilitating more air travel while protecting the environment. Forecasts of demand indicated that, without capacity constraints, passenger numbers could be expected to double or treble by 2030 (*ibid*: 21).[1] The extra capacity envisaged in the 2003 White Paper was estimated to meet the bulk of the increased demand to fly. As such, this policy framework was contentious: could it be practical, desirable and sustainable to allow air travel to grow to this scale?[2]

Continuing rapid increases in air travel clearly represent a cause for concern to climate change experts. By 2030, such growth is projected to more than double carbon dioxide emissions from UK aviation (Cairns and Newson, 2006). This is on top of CO_2 emissions having already nearly doubled between 1990 and 2000. By 2050, emissions from planes could account for roughly half the UK's total CO_2 budget (Tyndall Centre for Climate Change Research, 2005; Owen and Lee, 2006).

Until recently, there was no indication that large numbers of people were reining in their desire to fly, for this reason or any other. Indeed, in the years immediately following the White Paper's publication, demand further increased

* Sarah Butt is a Senior Researcher at the *National Centre for Social Research* and is Co-Director of the *British Social Attitudes* survey series. Andrew Shaw is a Research Group Director at the *National Centre for Social Research*.

in line with predictions. In 2004 alone, terminal passenger numbers rose by eight per cent. UK residents continued to embark upon more and more flights abroad, while, in 2007, a record number of visitors flew into the UK (Department for Transport, 2008a). Flying is something that many now take for granted and evidence from focus groups suggests that holidaymakers would be reluctant to give up the opportunities for air travel afforded in an era of cheap flights (Miller *et al.*, 2007).

However, there are some indications that the market for air travel may be starting to undergo a change. As the White Paper acknowledged:

> ... [the market] might mature more rapidly than we expect, causing the rate of growth to slow more quickly than forecast. Or the cost of flying may prove to be higher than projected ... due to rising oil prices or the costs of tackling global warming being higher than expected. (Department for Transport, 2003: 23)

Since 2004 the rate of increase in passenger numbers has fallen markedly. By August 2007, the annual rate of increase in trips aboard by UK residents was down to one per cent. In addition, the numbers of passengers on domestic flights is no longer rising. After 14 years of continuous annual growth, airlines recorded fewer domestic passengers in 2006 and 2007 compared with 2005 (Department for Transport, 2008a). Thus, aviation was growing more slowly even before fares started to rise significantly.

By the second half of 2008, higher fuel prices were having a substantial effect on the air travel industry. Though many airlines were initially protected from the surge in oil prices by hedge contracts for aeroplane fuel, the unfolding impact on prices and profits is expected to become highly visible to flyers. Fuel has generally accounted for no more than one third of operating costs. Modest rises in fuel prices have not prevented the lowering of fares by still profitable airlines. In July 2008, however, a leading budget airline announced that, with fuel costs having doubled within months and now amounting to nearly half of operating costs, it had become loss-making. Overall, reductions are anticipated in the number of both airlines and routes. The additional impact of the anticipated economic downturn in the UK is yet to be seen. However, it is likely that this will further reduce demand for flights, at least in the short term.

It is possible, of course, that economic factors will curtail air travel only temporarily. High levels of growth in air travel were restored quickly after Britain's two most recent recessions, as well as after the shock of 11th September 2001. The Civil Aviation Authority has argued that the recent slowdown in demand for air travel is similarly cyclical rather than indicative of a longer-term trend (CAA, 2008). However, compared with previous downturns in the market the policy context is now quite different. Following commitments to make massive reductions in carbon emissions by 2050, the government faces political pressure to limit the impact of flying on climate change. Though air travel contributes a relatively modest proportion of current emissions – six to seven per cent (Hansard, 2007) – forecasted growth in these emissions would raise the requirements for savings from other sectors to levels few judge attainable. Hence, the UK government and the European Union are pursing policies which will change the context in which airlines operate.

In February, 2007, UK Air Passenger Duty (APD) was doubled. This was followed by an announcement that APD would be replaced in November 2009 by an aviation duty levied on a per plane rather than a per passenger basis. At the time of writing, this remains under discussion, Nevertheless, the intention of policy is clear: the government intends the new duty to send "environmental signals and ensure aviation makes a greater contribution to covering its environmental costs" (HM Treasury, 2007: 123). While the new duty may in part prompt greater efficiency in the use of fuel and flights, it seems likely that, over time, the cost per passenger will also rise. The inclusion of airlines within Europe's carbon emissions trading scheme is likely to have a further impact on the cost of air travel. Inclusion is planned for 2012, though, again, the policy remains under discussion, having attracted interest from a number of non-EU countries who have voiced concerns over the policy and its application to their airlines.

It seems likely that air fares will rise as a result. Predicting the effect of such policy changes on consumers is difficult, especially given the fact that the real cost of flying has been falling for decades. Further declines in the non-fuel costs of air travel are predicted to continue, albeit at a declining rate, until 2020 (Department for Transport, 2007). This may help to offset cost increases for environmental reasons and limit the extent to which these are passed on to consumers through higher fares. However, combined recent developments certainly raise the possibility that air fares will have to rise considerably.

This, in turn, is likely to exert downward pressure on demand for flights. Certainly, there is widespread acceptance that falling prices over recent years have made a significant contribution to the increase in demand for air travel. It should be borne in mind that demand may be less responsive to price increases, as people become used to travelling by air and are reluctant to cut back on trips. Nevertheless, a range of estimates suggest that a 10 per cent change in fares would affect demand for flights by around five to 15 per cent (Cairns and Newson, 2006). Extending this analysis, calculations by Cairns and Newson (2006) further suggest that "an additional charge of £10 to £25 per ticket per year might be sufficient to stabilise the demand for flying".

How might the public react to increasing air fares? On the one hand, such developments could be so unpopular with the travelling public that political pressures start to build to prevent large fare rises, or at least to restrain the rate of increase. On the other hand, it is possible that higher fares and other measures to limit the growth in flying would actually be supported, or at least widely accepted, as a necessary change in an era of rapid man-made climate change (IPCC, 2007). This chapter attempts to shed light on which of these outcomes is the more likely by examining the public's changing attitudes towards air travel and exploring the characteristics of those in favour of raising fares to offset environmental damage.

Exploring attitudes towards air travel

There are a number of factors which might be thought likely to influence people's attitudes towards air travel and their willingness to accept restrictions on their ability to fly. Understanding where support for higher air fares is located is important in assessing both the likely attitudinal and behavioural responses to possible fare increases and the political feasibility of any government policy which might escalate these increases.

For example, the ability of a government to implement policies designed to offset the environmental damage of air travel is likely to depend on levels of support for such policies among those most affected by them. If users of air travel, especially frequent flyers, oppose higher fares or other policies designed to restrict air travel, this may in turn make any such policy harder to implement. On the other hand, to the extent that attitudes vary with people's level of environmental concern, growing awareness of the environmental impact of air travel leads to increased acceptance over time of the need for change in the market for air travel. The age profile of support is worth considering in this regard. If, for example, we find a generational shift towards more pro-environmental attitudes, this may make any policies introduced on environmental grounds more palatable.

It may also be important to take account of how support for pricing policies varies on the basis of income or other socio-economic characteristics. Such demographic factors are likely to be associated with the consumption of air travel and levels of environmental concern. Moreover, whilst it is strongly expected that fare rises of the magnitude anticipated will lead to reduced demand for air travel, the extent to which this occurs may vary on the basis of income and other socio-demographic characteristics.

Finally, an important consideration for political parties is the extent to which policies to address the environmental impact of flying are likely to be (un)popular among existing and potential supporters. It is often argued that environmental issues have the potential to cross-cut established political cleavages such as left and right and transcend traditional party politics (Dalton, 2006). Among Britain's three largest parties, the Liberal Democrats have for a long time been seen as the strongest advocates of green policies. However, in recent years, the environment has become an increased focus for all. It will be particularly interesting to examine the extent to which support for environmental policies is to be found among Conservative Party supporters given its leader David Cameron's recent attempts to reposition the party and establish its green credentials.

There are a number of difficulties associated with attempting to establish a link between attitudes and behaviour and, hence, with using attitudinal survey data to explore the likely response to environmental policy changes (Lyons *et al.*, 2008). First, attitudes are sensitive to variation in question wording and, in particular, the extent to which the risks of environmental damage are made explicit. This sensitivity may be due to a combination of factors including the generally low salience of the environment to people and people feeling social pressure to express pro-environmental attitudes when prompted. Second, we cannot automatically assume that pro-environmental attitudes will translate into action. This may reflect social desirability bias and a tendency to over-report levels of concern. Even if people are genuinely concerned and express a willingness to change their behaviour, they may be constrained in the extent to which they choose or are able to do so in practice. Nevertheless, by making use of attitudinal data available across a number of years we are able to explore whether and how attitudes to air travel are changing. Do people remain firmly committed to unlimited air travel or is there growing acceptance of the need for change in response to environmental pressures?

Reflecting the anticipated role that travel behaviour is likely to play in influencing support for policies which may restrict flying, this chapter begins by exploring the characteristics of flyers *versus* non-flyers. Similarly, it examines how concern for the environmental impact of air travel has changed over time and where this concern is located. The chapter then moves on to explore people's attitudes towards air travel and considers the extent to which people's acceptance of the need to restrict air travel has increased in recent years. The final part of the chapter compares how attitudes towards restricting air travel and raising fares vary among different groups of the population and discusses the likely implications of this in terms of policy outcomes.

Given that many of the factors influencing attitudes towards air travel are likely to be interrelated, this chapter makes use of multivariate analysis in the form of logistic regression. This allows us to isolate the effect of individual variables on attitudes and behaviour after taking account of other relevant factors. Full details of the regression analysis can be found in the appendix to this chapter.

Who flies, how often?

As we have already seen, there is some evidence that the British public's appetite and resources for flying may already have levelled off and this is supported by data from the *British Social Attitudes* survey series. Since 2003, we have asked respondents:

> How many trips did you make by plane during the last 12 months? Please count the outward and return flight and any transfers as one trip

As seen in Table 6.1, there has been no upward trend at all in the use of air travel reported by respondents between 2003 and 2007. The mean number of trips by air in the year before interview has remained stable, at 1.8 (2003–6) or 1.7 (2007).[3] In each year, around a third of respondents made one or two trips by air, while about one in five made three or more. Nearly half of respondents had not flown in the preceding 12 months. So, while flying is no longer for the few, it remains a long way from being an annual activity for all.

As one might expect, income is a key determinant of flying (Table 6.2). Only 25 per cent of people in households in the lowest income quartile have flown in the last year compared with 80 per cent of people in households in the highest income quartile. Over two-fifths of the latter group have made at least three trips by air in the last year.

Table 6.1 Consumption of air travel, 2003–2007

Number of trips in last 12 months	2003	2004	2005	2006	2007
	%	%	%	%	%
None	44	48	48	45	47
One	21	16	16	19	19
Two	15	15	16	16	15
Three	5	5	5	5	6
Four or more	14	17	15	15	14
Base	1155	1053	1100	3227	3085
Mean number of trips	1.8	1.8	1.8	1.8	1.7
Base	1148	1049	1099	3210	3081

Table 6.2 Characteristics of flyers *versus* non-flyers

		Number of trips in last 12 months			
		None	One or two	Three or more	Base
All	%	47	34	19	3094
Household income					
Lowest quartile	%	75	21	4	617
2nd quartile	%	59	32	10	766
3rd quartile	%	37	42	21	693
Highest quartile	%	20	38	42	581
Social class					
Managerial & professional	%	31	37	32	1120
Intermediate	%	42	39	19	358
Self-employed	%	48	35	17	298
Lower superv. & technical	%	55	34	11	345
Manual	%	62	28	10	881
Employment status					
In paid work	%	36	39	26	1616
Not in paid work	%	61	27	11	1478
Region					
North of England	%	46	36	19	845
Midlands	%	52	32	15	779
Wales and SW	%	51	35	14	437
London	%	41	33	26	298
South East England	%	45	31	24	441
Scotland	%	38	35	27	292

Even after controlling for income, social class and employment status remain significant predictors of air travel, with those employed in professional and managerial occupations most likely to have flown (see the appendix to this chapter for full details). This probably reflects that these groups are more likely to have flown for business. Business travel accounts for around a fifth (22 per cent) of all trips through UK airports (Cairns and Newson, 2006).

The multivariate analysis also confirms that there are modest regional differences in air travel behaviour. People in London and Scotland are the most likely to have flown and, especially, to have taken multiple trips. In the case of Londoners this may reflect proximity to airports and the fact that people in London are more likely than people living in other parts of the UK to have family connections abroad. In Scotland, distance from other UK and European destinations increases demand for flights.

Flying and climate change

Any concerns about environmental effects clearly have not prevented the rapid growth of aviation in recent decades. However, the prominence of climate change as an urgent global issue has increased considerably in the last few years. Growing awareness of climate change and its contributing factors may or may not lead directly to changes in individual behaviour. Nevertheless, one would anticipate that awareness and understanding of environmental impact will be a key factor underpinning change either through choice or the acceptance of constraints such as higher prices. So to what extent are the concerns of climate change experts about current and, especially, projected levels of air travel already reflected in public perceptions?

Respondents were asked several questions regarding their attitudes towards transport and climate change. Specifically, we asked how much people agree or disagree with the following statements:

The current level of car use has a serious effect on climate change

The current level of air travel has a serious effect on climate change

As seen in Table 6.3, in 2007, 70 per cent of people either agree or strongly agree that air travel has a serious effect on climate change. This is only marginally lower than the proportion of people who agree that car use has a serious effect on climate change (72 per cent). Attitudes towards the environmental impact of air travel and car use appear to have converged in recent years; agreement that air travel affects climate change has risen from 64 per cent in 2005 whilst agreement that car use affects climate change has fallen from 77 per cent. Even though, at present, aircraft are relatively modest contributors to total global emissions, perceptions have already shifted: both car use and air travel are believed by a large majority of people to be having a serious effect on climate change.[4]

Of course, recognising a serious effect does not imply being concerned about that effect or, indeed, climate change at all. Therefore we also asked the question:

> How concerned are you about the effect of transport on climate change?

In fact, levels of concern about the effect of transport on climate change are also high with 76 per cent of people saying that they are either very or fairly concerned.

Combining the two measures enables us to confirm that a clear majority (almost two-thirds) of the British public are both concerned about the effect of transport on climate change *and* think that air travel has a serious effect. The high and growing level of recognition and concern for the environmental damage caused by air travel raises the possibility that people may take steps to cut back on air travel and be supportive of policies designed to encourage this.

Table 6.3 Concern about the effect of transport on the environment, 2005–2007

	2005	2006	2007
% agree car use has a serious effect on climate change	77	80	72
% agree air travel has a serious effect on climate change	64	74	70
% concerned about the effect of transport on climate change	80	81	76
% concerned about effect of transport on climate change *and* agree air travel has serious effect on climate change	57	67	62
Base	*1101*	*3228*	*3094*

Table 6.4 shows that majorities of all major social groups are both concerned about the climate change impact of travel and agree that flying has a serious effect. The size of these majorities does vary across groups. Multivariate analysis confirms that flyers (especially frequent flyers) are less likely to recognise and be concerned about the environmental impact of air travel than non-flyers. Having educational qualifications to A-level standard or above and being female are also associated with a greater level of environmental concern. Multivariate analysis also highlights some notable differences on the basis of party identification. Despite recent attempts to position the Conservative Party as a party for the environment, the attitudes of Conservative identifiers remain less green than the attitudes of Labour and Liberal Democrat supporters. Those with no party identification are least likely to agree that air travel has an impact on climate change and to be concerned about it, perhaps reflecting a general sense of disengagement amongst this group. Nevertheless, there is widespread support across all sections of the population for the view that the negative environmental impact of air travel is cause for concern.

Table 6.4 Concern about the environmental impact of air travel, by respondent characteristics

	% concerned about effect of transport on climate change *and* agree air travel has a serious effect on climate change	Base
All	62	3094
Sex		
Male	59	1373
Female	65	1721
Highest educational qualification		
Higher education	69	872
A level	68	404
GCSE/O level	60	730
None	55	793
Party identification		
None	49	496
Conservative	59	819
Labour	68	1058
Liberal Democrat	73	293
Number of trips		
None	63	1263
One or two	66	875
Three or more	60	501

Free to fly?

As previously discussed, concern about the impact of air travel on climate change does not necessarily mean that people would be willing to cut back on flights or would support policies raising the cost of air travel.[5] In order to explore this issue we measured how much people agree or disagree with the following statements regarding unlimited air travel:

People should be able to fly as much as they like

People should be able to fly as much as they like even if new terminals or runways are needed

People should be able to fly as much as they like even if it harms the environment

As seen in Table 6.5, responses to the first unqualified statement reveal that a majority of people (63 per cent) still spontaneously agree with the principle of unrestricted air travel. However, views on this issue are highly sensitive to context. Once people are reminded of the possible implications of air travel (the potential, firstly, to have to build new terminals and runways and, secondly, for environmental harm), support for unrestricted flying drops sharply. Under a fifth of respondents agree that people should be allowed to travel by plane as much as they like, even if it harms the environment.

This raises the question of why, especially given reported high levels of concern for the environment, more people do not reject the notion of unrestricted air travel from the outset. Perhaps the initial unqualified statement elicits more general attitudes regarding state restrictions on individuals' freedom of action. Perhaps, for many, the salience of their environmental concerns remains low, requiring a reminder that they may wish to take these concerns into account. Whatever the reasons, remarkably high numbers do not automatically acknowledge the need to constrain flying and have to be specifically reminded of environmental consequences before doing so.[6]

There is, however, some evidence of the beginnings of a shift towards more consistently environmentally conscious attitudes towards air travel. Between 2003 and 2007, the level of agreement that people should be allowed to fly as much as they like fell sharply from 78 per cent to 63 per cent. Meanwhile, there was no net change in the level of support for unrestricted air travel, even with the environmental caveat (19 per cent). There is always a risk that people will over-report their support for green policies, feeling social pressure to do so, especially if the possibility of environmental damage is explicitly mentioned in the question. However, changing levels of support for the unqualified statement, and the lessening in the apparent dissonance between responses regardless of whether the environment is explicitly mentioned, suggests that the salience of the environment as a factor shaping opinions may be increasing.

Table 6.5 Attitudes towards air travel, 2003–2007

	2003	2004	2005	2006	2007
% agree people should be able to travel by plane ...					
... as much as they like	78	77	70	69	63
... as much as they like, even if new terminals or runways are needed	52	43	43	44	40
... as much as they like, even if it harms the environment	19	15	18	19	19
Base	972	872	903	932	847

Reduced levels of support for unqualified freedom to fly and heightened perceptions that flying has negative effects do not, of course, imply widespread agreement with any specific policy framework for aviation. Since 2004, we have been gauging reaction to one leading option: linking the price of flying to the environmental cost. We asked respondents how much they agreed or disagreed with the following statement:

The price of a plane ticket should reflect the environmental damage that flying causes, even if it makes air travel much more expensive[7]

Initially, in 2004, only a minority – albeit a sizeable one of around a third – were prepared to agree with the idea that ticket prices should reflect environmental damage, as shown in Table 6.6. A similar percentage disagreed. However, in subsequent years, the proportion in agreement with the potential need for higher fares has risen to virtually half. Only just over a quarter of respondents actually disagree with the idea that ticket prices should reflect environmental damage, with the remainder expressing a neutral view towards the idea. Even amongst those who agree in principle that people should be able to fly as much as they like, agreement that ticket prices should reflect environmental damage is a common response (45 per cent). If people are indeed willing to accept increases in the cost of flying, this perhaps points to an evolving recognition that, however convenient, unrestricted access to very cheap air travel is unlikely to continue.

Table 6.6 Attitudes towards ticket prices and environmental damage, 2004–2007

	2004	2005	2006	2007
Price of ticket should reflect environmental damage that flying causes	%	%	%	%
Agree	36	42	48	49
Neither agree nor disagree	25	25	29	22
Disagree	34	23	24	28
Base	*872*	*903*	*932*	*847*

The shift over time in attitudes towards unlimited air travel in part reflects the increasing numbers of people who recognise that air travel has an impact on climate change and who say they are concerned about it. As Table 6.7 illustrates, people who are concerned about the environmental impact of air travel are more likely to disagree that people should be able to fly as much as they like and more likely to agree that ticket prices should reflect environmental damage.

Table 6.7 Attitudes to air travel, by level of environmental concern

	Believes air travel has impact and is concerned	Does not believe air travel has impact and/or not concerned
% agree …		
… people should be able to travel by plane as much as they like	55	79
… people should be able to travel by plane as much as they like, even if new terminals or runways are needed	32	55
… people should be able to travel by plane as much as they like, even if it harms the environment	12	31
… ticket prices should reflect environmental damage	60	31
Base	*541*	*306*

At the same time, there is also evidence of a shift in attitudes over time amongst those people who express concern. For example, the proportion of people concerned about the environmental impact of air travel who nevertheless agree that people should be able to fly as much as they want has fallen since 2005 (from 65 per cent to 55 per cent). Similarly, the proportion of people in the concerned group agreeing that ticket prices should reflect environmental damage has risen (from 49 per cent to 60 per cent). This change in attitudes perhaps suggests the beginnings of a move towards people not only being concerned about the environmental effects of air travel but also recognising the need to take action to do something about it.

In this respect, there is a contrast to be drawn between attitudes towards raising the cost of flying and attitudes towards increases in the cost of motoring. Previous *British Social Attitudes* reports have considered the feasibility of introducing pricing strategies to influence behaviour in relation to car use and highlighted the challenges this presents to the government in the face of widespread public opposition (Exley and Christie, 2003). Such opposition continues; 61 per cent of people disagree that car users should pay higher taxes for the sake of the environment. People's greater willingness to pay more for flying but not motoring is likely to be down to a combination of factors. In part it may reflect slight differences in question wording; the car use question talks about higher taxes rather than prices and people may be particularly resistant to any suggestion of raising taxes.[8] More substantively, however, differences in attitudes probably reflect the fact that air travel is far from being a necessity for most people in the way that travelling by car has become. Furthermore, air travel remains largely concentrated amongst high-income groups who are best placed to absorb higher costs. One of the most important differences may be the fact that whilst the cost of motoring is already perceived as being too high by many and to be increasing, air passengers have enjoyed a number of years of falling fares in the wake of the growth of budget airlines and increased competition. Whatever the reason, there appears to be more scope for government to introduce policies which may raise the cost of air travel compared with raising the cost of motoring.

Who would be willing to pay higher fares?

In order to assess fully the feasibility of introducing environmental pricing policies, and their likely impact on behaviour, it is important to look in more detail at exactly where acceptance for such policies is located. The rest of this chapter, therefore, looks at variations across population subgroups in the level of support for restrictions on air travel and, specifically, for the idea that ticket prices should reflect environmental damage.

Generally speaking, those groups most likely to agree that ticket prices should reflect environmental damage are also the groups least likely to agree that people should be able to fly as much as they like. However, as discussed above, many people who are pro-flying also appear to recognise the need for action to offset environmental damage and may be willing to bear the cost of higher fares. On the one hand, this may mean that pricing policies are easier to introduce than it might at first appear. On the other hand, it needs to be borne in mind that higher fares will not automatically lead to a reduction in flying – those who can afford it may simply accept that they have to pay more. We did not ask respondents any questions relating to how fare increases might impact on their own travel behaviour. However, as discussed in the introduction to this chapter, if fare increases are large enough, it seems fair to assume that an overall reduction in air travel is the likely outcome.

The next set of tables compare both the proportions of different subgroups who agree or disagree that people should be able to fly as much as they like and the proportions who agree or disagree that the price of air travel should reflect environmental damage.[9] In order to maximise the number of cases available for analysis we have pooled data from 2006 and 2007.[10] People's attitudes towards air travel have already been shown to be strongly related to their level of environmental concern. After controlling for people's level of environmental concern, the multivariate analysis showed that attitudes towards air travel additionally appear to be related to: the consumption of air travel, education, socio-economic status, and age. There is limited variation in attitudes on the basis of party identification. Full details of the multivariate analysis can be found in the appendix to this chapter.

Flyers and non-flyers

Perhaps unsurprisingly, Table 6.8 shows that people who have flown in the last year are significantly more likely than those who have not flown to agree that people should be able to travel by plane as much as they like. Frequent flyers, i.e. those taking three or more trips in the last 12 months, are particularly likely to agree with the principle of unlimited air travel.

At the same time, however, agreement with the idea that ticket prices should reflect environmental damage is relatively high regardless of whether respondents are non-flyers, once-a-year flyers or more frequent flyers. When combined with the fact that only around half of the population have flown in the last year, this suggests that higher air fares may not prove too contentious.

Frequent flyers are more likely than non-flyers to disagree with the need for prices to reflect environmental damage, reflecting the fact that they will be the ones bearing the higher costs. However, even among flyers, levels of opposition to ticket prices reflecting environmental damage remain low, with less than a third of respondents actually expressing disagreement with the idea. The lack of stronger opposition to potentially higher ticket prices among flyers may well reflect the fact that flyers tend to come from higher income groups. It remains to be seen whether higher fares would impact on people's flying behaviour or simply be accepted as the necessary cost of air travel.

Table 6.8 Attitudes to air travel, by consumption of air travel, 2006/07[+]

	Number of trips by air in past 12 months		
	None	One or two	Three or more
People should be able to travel by plane as much as they like	%	%	%
Agree	62	67	76
Disagree	13	13	7
Price of a plane ticket should reflect environmental damage	%	%	%
Agree	50	48	46
Disagree	21	29	31
Base	*821*	*624*	*323*

[+] Data pooled from 2006 and 2007 surveys

Socio-economic status

There is relatively little variation on the basis of either social class or income in the proportion of people who agree with the principle of unlimited air travel; a majority of all groups agree that people should be able to travel by plane as much as they want. The lack of an overall relationship probably reflects the fact that higher socio-economic status is associated, on the one hand, with greater environmental concern but, on the other, with more frequent consumption of air travel.

Nevertheless, high earners and those in professional and managerial occupations are significantly *more* likely to agree that ticket prices should reflect environmental damage. The fact that socio-economic status remains a significant factor even after controlling for levels of environmental concern suggests that to some extent agreement also reflects ability to pay. This finding, coupled with the fact that higher socio-economic groups are just as likely as other people to support unlimited air travel, raises the possibility that raising ticket prices need not necessarily constrain demand for flights as markedly as some projections suggest. Those groups who can afford higher fares may choose to accept the additional costs of flying rather than cutting back a great deal on flights. However, it does need to be borne in mind that most of the debate is about curtailing expected *growth* in flights rather than cutting current consumption. It remains to be seen whether even the higher-income groups could and would afford to fly more often if price rises are sustained.

Table 6.9 Agreement that ticket prices should reflect environmental damage, by household income, 2006/07[+]

	Household income			
	Lowest quartile	**2nd quartile**	**3rd quartile**	**Highest quartile**
People should be able to travel by plane as much as they like	%	%	%	%
Agree	65	64	66	69
Disagree	13	13	10	12
Price of a plane ticket should reflect environmental damage	%	%	%	%
Agree	44	45	49	57
Disagree	21	27	29	25
Base	*335*	*459*	*427*	*330*

[+] Data pooled from 2006 and 2007 surveys

Age

People in the youngest age group are the least likely to agree that ticket prices should reflect environmental damage as seen in Table 6.10. This remains the case even after taking account of the fact that those under the age of 35 are less likely than older age groups to be concerned about the environmental impact of air travel. The finding is consistent with other research studies which have found not only that the level of environmental concern tends to be lower amongst the youngest age groups but that, even when they express concern, young people tend to be less supportive of policies to tackle environmental problems (Anable *et al.*, 2006; Department for Transport, 2006). Given the large overall increase in pro-environment attitudes over time, it is unlikely that this represents a generational shift towards less green attitudes among the young. It is more probable that the differences observed are a function of age, with people tending to become more environmentally concerned as they get older, gain more experience of the world, form their own families and perhaps develop a stronger sense of community and public responsibility.

Table 6.10 Agreement that ticket prices should reflect environmental damage, by age, 2006/07[+]

	Age				
	18–34	35–44	45–54	55–64	65+
People should be able to travel by plane as much as they like	%	%	%	%	%
Agree	68	71	64	64	63
Disagree	10	11	12	15	13
Price of a plane ticket should reflect environmental damage	%	%	%	%	%
Agree	42	48	49	58	52
Disagree	29	29	28	20	21
Base	*422*	*335*	*337*	*287*	*394*

[+] Data pooled from 2006 and 2007 surveys

Political attitudes

Supporters of the two largest political parties display very similar attitudes towards restrictions on air travel as shown in Table 6.11. Overall, Liberal Democrat identifiers display the most pro-environmental attitudes towards air travel whilst non-partisans are the least likely group to agree that ticket prices should reflect environmental damage. However, after controlling for differences in the level of environmental concern, partisanship was not significantly associated with attitudes to air travel. The fact that around half of both

Conservative and Labour identifiers support the idea of ticket prices reflecting environmental damage suggests that a government formed of either party could feasibly pursue environmental pricing policies.

However, although there is no difference between Conservative and Labour identifiers on the specific issue of ticket prices, it is worth bearing in mind that, as previously discussed, these two groups do differ in terms of green attitudes more generally. Overall, Conservative identifiers are significantly less likely to say they were concerned about the effects of transport on the environment compared with either Labour or Liberal Democrat supporters. It appears that David Cameron has further work to do in terms of convincing Conservative supporters to care about green issues. It also means that playing on voters' fears for the environment is less likely to be an effective strategy for a Conservative government seeking to influence the market for air travel compared with a Labour government seeking to introduce similar policies.

Table 6.11 Agreement that ticket prices should reflect environmental damage, by party identification, 2006/07[+]

| | Party identification | | | |
	None	Cons	Labour	Lib Dem
People should be able to travel by plane as much as they like	%	%	%	%
Agree	73	70	67	53
Disagree	6	9	12	22
Price of a plane ticket should reflect environmental damage	%	%	%	%
Agree	34	52	50	61
Disagree	34	26	24	20
Base	*259*	*480*	*589*	*199*

[+] Data pooled from 2006 and 2007 surveys

Overall, these findings comparing attitudes to air travel across different groups point to two things. On the one hand, a majority of all groups support the principle of unlimited air travel. On the other hand, opposition towards the idea that ticket prices should reflect environmental damage remains relatively low, around 30 per cent, amongst all groups in the population regardless of age, sex, income, education or party identification. This, in turn, suggests that there is no obvious group that would be likely to mount a challenge against rising air fares.

Conclusions

An era in which very cheap flights have been widely available is under threat from a combination of higher oil prices and government-led plans to ensure fares reflect the environmental damage from air travel. The purpose of this chapter has been to gauge levels of public support or opposition towards what potentially could be large increases in the price of air travel and to explore the extent to which the government might come under pressure to prevent further increases.

At present, there are a number of factors working in favour of policies designed to reduce the environmental impact of air travel. First, it appears that the growth in passenger numbers had stalled *before* 2008's 'double whammy' of higher fuel prices and an economic downturn. Coupled with this is, secondly, the growing concern by the public about the effect of air travel on climate change. The majority who still spontaneously think that people should be allowed to travel by plane as much as they like is weakening; and, in any case, only a small minority retain this view when prompted with the potential environmental impacts of unconstrained air travel.

Moreover, opposition to unlimited air travel is linked with concern about the environmental effects. This suggests that government arguments based on the environmental damage caused by air travel may well persuade many that higher ticket prices are necessary. Already, we found remarkably low levels of opposition to the idea that ticket prices may have to rise in order to offset environmental damage. This remains the case amongst current flyers as well as non-flyers and holds across the political spectrum. There appears to be a growing recognition that the recent trend towards ever cheaper flights cannot continue. It would appear, therefore, that higher air fares will not be widely resisted by the public or present a particular political headache for either the current Labour government or a future Conservative government.

It remains to be seen, however, whether higher ticket prices will have the effect of reducing demand for air travel. Although fare increases are expected to be substantial in percentages terms, it needs to be borne in mind that they are rising from historically low levels. It is possible that, if robust economic growth is restored, people will simply pay the extra and continue to fly more often. It is noteworthy that high earners are more supportive of higher air fares than low earners – presumably because they know they can probably afford to pay more. It is also worth noting that there is no evidence of the young turning against flying, so no suggestion of a generational shift in favour of limiting travel on environmental grounds.

Nevertheless, given the extent of the fares increases currently being touted, it seems fairly certain that some people will be forced to reconsider their flying behaviour. This is particularly likely in the short run as rising prices coincide with an economic downturn. However, experts have suggested that year-on-year increases in fares will be needed to continue to constrain demand as people become used to and start to absorb one-off increases in cost. This, of course, then raises the question of how long public support will hold up should fares continue to increase.

Notes

1. For the latest forecasts from the Department for Transport see Department for Transport (2007).
2. As the *Guardian* reported at the time, the planned expansion of capacity outlined in the White Paper "sparked fury among environmentalists" ("Huge airport expansion given the green light", *Guardian*, 17th December 2003).
3. Cases where number of flights was above 50 were excluded from calculation of the mean.
4. Attitudes on the effect of transport on climate change are sensitive to question wording. An ONS study employing an alternative question which asked people to select the causes of climate change from a multiple-choice list found that people are still more likely to pick car use (69 per cent) than air travel (43 per cent) as a contributing factor (Department for Transport, 2008b). Nevertheless, air travel was the second most commonly cited cause after car use.
5. Although the multivariate analysis in Table A.2 points to a relationship between air travel behaviour and environmental concern, we cannot necessarily assume a causal relationship, i.e. that non-flyers choose not to fly as a result of their concern for the environment. Other research suggests that non-flyers' reasons for not having flown are much more likely to be related to situational constraints such as lack of time or money, or poor health (Department for Transport, 2006).
6. The large effect on responses of adding the words "even if new terminals or runways are needed" or "even if it harms the environment" appeared even though the questions were positioned one after the other on the self-completion questionnaire, so that respondents were free to consider the three statements together.
7. Other studies have found similar levels of support for more-specific fare increases. For example, in 2006 the ONS Omnibus asked people whether they would be willing to pay an additional 20 per cent, 10 per cent, five per cent or nothing at all. Almost seven in ten (69 per cent) said they would be willing to pay some additional charge to reflect environmental costs, with half (52 per cent) saying they would be willing to pay an additional 20 per cent (Department for Transport, 2006).
8. The precise wording of the agree/disagree statement relating to higher taxes for car users is "[Agree/disagree] For the sake of the environment, car users should pay higher taxes".
9. Analysis was also run looking at factors influencing the extent to which people agreed with the idea that "people should be able to travel by plane as much as they like" once the potential costs in terms of environmental damage were explicitly pointed out to them. Agreement with the statement that "people should be allowed to travel by plane as much as they like, even if new terminals or runways are needed to meet the demand" varied in a very similar way to agreement with the unqualified statement. In contrast, agreement with the idea that "people should be able to travel by plane as much as they like, even if this harms the environment" showed very little variation across subgroups. The one significant finding was that people saying they were concerned about the environmental impact of air travel were more likely to disagree with this statement. This lack of variation probably reflects the fact that

this qualified statement generally encourages people to give a pro-environment response regardless of their underlying attitude towards air travel.

10. Attitudes towards ticket prices were unchanged between 2006 and 2007. There was an overall decline in the proportion of people agreeing that people should be able to travel by plane as much as they like. However, the patterns of subgroup variation remain broadly consistent across both years.

References

Anable, J., Lane, B. and Kelay, T. (2006), *An Evidence Base Review of Public Attitudes to Climate Change and Transport Behaviour. Final Report to the Department for Transport*, London: Department for Transport

Cairns, S. and Newson, C. (2006), *Predict and decide: Aviation, climate change and UK policy*, Oxford: Environmental Change Institute

Civil Aviation Authority (2008), *Recent Trends in Growth of UK Air Passenger Demand*, London: Civil Aviation Authority

Dalton, R. (2006), *Citizen Politics: Public opinion and political parties in advanced industrial democracies*, Washington, DC: CQ Press

Department for Transport (2003), *The future of air transport*, White Paper, London: The Stationery Office

Department for Transport (2006), *Public Experiences of and Attitudes to Air Travel*, London: Department for Transport

Department for Transport (2007), *UK Air Passenger Demand and CO_2 Forecasts*, London: The Stationery Office

Department for Transport (2008a), *Transport Statistics Great Britain*, London: The Stationery Office

Department for Transport (2008b), *Public Attitudes to Climate Change and the Impact of Transport (2006 and 2007)*, London: Department for Transport

Exley, S. and Christie, I. (2003), 'Stuck in our cars? Mapping transport preferences', in Park, A., Curtice, J., Thomson, K., Jarvis, L. and Bromley, C. (eds.), *British Social Attitudes: the 20th Report – Continuity and change over two decades*, London: Sage

Hansard (2007), House of Commons 2 May 2007 Vol 459, col. 1670W

HM Treasury (2007), *Meeting the aspirations of the British people 2007 Pre-Budget Report and Comprehensive Spending Review*, London: The Stationery Office

IPCC (2007), *Climate change 2007: Synthesis report. Contribution of working groups I, II and III to the fourth assessment report of the Intergovernmental Panel on Climate Change*, Geneva: Intergovernmental Panel on Climate Change

Lyons, G., Goodwin, P., Hanly, M., Dudley, G., Chatterjeee, K., Anable, J., Wiltshire, P. and Susilo, Y. (2008), *Public Attitudes to Transport: Knowledge Review of Existing Evidence*, London: Department for Transport

Miller, G., Rathouse, K., Scarles, C., Holmes, K. and Tribe, J. (2007), *Public Understanding of Sustainable Leisure and Tourism: A Report to the Department for Environment, Food and Rural Affairs*, London: Department for Environment, Food and Rural Affairs

Owen B. and Lee, D. (2006), *Allocation of international aviation emissions from scheduled air traffic – future cases, 2005–2050*, London: Department for Environment, Food and Rural Affairs

Tyndall Centre for Climate Change Research (2005), *Decarbonising the UK: Energy for a climate conscious future*, Norwich: Tyndall Centre for Climate Change Research

Acknowledgements

The *National Centre for Social Research* is grateful to the Department for Transport for their financial support which enabled us to ask the questions reported in this chapter, although the views expressed are those of the authors alone.

Appendix

The multivariate analysis technique used is logistic regression, about which more details can be found in Appendix I of the report. Results are presented in terms of odds ratios. For categorical variables, an odds ratio greater than one indicates that the odds of the specified outcome occurring are higher for that group compared with the reference group (shown in brackets after the category heading). An odds ratio less than one indicates the odds of the specified outcome occurring are lower for that group compared with the reference group.

Table A.1 Flown in the last 12 months (*versus* not flown)

	Odds ratio
Sex (Male)	
Female	*1.24
Age (18–34)	
35–44	1.03
45–54	1.05
55–64	*1.48
65+	1.17
Social class (Professional and managerial)	
Intermediate	0.87
Self-employed	0.72
Supervisory and technical	**0.60
Manual	**0.52
Education (Highest education qualification)	
A level	0.97
GCSE/O Level	**0.66
None	**0.49
Household income (Lowest quartile)	
2nd quartile	*1.48
3rd quartile	**3.02
Highest quartile	**5.32
Employment status (Not in paid work)	
In paid work	**1.44
Region (Midlands)	
North of England	**1.61
Wales and South West	1.12
London	*1.65
South East England	1.24
Scotland	**2.24
Party ID (None)	
Conservative	0.95
Labour	0.92
Liberal Democrat	0.83
Other	0.86
R^2	0.24
Base	2715

2007 data
 * = significant at 95% level; ** = significant at 99% level

Table A.2 Believe air travel has serious effect on climate change and concerned (*versus* don't believe has an effect/not concerned)

	Odds ratio
Flights in last 12 months (None)	
One or two	0.94
Three or more	**0.66
Sex (Male)	
Female	**1.41
Age (18–34)	
35–44	1.14
45–54	1.25
55–64	1.26
65+	1.21
Social class (Professional and managerial)	
Intermediate	0.82
Self-employed	0.87
Supervisory and technical	0.91
Manual	0.98
Education (Highest education qualification)	
A level	1.10
GCSE/O Level	*0.73
None	**0.52
Household income (Lowest quartile)	
2nd quartile	1.16
3rd quartile	0.97
Highest quartile	1.20
Region (Midlands)	
North of England	1.09
Wales and South West	1.17
London	1.38
South East England	1.27
Scotland	0.84
Party ID (None)	
Conservative	*1.44
Labour	**2.11
Liberal Democrat	**2.43
Other	*1.64
R^2	0.08
Base	2347

2007 data
* = significant at 95% level; ** = significant at 99% level

Table A.3 Agree people should be able to fly as much as they like (*versus* neither/disagree)

	Odds ratio
Flights in last 12 months (None)	
One or two	*1.42
Three or more	**2.24
Attitudes to environment (Not concerned)	
Believe air travel has effect and concerned	**0.38
Sex (Male)	
Female	0.92
Age (18–34)	
35–44	1.27
45–54	0.75
55–64	0.85
65+	0.75
Social class (Professional and managerial)	
Intermediate	1.31
Self-employed	1.02
Supervisory and technical	1.15
Manual	1.20
Education (Highest education qualification)	
A level	1.28
GCSE/O Level	**1.85
None	**1.93
Household income (Lowest quartile)	
2nd quartile	1.03
3rd quartile	*1.06
Highest quartile	1.24
Region (Midlands)	
North of England	0.95
Wales and South West	1.28
London and South East	0.85
Scotland	0.97
Party ID (None)	
Conservative	1.07
Labour	1.02
Liberal Democrat	*0.65
Other	0.79
R^2	0.14
Base	1622

Data pooled from 2006 and 2007 surveys
* = significant at 95% level; ** = significant at 99% level

Table A.4 Agree ticket prices should reflect environmental damage (*versus* neither/disagree)

	Odds ratio
Flights in last 12 months (None)	
One or two	0.10
Three or more	**0.54
Attitudes to environment (Not concerned)	
Believe air travel has effect and concerned	**3.03
Sex (Male)	
Female	*0.76
Age (18–34)	
35–44	1.12
45–54	1.25
55–64	**1.85
65+	**1.59
Social class (Professional and managerial)	
Intermediate	0.71
Self-employed	0.71
Supervisory and technical	*0.57
Manual	**0.55
Education (Highest education qualification)	
A level	*0.68
GCSE/O Level	*0.70
None	*0.65
Household income (Lowest quartile)	
2nd quartile	0.84
3rd quartile	1.02
Highest quartile	1.33
Region (Midlands)	
North of England	0.87
Wales and South West	1.09
London and South East	1.21
Scotland	0.78
Party ID (None)	
Conservative	1.39
Labour	1.46
Liberal Democrat	1.87
Other	1.45
R^2	*0.16*
Base	*1622*

Data pooled from 2006 and 2007 surveys
* = significant at 95% level; ** = significant at 99% level

7 Therapy culture? Attitudes towards emotional support in Britain

Simon Anderson, Julie Brownlie and Lisa Given[*]

> The triumph of therapeutic culture is most striking in Britain, a society that was formerly associated with reserve, understatement and reticence. (Furedi, 2004: 18)

Recent years have seen a growing interest within the social sciences in the idea of an emerging 'therapeutic culture'. Some see evidence for this in the expansion of the therapeutic professions and an apparent tendency to frame social problems as problems of the 'self', rather than as reflecting structural issues such as inequality or poverty. For others, it can be seen in the spreading of therapeutic talk and beliefs beyond the realm of the therapeutic (Cloud, 1998). Consequently, even though few of us may be 'in therapy', we are all exposed to therapeutic precepts through various channels, including self-help literature, the confessional milieu of the media, and public health information (Cameron, 2000). The concept of a therapeutic culture has also been invoked as a way of characterising an increased concern with the expression and management of emotions; a stigmatising of informal relations of dependency so that our reliance on these falls as our dependency on formal relations increases (Furedi, 2004); and an extension of the therapeutic sensibility beyond those involved in therapy or counselling services, to shape all institutions in society such as the legal and education systems (Nolan, 1998).

For sociologists, this interest in the therapeutic is part of a wider concern with the relationship between the public and private sphere, and the balance between formality and informality. Various theorists from the 1960s onwards (such as Rieff, 1966; Lasch, 1979; and, more recently, Berlant, 2000) have addressed the 'rise of the therapeutic' in terms of its potential costs for both spheres. While some, like Giddens (1991), highlight the opportunities rather than the costs of therapeutic engagement, for the most part, theorists have taken a less rosy view

---

[*] Simon Anderson is Director of the *Scottish Centre for Social Research*, part of NatCen. Julie Brownlie is Senior Lecturer in Sociology, Department of Applied Science, Stirling University. Lisa Given is a Senior Researcher at the *Scottish Centre for Social Research*.

of the therapeutic turn. A particularly bleak and well-publicised version of this has recently come from Frank Furedi in his book, *Therapy Culture* (2004). For Furedi, the prevalence of a therapeutic ethos has brought about what he terms 'the disorganisation of the private sphere' through creating a sense of a vulnerable self, dependent on professionals.

This theoretical work has been paralleled by a growing interest within policy circles in the UK in issues relating to people's emotional lives and well-being. In February 2008, for example, the Health Secretary Alan Johnson announced a major new programme to train 3,600 psychological therapists. With a budget of £170m, this 'Improving Access to Psychological Therapies' programme is designed to give people with depression and anxiety disorders from mild to severe forms of these conditions access to cognitive behavioural therapies. This development can be traced back to Richard Layard's argument, presented to the No. 10 Strategy Unit in 2005, that the socio-economic as well as personal cost of mental illness makes it Britain's main social problem (Layard, 2004).

Yet these theoretical and policy developments have taken place against a backdrop of scant empirical evidence. Most of the work that has been conducted on the theme of emotions talk and emotional support has been either small scale and qualitative, or has focused on populations of service users (for example, in relation to mental health).

So has Britain actually witnessed the "triumph of the therapeutic", to coin Rieff's phrase (1966), as Furedi and others would have us believe? This is the question that our chapter seeks to address. It does so as part of a mixed method, ESRC-funded research project which examines public views and experiences of emotional support. The project included developing a set of questions about emotional support which were asked as part of the 2007 *British Social Attitudes* survey. They allow us, for the first time, to examine a number of specific questions to have emerged from current debates about Britain's so-called 'therapeutic culture'.

Firstly, we will examine whether there is evidence of an emerging cultural consensus that it is 'good to talk' about emotions in general, regardless of professional therapeutic input. Secondly, we assess the extent to which the British public is now aware of, and comfortable with, the notion of formal therapeutic intervention to help with difficulties in their emotional lives. Next, we examine how many people are actually using such services (particularly those which are explicitly talk-based), and whether there is a groundswell of demand for the further provision of such services. Finally, we assess whether there is an inverse relationship between formal and informal emotional support; does use of formal emotional support tend to result in lower levels of reliance on more traditional, informal, support networks?

Since this is the first time that a national survey has explicitly addressed these issues, we do not have any earlier data against which we can compare our findings. This means we cannot demonstrate conclusively the pace and direction of social change. Nevertheless, our analysis does allow us to examine the impact of age on attitudes and beliefs (since one might expect an emerging culture to leave its mark more clearly on younger than older people); and the nationally representative character of the sample also allows us to ask whether such developments can really be said to be universal and to explore the ways in which experiences of therapeutic culture may vary between different social groups.

It's good to talk?

We start by examining general attitudes towards talking about emotions (or what we will call 'emotions talk'). To examine this, the survey included a number of attitude statements to tap not only individuals' own orientation towards talking about their feelings but also perceptions of whether such practices are now more common than in the past. Respondents were asked to show the extent to which they agreed or disagreed with each statement. The wording of the statements is shown in Table 7.1.

The table shows significant support for Furedi's assertion (2004) that British society is no longer characterised by "reserve, understatement and reticence". Just over a half of people say they find it easy to talk about their feelings (although a quarter do not) and around two-thirds indicate that it is important to them to be able to do so. Views are relatively evenly balanced on the issue of whether people "spend too much time talking about their feelings". There is certainly no evidence of widespread unease about the extent of 'emotions talk', though there is a sizeable minority (two-fifths) who do express such a view.

It is striking that two-thirds agree that "people nowadays spend more time talking about their feelings" while a half indicate that they grew up in a household where "people didn't talk about their feelings". Both these findings suggest that, regardless of changes in actual 'emotional practice', there is a widespread perception that emotions are now discussed more freely than in the past.

Table 7.1 General attitudes towards 'emotions talk'

		Agree	Neither	Disagree
I find it easy to talk about my feelings	%	55	20	25
People spend too much time talking about their feelings – they should just get on with things	%	35	25	40
It's important to me to be able to talk about my feelings	%	68	18	14
I grew up in the sort of household where people didn't really talk about their feelings	%	48	14	37
People nowadays spend more time talking about their feelings than in the past	%	66	19	12

Base: 2102

To examine attitudes towards talking about emotions in more detail, we constructed a scale to act as a summary measure of people's responses to the first three questions shown in Table 7.1. The scale is scored from three to 15, with low scores indicating a positive attitude to emotions talk and high scores more negative orientations. We then split respondents into three equally sized groups: 'most talkative', 'intermediate' and 'least talkative'.

The results are shown in Table 7.2, which summarises how attitudes to emotions talk vary between different groups. The first and most obvious thing to note is the stark difference between men and women. Women are much more likely than men to belong to the 'most talkative' group; nearly four in ten fall into this category, almost double the proportion found among men. While this is hardly surprising in terms of popular stereotypes, it does highlight a dimension that is curiously absent from much theorising about the emergence of therapeutic culture. We return to how one might understand these gender differences below.

Table 7.2 General attitudes towards emotions talk, by gender, age, education, well-being and experience of serious mental health problems

		Most talkative	Intermediate	Least talkative	Base
Gender					
Male	%	22	35	44	944
Female	%	39	31	30	1158
Age group					
18–24	%	35	39	26	142
25–44	%	35	33	32	732
45–59	%	32	32	36	499
60+	%	22	30	48	706
Highest educational qualification					
Degree	%	38	29	33	393
No degree	%	21	33	46	1709
Well-being scale					
Highest	%	36	33	31	573
Intermediate	%	32	30	38	529
Lowest	%	25	32	43	588
Experience of serious mental health difficulties in last five years					
Yes	%	42	28	30	221
No	%	30	33	37	1869

If there is an emerging therapeutic culture, one would expect to see an age-related gradient, with younger people more likely than older people to exhibit positive attitudes towards talking about one's emotions. This is partly the case; people aged under 60 are much more likely than those aged 60 or over to be in the 'most talkative' group. Beyond this, however, there are few other age differences. And what is not evident in the table is the way that age and gender interact with one another; the gap between men and women is at its greatest among the two youngest age groups. So while 23 per cent of young men aged 18–24 fall into our most talkative group, so too do 49 per cent of young women. One possible interpretation of this is that young men become more comfortable with emotions talk as they enter into long-term intimate relationships, whereas young women have often developed relationships of emotional inter-dependence with female friends before establishing such longer-term ties.

As with gender and age, a number of other characteristics are independently associated with belonging to the 'most talkative' group, suggesting that if any shift towards a therapeutic culture is taking place, it is less powerful than Furedi and others have implied. There is, for example, an education effect, with graduates being significantly more likely than non-graduates to belong to the most talkative group.

Attitudes towards talking about emotions also vary according to subjective well-being[1] and past experience of mental health difficulties. Reassuringly, perhaps, for proponents of emotion talk, those with high levels of well-being are more likely than average to be in the most talkative camp, and those with low levels are the most likely to be in the least talkative group (nearly half fall into this category). Interestingly, however, those with experience of serious mental health difficulties are relatively *more* likely to have a positive orientation towards emotions talk. One possible explanation of this might be that their attitudes have been shaped by the experience of formal, talk-based treatment.

Attitudes towards therapy and counselling

One might expect another feature of an emergent therapeutic culture to be a widespread sense of familiarity with the idea of counselling or therapy, and a sense that individuals would feel comfortable engaging with this type of formal emotional support. But as Table 7.3 shows, this does not appear to be the case. The table shows responses to a set of questions about counselling or therapy. These were introduced to respondents as follows:

> *Sometimes when people are feeling especially worried, stressed or down, they choose to talk about it to someone who is trained to help or to listen. Here are some things people say about that.*
>
> *If I was feeling worried, stressed or down I'd feel comfortable talking to my GP about it*
>
> *If I was feeling worried, stressed or down I'd feel comfortable talking to a therapist or counsellor about it*
>
> *I'd know how to go about finding a counsellor or therapist if I needed to*
>
> *Counselling or therapy is only for people with really serious problems*
>
> *I don't really know anything about counselling or therapy*
>
> *If I had seen a counsellor or therapist, I wouldn't want anyone to know about it*

While it is true that around four in ten would feel comfortable talking to a therapist or counsellor in these circumstances, almost as many disagree. Moreover, a markedly larger proportion say they would feel comfortable talking to their GP – a more traditional form of help-seeking, without the same associations with talk-based therapeutic culture. A sizeable minority also indicate that they would not want anyone to know if they had seen a therapist or counsellor (just over four in ten), that they would not know how to find a therapist or counsellor (just over three in ten), that they feel counselling or therapy is only for people with really serious problems (three in ten) and that they don't really know anything about therapy or counselling (around three in ten). Taken together, these findings certainly do not seem to paint a picture of a culture in which therapeutic ideas and practices are universally accepted or understood.

Table 7.3 Attitudes towards therapy and counselling

		Agree	Neither	Disagree
Would feel comfortable talking to GP if feeling worried, stressed or down	%	58	14	25
Would feel comfortable talking to a therapist or counsellor if feeling worried, stressed or down	%	38	23	35
Would know how to find counsellor/ therapist if needed	%	50	12	33
Counselling or therapy only for people with really serious problems	%	31	23	42
Doesn't really know anything about counselling or therapy	%	35	19	43
Wouldn't want anyone to know if had seen a counsellor or therapist	%	43	27	26

Base: 1025

These aggregate figures obscure some wide differences by age, which suggest that older people are much more likely than younger groups to feel comfortable discussing these sorts of issues with their GP but are not nearly as enthusiastic about doing so with a therapist or counsellor. This is illustrated in Figure 7.1. The smallest proportion agreeing that they would feel comfortable talking to a counsellor or therapist is found among those in the youngest age group (27 per cent), followed by those in the oldest (31 per cent). It is those in the middle two age groups who are least resistant to this idea. Again, the relationship between attitudes and age suggests a slightly more complex picture than might be expected from a simple narrative of a growing cultural acceptance of therapeutic ideas developing over time. There may, for example, be a life-stage effect which delays, for young men in particular, the acceptability of discussing one's emotions with those outside one's immediate family or social network.

Figure 7.1 Agree would feel comfortable talking to GP or therapist/counsellor, by age group

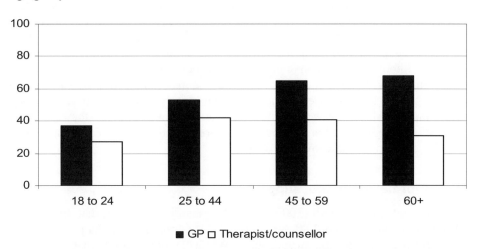

■ GP □ Therapist/counsellor

Not surprisingly, responses to the three other attitude statements included in Table 7.3 followed a similar pattern, with those aged 25–44 showing the highest levels of understanding and awareness, and those in the youngest and oldest age groups showing the lowest. And again, the contrast between those aged 45–59 and those aged 60 and over is very striking: for example, only 30 per cent of the former say they "don't really know anything about counselling or therapy" compared with 52 per cent of the latter. This provides more evidence of an important generational shift in cultural sensitivities to the talking therapies that can be dated, more or less, to the transition between the pre- and post-war generations. It is less clear, though, that this forms part of an inevitable march towards the therapeutic, with each generation more predisposed to such ideas and practices than the last. In fact, the youngest age group – those who would arguably have been most exposed to therapeutic precepts throughout their lifetimes – are the group least likely to say they would feel comfortable talking to either a GP *or* a therapist or counsellor.

On all the measures shown in Table 7.3, women are again more likely than men to have a positive orientation towards counselling and therapy. Men are *more* likely than women to think counselling is only for people with very serious problems (35 and 28 per cent respectively) and to say they don't really know anything about it (38 and 32 per cent respectively). Conversely, men are *less* likely than women to say they would feel comfortable talking to a therapist or counsellor (35 and 40 per cent respectively) or know how they would find one (46 and 55 per cent).

There are also clear educational and income effects here, with those educated to degree level and living in more affluent households being markedly more likely to be aware that therapy/counselling is not only for those with serious problems, to say they know something about it and that they would know how to find a therapist or counsellor. For example, 51 per cent of graduates would feel comfortable talking to a therapist or counsellor, and 62 per cent would know how to find one. This compares with figures of just 35 and 48 per cent respectively among non-graduates. While such a finding is not unexpected, it nevertheless could signal a degree of cultural resistance to the idea of therapy or counselling among groups who may actually have significant need of such services. This suggests that the simple expansion of provision may not be enough without work to change prevailing attitudes and awareness.

Agreement with the statement, "If I had seen a counsellor or therapist, I wouldn't want anyone else to know" is also clearly related to awareness and understanding. In other words, those whose responses suggest they know or understand more about therapy/counselling are *less* likely to be concerned about the idea of anyone else knowing about it.

Use of formal emotional support

In *Therapy Culture*, Furedi (2004) refers to research suggesting that, by the turn of the 21st century, around 80 per cent of the American public had experienced some form of therapeutic intervention. While acknowledging that therapy is sometimes depicted as an American eccentricity, he goes on to assert that "the impact of therapeutic intervention on British society is *no less significant*" (2004: 9). It is not entirely clear whether he means to suggest that levels of 'therapeutic intervention' are at a similar level in the UK – what is striking, however, is that he offers no evidence from studies of the general population in the UK in support of this general assertion.

So what do our data tell us about how many people are actually accessing formal emotional support in the UK? It needs to be remembered that – unlike most previous studies which have focused on service user populations – this is based on a nationally representative sample of the British adult population. We asked:

> *Again thinking specifically about times when you have felt especially worried, stressed or down, have you ever actually talked to any of the people on this card about how you were feeling?*

We then showed respondents the list of people shown in Table 7.4. As the table shows, there is little evidence of current widespread reliance on professionalised or formal emotional support in Britain. A substantial minority of all adults, two-fifths, have certainly discussed their emotional lives at some point with a health professional or one of the other people listed in the table. Indeed, around a quarter have done so within the past year. But it is also clear that this contact is overwhelmingly associated with GPs rather than involving more explicitly 'talk-based' forms of therapy or counselling. Three in every ten people have discussed their emotional lives with their GP at some point, nearly double the proportion (16 per cent) who have ever spoken to a 'talk-based' professional (that is, a psychologist, psychiatrist, counsellor or therapist). The discrepancy between these two sources of advice and support is even greater if we focus only on those who have sought support in the last year; while two in ten have spoken to their GP, only six per cent have spoken to a talk-based professional.

Table 7.4 Contact with formal emotional support – ever and in the last year

	% contact ever	% contact in last year
GP	31	19
Psychologist	2	1
Psychiatrist	4	2
Therapist or counsellor (in person)	13	4
Therapist or counsellor (by telephone)	2	1
Someone from a support service who is trained to help people or to listen	3	1
Social worker or care worker	2	2
Minister/priest/other religious leader	4	2
Some other kind of professional	2	1
Any of the above	40	25

Base: 2102

So among the population as a whole, then, we have found little evidence of a widespread involvement in formal emotional support. But does this hold true across different groups within the population or are some much more likely than others to have turned to these sources of support?

In terms of age, the pattern across the first three age groups is generally what one might expect: experience accumulates with age. This is shown in Figure 7.2. What is striking, however, is the way that the use of all types of formal support (but especially those associated with the talking therapies) drops sharply among those in the oldest age group. In other words, there appears to be something fundamentally different about the experiences (and, as we have seen, attitudes) of the pre-war generation. However, the pattern is slightly different for contact with GPs and for 'talk-based' professionals. Older people's relationships with their GP is often rather different from that of young people – partly because they tend to experience poorer health and so simply see their GP more often, but also because they are more likely to have built up a relationship with their GP over a number of years. So it is perhaps not surprising that the fall-off in use of GP services for emotional support among the 60-plus age group is less pronounced. It is clear, however, that older people are markedly less likely than younger age groups to have contact with professionals from the 'talk-based' therapies. It is also noticeable that those in the youngest age group are significantly less likely than the oldest to have sought support from their GP, but much *more* likely to have experienced talk-based therapy of some kind.

Figure 7.2 Contact with formal emotional support ever, by age group

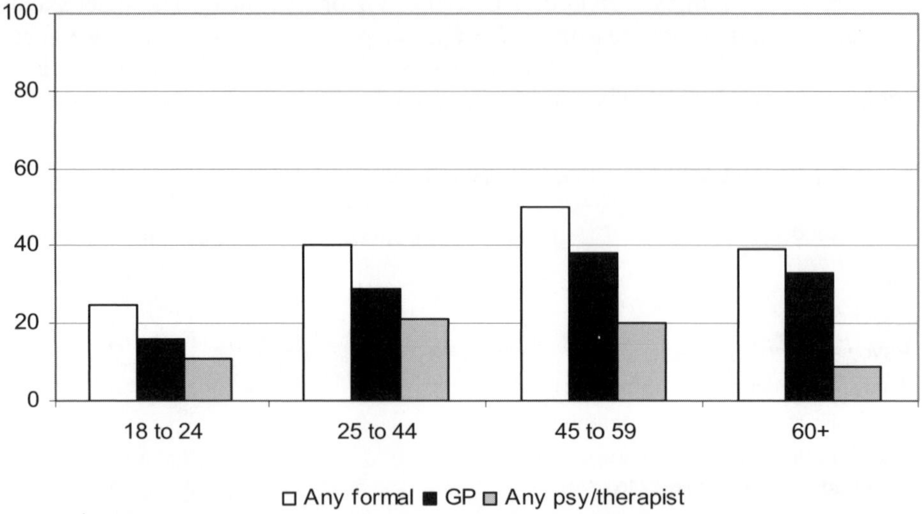

□ Any formal ■ GP □ Any psy/therapist

If we focus only on formal service use in the past year, a similar pattern emerges. It shows a clear peak in formal service use in middle age (specifically 45–59), perhaps reflecting need. After all, numerous studies have identified a 'u-curve' in well-being that suggests that one's middle years are the most difficult in emotional terms (Clark, 2007; Blanchflower *et al.*, 2008). However, it is likely that there is also a cohort effect here; in other words, that the emotional difficulties experienced in mid-life by those born in the period between, roughly, 1945 and 1965 may be combining with a greater sensitivity to, and awareness of, counselling and its possibilities. The figures for 'last year' use of talk-based therapies among the youngest age group suggest that demands on these services will continue to rise, as larger numbers of people enter their 'difficult' middle years with existing experience of talk-based emotional support. In this respect, it could be argued that those who identify an emergent therapeutic culture are simply anticipating future developments. There is, however, no doubt that they overstate the extent to which it currently defines contemporary experience.

However, age is not the best predictor of past use of formal emotional support. The most powerful predictor of use is a low score on our mental well-being scale, or having had experience of serious mental health problems within the last five years. So formal service use appears to be associated more with actual need rather than with what might be characterised as a more voluntaristic "project of the self" (Giddens, 1991). This may partly explain why gender does not predict use of formal emotional support, as despite the fact that women are generally much more predisposed to emotions talk, men and women do not differ significantly in terms of mental health problems or their mental well-being.

Given this link, we might expect to find a higher level of service use among poorer groups, as they are more likely than affluent ones to experience mental ill health and/or lower mental well-being. To some extent this is true; a half of those in the lowest income quartile (household income less than £12,000) have used formal sources of emotional support at some point, compared with 38 per cent of those in the highest income quartile (household income of £38,000 or more). But these differences are not as great as we might expect, even once we take account of age; and there is no difference at all in relation to levels of use of more overtly talk-based therapies (such as psychology, psychiatry and counselling). By contrast, poorer people *are* much more likely to have experience of using prescription medication to deal with emotional problems. We asked:

> *At times when you may have felt especially worried, stressed or down, have you ever used prescribed medication, for example, anti-depressants, sedatives or sleeping tablets?*[2]

Three in ten (31 per cent) of those in the lowest income quartile had used medication of this sort, nearly double the rate found among the most affluent quartile (17 per cent). This does not appear to be driven by higher levels of need. Looking only at the experience of those with the lowest mental well-being scores, use of medication stood at 42 per cent in the lowest income quartile, compared with 27 per cent in the highest. Consequently, it seems that among the poorest sections of British society there may be a substitution of a pharmaceutical for a talk-based response to emotional problems.

Potential demand for formal emotional support

We also examined the extent to which there is hidden demand for formal support, by asking:

> *Have there ever been (any other) times when you were feeling especially worried, stressed or down when you thought about talking to any of the people on this card but didn't actually do so?*

Responses to this question allow us to assess whether there is widespread potential demand for such services over and above the level of use we have already found. Overall, around one person in five (22 per cent) indicated that there had been at least one previous occasion on which they had considered contacting some kind of formal support but had not actually done so. Those with previous experience of this sort of support were twice as likely as those without to say they had considered talking to a professional but had not actually done so (31 per cent compared with 16 per cent). It is particularly striking that among those who had ever talked to a psychologist, psychiatrist, therapist or counsellor, one in five (19 per cent) said there had been other occasions on which they had considered contacting such services but had not actually done so. This is five times the rate found among those with no previous experience of contact with these professions, only four per cent of whom had thought about contacting similar services. This suggests that, while there is a reasonable level of additional potential demand, so far it comes mainly from those who already have experience of using such services.

People give a variety of reasons for not actually contacting emotional support services, despite having considered doing so. As Table 7.5 shows, there is little evidence of concrete barriers to the use of such services (such as problems of access or awareness of where or how to contact them). There is some evidence of people worrying about confidentiality or feeling awkward or embarrassed, but by far the main reasons given were that they did not ultimately believe that talking to someone else would help the situation, or that the problem resolved itself in other ways. This reinforces the suggestion that professional therapeutic intervention is not routinely seen as a useful or viable response to everyday emotional difficulties.

Table 7.5 Reasons given for not contacting formal emotional support services

	% mentioning
The problem resolved itself	31
Didn't believe it would make any difference	29
Didn't feel up to it	15
Felt embarrassed or shy	12
Didn't know how to put it into words	9
Didn't really know who to contact	7
Nervous about /afraid of contacting them	7
Worried it would appear on medical record	6
Felt ashamed	5
Didn't feel it was for people like me	5
Couldn't afford it	5
Didn't really know how to contact them	3
Was worried about someone finding out	3
Too difficult to get to	1
Too far to travel	*
Some other reason	7
No particular reason	7
Base	*471*

Base: those who had considered contacting formal emotional support but had not done so

The relationship between formal and informal emotional support

Furedi (2004) identifies a profound antagonism between therapeutic culture and informal relations and support. Indeed, as he puts it:

> ...the greatest hostility of therapeutic culture is reserved for the sphere of informal relations. Indeed [...] the disorganisation of the private sphere is probably the main accomplishment of therapeutic culture. (Furedi, 2004: 21)

There are limits to the extent to which we can test this thesis. Ideally, one would map the level and pattern of use of both formal and informal support over time and establish whether, as Furedi suggests, the former is on an upward and the latter on a downward trajectory. In the absence of time-series data, however, only more tentative analyses are possible. If Furedi is right, we might expect to find evidence that informal relationships and support are ceasing to play a major role in contemporary emotional life. But, like other recent studies (see, for example, Park and Roberts, 2002; Pahl and Spencer, 2006), our data suggest that webs of informal emotional support continue to play a major role in the lives of the majority of the population. There are several clear indicators of this. First of all, when asked how often in the last year they have spoken to a friend or relative "because you were feeling especially worried, stressed or down", around half (47 per cent) say they have done so at least once a month. Among those in relationships, a slightly larger proportion (56 per cent) say they have talked to their spouse or partner with the same frequency. Of course, to some extent these figures may simply reflect need: in other words, many people may *not* have found themselves in situations in which they wanted such support. So an alternative hypothetical measure is how likely people would be to talk to those close to them *if* they found themselves facing emotional difficulties. Fully two-thirds of those in a relationship (67 per cent) say they would be "very likely" to talk to their spouse/partner if they were feeling "especially worried, stressed or down", while a further 24 per cent say they would be "fairly likely" to do so. Four in ten (43 per cent) say they would be very likely to talk to a close friend or relative, and 39 per cent that they would be fairly likely to do so.

On both our actual and hypothetical measures of informal emotional support, women were markedly more likely than men to show a willingness to turn to those close to them. Among those in relationships, for example, two-thirds (66 per cent) of women said they had sought support from their partner at least once a month over the past year, compared with just under a half (47 per cent) of men. By contrast, a quarter of men (25 per cent) said they had *never* sought support from a close friend or relative, compared with only 10 per cent of women.

Whether in a relationship or not, most people – both male and female – continue to have other people around them to whom they say they could and would talk if they were feeling worried, stressed or down. We asked respondents how many people they have in their lives that might fill that role:

> *Some people have someone in their life they can talk to if they are feeling especially worried, stressed or down, others do not. Roughly how many people, if any, do you have whom you could talk to if you were feeling like that?*

Seven in ten (70 per cent) indicated that they had at least three such sources of informal support, while 40 per cent had five or more. The average number was 4.6.

An alternative way of looking at this issue is to consider networks of *potential* support. One measure of this is the frequency with which people are in contact or communication with those close to them. While such contact may not, in itself, constitute active emotional support, it could be argued that it is a form of *extant* support. Moreover, it is in the course of such everyday contact that individuals often seek and receive support of various kinds. In recognition of the wide variety of ways in which people keep in touch with one another, we asked how often people were in contact with family or friends "about how you're feeling or just to catch up". We asked about face-to-face contact, as well as contact by telephone, text, e-mail or letter, or via social networking or internet chat sites.

There is considerable variation here in the use of different forms of communication across different groups (and especially by age), but what is abundantly clear is that the vast majority of those interviewed tend to talk to friends or family (face to face or by phone) at least once a week. Moreover, over four in ten (44 per cent) talk face to face to friends or relatives every day, slightly higher than the proportion who talk to this group on the phone each day (37 per cent).

Age and gender are key predictive variables here, with very striking patterns especially evident in relation to use of communications technology (phone, text, e-mail, web). Overall, it is clear that younger people tend to have a much denser network of regular communication with friends or family and that – across all types of communication and among both men and women – the extent of such contact decreases with age. So, for instance, seven in ten (69 per cent) 18–24 year olds talk face to face to friends or family every day, falling to just under four in ten (38 per cent) of those aged 60 and above. While this tells us nothing about the quality or content of that communication, it does suggest that potential *opportunities* for emotions talk are greater for younger than older people, simply because of frequency of contact.

Overall, then, it appears that informal relationships of support (mediated in a variety of ways) continue to play a major role in most people's lives. Indeed, if one compares the proportion of those who say they have talked to close friends or family when feeling worried, stressed or down in the last month, we find that it remains higher than the proportion who have used any kind of formal emotional support ever (45 compared with 40 per cent). While this is not, of course, a like-for-like comparison, it is a useful corrective to the image of an all-pervasive therapeutic culture. For most people, emotional support continues to be sought and given against a backdrop of relationships with partner, friends and family rather than contact with therapeutic professionals.

Perhaps even more importantly, though, is the relationship between use of formal and informal support. Again, if Furedi is correct, one might expect to see less reliance upon friends and family among users of formal emotional support. In fact, the opposite is true. Those who have experience of talking to GPs, counsellors and other professionals are markedly *more likely* to say they would be likely to talk to friends or family, and actually to have done so. So, among those who have used formal support in the past, one in five (22 per cent) talk to friends and family at least once a week (compared with 14 per cent of those who have not used formal support), and one in three (33 per cent) talk to their spouse or partner this often (compared with 21 per cent who have not used formal support).

Conclusions

Furedi and others have posited a society in which therapeutic ideas and practices have become all-pervasive. In the critical realm of emotional support, however, this does not yet appear to be the case. There is undoubtedly an emerging consensus about the general value of 'talking about things' and a sense that we are now more open about difficulties in our emotional lives than we once were. But this does not translate into a universal or even widespread acceptance of formal therapeutic intervention. A sizeable proportion of the population remains wary of the idea of therapy or counselling, or simply understands very little about it. Meanwhile, the number with direct experience of 'professional' emotional support (with the exception of that offered by GPs) remains relatively low, certainly by comparison with the figures Furedi himself cites for the United States, and there is little evidence of a groundswell of unmet everyday demand.

But perhaps more interesting than the idea of a universal or dominant 'therapeutic culture' is the notion of one that is highly patterned or differentiated. Gender is obviously a key dimension here. While there may be evidence from elsewhere that, despite popular stereotypes, men and women have similar communication skills even if they choose to *behave* differently (Cameron, 2007), these findings suggest that women do tend to be more positive about the value of emotions talk and more attuned to the possibilities of formal emotional support – even if they are no more likely than men to make actual use of talk-based therapies. The point here is to highlight how continuing inequalities within interpersonal relationships – and powerful constructions about how we should act as men and as women – shape our beliefs and practices when it comes to talking about our emotions. The findings also suggest, however, that significant variations between different groups of men and women need to be taken account of.

There is also a clear cohort effect that can be traced, roughly, to the experiences of the post-war generation. This group is far more positive than its immediate predecessor about emotions talk in general and the use of counselling or therapy in particular. However, this cultural predisposition also appears to be combining with life-stage effects as the baby-boomers confront the difficulties of middle and old age. As the current 'mustn't grumble' generation of older people dies off, will it be replaced by a cohort that places much greater demands on talk-based therapies? Moreover, those currently aged 60 and over tend to have a very different relationship to their GP – one characterised by greater continuity and trust than is perhaps the case for younger generations. Does this mean that the demands placed on GPs (many of which relate – directly or indirectly – to emotional difficulties) will lessen as current generations age? Or will younger generations become more reliant on their GPs as they get older and their health worsens?

Important questions can also be asked about what lies ahead in terms of the emotional lives and needs of the youngest age group we studied. Will the gap between young men and women in terms of their general orientations towards emotions talk narrow, or is there something about the current generation of young men that means they will continue to resist such attitudes and practices, even as they enter long-term relationships and their more emotionally challenging middle years? To what extent is the very high level of social contact among young people (relative to older age groups) simply a function of life-stage and to what extent is it driven by technology? What are the implications of the development of new communications technologies for the maintenance of strong informal networks into one's 30s and beyond?

Finally, it is worth considering the ways in which economic disadvantage and need intersect in relation to the use of different kinds of formal emotional support. In general, the clearest predictor of the use of formal emotional support is need, whether defined in terms of lower levels of 'well-being' or actual experience of serious mental health difficulties. But, despite the fact that poorer people are much more likely to experience serious mental ill health and lower subjective well-being, they are more likely to seek support from their GP than from the 'talking therapies' and remain relatively more likely to be offered drugs than talk.

In summary, our findings suggest that contemporary Britain is now characterised by a relative openness to talking about emotions and there is a widespread perception that this is part of a generational or cultural shift. It is also clear that the attitudes and experiences of those born in the second half of the last century are very different from those of their predecessors. But the conclusion that professional emotional support has come to occupy a dominant or even central role in our lives appears premature. Informal social relationships continue to occupy a hugely important role in most people's lives, while formal emotional support – and especially the use of talk-based therapies – remains relatively rare. Those who do access such support appear to be driven largely by experience of significant mental health problems rather than a reflexive and voluntaristic 'project of the self'. Most people remain wary of (or oblivious to) the possibilities of talk-based therapeutic intervention, while for many of those in most need – especially in our poorer communities – the problem may still be one of failing to address the structural adversities which produce such needs and of excessive medication. In such circumstances, talk of the triumph of the therapeutic has a particularly hollow ring.

Notes

1. Subjective mental well-being was measured using the Warwick Edinburgh Mental Well Being Scale (WEMWBS), a recently developed and validated scale for assessing positive mental health (mental well-being). WEMWBS is based on 14 positively worded items with five response categories and covers most aspects of positive mental health (positive thoughts and feelings) currently in the literature, including both hedonic and eudaimonic perspectives. The questions can be found at www.natcen.ac.uk/bsaquestionnaires (see self-completion questionnaire version C, Q.25a-n or version D, Q.29a-n).
2. This question included an interviewer instruction that read as follows "INTERVIEWER - IF ASKED, ONLY INCLUDE MEDICATION PRESCRIBED BY A DOCTOR OR OTHER MEDICAL PROFESSIONAL. DO NOT INCLUDE THINGS BOUGHT OVER THE COUNTER."

References

Berlant, L. (2000), 'The Subject of True Feeling: Pain, Privacy, Politics', in Ahmed, S., Kilby, J., Lury, C., McNeil, M. and Skeggs, B. (eds.), *Transformations: Thinking Through Feminism*, pp. 33–48, London: Routledge

Blanchflower, D.G and Oswald, A.J. (2008), 'Is well-being U-shaped over the life cycle?', *Social Science & Medicine* **66**: 1733–1749

Cameron, D. (2000), *Good to Talk? Living and Working in a Communication Culture,* London: Sage

Cameron, D. (2007), *The Myth of Mars and Venus. Do men and women really speak different languages?,* Oxford: Oxford University Press

Clark, A.E. (2007), 'Born To Be Mild? Cohort Effects Don't (Fully) Explain Why Well-Being Is U-Shaped in Age', *IZA Discussion Papers*, **3170**, Institute for the Study of Labor (IZA)

Cloud, D. (1998), *Control and consolation in American politics and culture: Rhetorics of therapy,* London: Sage

Furedi, F. (2004), *Therapy Culture: Cultivating Vulnerability in an Uncertain Age,* London: Routledge

Giddens, A. (1991), *Modernity and Self Identity: Self and Society in the Late Modern Age*, Cambridge: Polity Press

Lasch, C. (1979), *The Culture of Narcissism: American Life in an Age of Diminishing Expectations,* New York: Warner Books

Layard, R. (2004), *Mental Health: Britain's Biggest Social problem?,* paper presented to Strategy Unit, available at http://www.cabinetoffice.gov.uk/strategy/seminars/mental_health.aspx

Nolan, J.L. (1998), *The Therapeutic State: Justifying Government at Century's End,* New York: New York University Press

Park, A. and Roberts, C. (2002), 'The ties that bind', in Park, A., Curtice, J., Thomson, K., Jarvis, L. and Bromley, C. (eds.), *British Social Attitudes: the 19th Report,* London: Sage

Pahl, R. and Spencer, L. (2006), *Re-Thinking Friendship: Hidden Solidarities Today,* Oxford: Princeton University Press

Rieff, P. (1966), *The Triumph of the Therapeutic: Uses of Faith After Freud,* London: Chatto and Windus

Acknowledgements

The *National Centre for Social Research* and the authors would like to thank the Economic and Social Research Council (ESRC) for providing the funding that allowed us to include questions in the 2007 *British Social Attitudes* survey, grant number RES-062-23-0468. However, the views expressed are those of the authors alone.

8 Britain at play: should we 'do' more and view less?

Rossy Bailey and Alison Park[*]

The concept of 'leisure' came to prominence in Victorian Britain, as working hours fell and the work-free 'weekend' arrived. Later, leisure became a symbol of development, "an attribute of the progress of civilisation, in which we move, step by step, from a primitive world of unremitting toil toward a future of uninterrupted play" (Gershuny and Fisher, 2000: 620). But debates in the 1960s about the rise of the "leisure society" (Dumazedier, 1967) have given way to concerns about work–life balance and ever-increasing working hours (Schor, 1992; Mulgan and Wilkinson, 1995; Bunting, 2004). Despite these fears, the time we have to spend on leisure activities has grown over the last four decades, albeit at a snail's pace. Comparing working hours in Britain at the end of the 1990s with those at the middle of the 20th century, reveals that the time we spend at paid work has fallen by two hours and forty minutes per week, most of which has been accounted for by an increase in leisure time of two hours and twenty minutes (Gershuny and Fisher, 2000). Nearly a quarter of the 'average' person's day can now be classed as 'free time', although this varies enormously between one group and another (Lader *et al.*, 2006).

This chapter focuses upon what Britain does with the leisure time it now has, and upon the implications of these choices, both for individuals and for society as a whole. By leisure time we mean time left over after fulfilling obligations such as paid work, domestic chores, childcare, and so on. We begin by outlining why people's leisure choices might be important, and which types of leisure activities might be of particular interest. We then describe who does what, exploring the extent to which different groups spend time doing different things. In so doing, we also consider the extent to which people's leisure choices *really* are choices. Or do constraining factors, such as cost, location or domestic responsibilities, have a significant impact on the decisions people are able to make? Finally, we assess whether the way people spend their leisure time actually matters, either on an individual level or for society as a whole. Are

[*] Rossy Bailey is a Senior Researcher; Alison Park is a Research Group Director, both at the *National Centre for Social Research*. The authors are both Co-Directors of the *British Social Attitudes* survey series.

certain leisure pursuits associated with good health or happiness? Do they promote 'social capital', the bonds of trust and reciprocity that help societies function?

Is leisure important?

Many claims have been made as to how leisure can be of individual and collective benefit. This is particularly true when it comes to sport:

> Sport has the ability to overcome social barriers and empower individuals. It can help to reduce social exclusion, promote lifelong learning, and provide opportunities for engagement in community life through voluntary work. (Sport England, 1999)

Physically active activities are associated with improved general physical and mental health and are also seen to prevent cardiovascular and other major diseases such as obesity, diabetes and certain cancers (Pagano, 2006). These are not just individual misfortunes; such problems cost government an estimated £8.2 billion a year (Craig and Mindell, 2008). But the individual benefits of leisure do not relate to physical exercise alone; active and social leisure pursuits have been found to be associated with higher levels of life satisfaction, while more passive activities seem to be weakly or negatively associated with life satisfaction (Donovan and Halpern, 2002). Donovan and Halpern suggest that leisure activities may increase life satisfaction as they allow people to switch off and provide them with opportunities for socialising.

As well as having benefits for the individuals who engage in particular leisure activities, leisure may also have wider benefits for society. The collective implications of a healthier and happier population are obvious, but leisure can also be seen to have less direct social benefits, too. Of particular note is the fact that sociability is at the centre of many leisure activities, both structurally and motivationally. This means that leisure activities can provide a significant arena for social interactions and for creating or strengthening networks which may develop 'social capital' (Glover and Hemingway, 2005). Robert Putnam describes social capital as the "networks, norms, and trust that enable participants to act together more effectively to pursue shared objectives" (1996: 56). And the last decade has seen increasing attention paid by government to the possible links between leisure and issues such as civic renewal (Keaney, 2006; Rojec et al., 2006).

This discussion already hints at a number of ways in which we might classify different leisure pursuits. In particular, we can distinguish between those that are *passive*, requiring little more from participants than watching or listening. By contrast, others are far more mentally or physically active and engaging. This distinction is important; we might expect to find that physically or mentally *active* pursuits have more desirable outcomes in terms of health or mental well-being than passive consumption. The extent to which leisure activities are *sociable* is also a crucially important factor, as it is these forms of leisure that might be expected to play the most important role in promoting linkages between people and helping ensure community cohesion.

The fact that leisure has a number of possible benefits makes it important to understand social variation in people's leisure choices. Of course, we would expect different people to do different sorts of things in their free time. Perhaps most obviously, we might expect people's choices to change as they get older, perhaps because they have accumulated more responsibilities; a job, for instance, or a partner and children. These might have a bearing on the amount of time that people can spend on leisure pursuits. Age might also have a bearing on the sorts of activity people can participate within or enjoy. Gender is another obvious candidate, reflecting both the different interests that men and women might have and differences in the leisure opportunities available to them. Equally obviously, a person's financial resources will no doubt have a bearing on what they do in their spare time; not everybody can afford a computer, for instance, or pay the necessary ticket prices to go to the cinema regularly. A person's educational background might also have an impact, because it may influence their physical or mental skills, as well their 'cultural capital' (that is, an individual's cultural resources and patterns of cultural consumption, most often transmitted through education). We might also expect a person's religious or ethnic background to have an effect, perhaps by emphasising certain types of leisure activity over others. Finally, physical access may also matter; people living in rural areas will have access to very different facilities to those available to people living in more urban areas.

Britain at play

Leisure is clearly important to people. More time spent on leisure activities, along with more time spent with the family, are the most common choices when people are asked which daily activities they would like to do more of. Six in ten (60 per cent) would like to spend more time on leisure activities than they currently do (and around the same proportion – 62 per cent – say they would like to spend more time with their family). Perhaps not surprisingly, only 15 per cent would like to spend more time doing household work, while 16 per cent of those in paid work say they would like to spend more time at work.

Our leisure choices

To find out what people do in their free time, we showed respondents a list of different activities and asked them to say how often, if at all, they did each one. We defined 'free time' as "time you are not occupied with work or household duties or other activities that you are obliged to do". The results are shown in Table 8.1, grouped into four broad categories.

The first category comprises activities that people tend to do at home (though not necessarily in their own homes): watching television, reading, spending time on a computer, and so on. These are by far the most common leisure pursuits among those we asked about; indeed, nine in ten people do the most common of all, watching television, a DVD or video, several times a week or more (74 per cent do this every day). Next most common is listening to music, reported by around three-quarters of people. The importance of these two activities should not be underestimated; after all, the 2005 Time Use Survey found that "the three main activities carried out by people in Great Britain were sleeping, working, and watching TV and videos/DVDs or listening to music" (Lader *et al.*, 2006: 9). It is notable that these are largely passive activities, which participants consume rather than actively engage with. Next most common is spending time on the internet or on a computer, with just over a half of people doing this each week (30 per cent do so on a daily basis), while four in ten read books this often. We also asked about two other less common home-based activities: playing cards or board games and doing handicrafts. Though only a small minority do these on a weekly basis, just under one in five do them at least several times a month.

Table 8.1 Frequency of leisure activities[+]

		Daily/ Weekly	Monthly	Annual or less often	Never
Staying in					
Watch TV, DVDs, videos	%	91	5	1	1
Listen to music	%	76	13	5	3
Spend time on internet/PC	%	52	12	6	27
Read books	%	42	18	25	12
Do handicrafts such as needle-work, woodwork etc.	%	7	12	22	55
Play cards or board games	%	6	13	41	33
Physical activities					
Take part in physical activities such as sports, going to the gym, going for a walk	%	51	22	11	11
Socialising					
Get together with friends	%	37	40	17	2
Get together with relatives	%	26	35	32	4
Going out					
Attend cultural events such as concerts, live theatre, exhibitions	%	*	9	60	27
Go to the movies	%	1	8	57	28
Spectator at sporting events	%	4	9	35	49

Base: 906

[+] 'Weekly'/'Monthly'/'Annual' = "several times" a week/month/year

Physical activity, such as playing sports or going to the gym, is a popular leisure pursuit, with around a half of people doing it each week (21 per cent do so every day). However, a significant minority, 22 per cent, never take part in physical activities like this or do so very infrequently. Socialising is also clearly an important element of people's free time. As Table 8.1 shows, nearly four in ten report getting together with friends several times a week or more, while a quarter see relatives this often.

Events that involve 'going out' are far less common than those that involve staying in. Around one in ten people go to some form of cultural event (such as a concert, play or exhibition) several times a month or more, and a similar proportion go to the cinema or go to see a sporting event this often. But significant minorities *never* do these sorts of activity – half never go to watch sporting events, and over a quarter never go to the cinema or a cultural event.

To find out more about physical leisure pursuits, we asked people to indicate which sport or physical activity they take part in most frequently. Six in ten (61 per cent) gave a response, while three in ten (31 per cent) said they do not take part in *any* sport or physical activity. A huge range of activities were mentioned, from bowling and curling, to badminton, dancing and cricket, but only a few are done by more than a handful of people. The most common activity is walking (including climbing and trekking); of those who took part in a sport or physical activity, this was chosen by nearly four in ten. This was followed by: fitness training, such as aerobics classes, or working out at the gym; swimming, snorkelling and diving; football; and cycling and athletics.

Table 8.2 Participation in sport or physical activity (activities selected by four per cent or more)

% takes part in sport or physical activity	61
Sport or physical activity taken part in most frequently	%
Walking	38
Fitness training	14
Swimming	9
Football	8
Cycling	4
Athletics	4

Base: 547

Who does what?

Earlier we identified a number of ways in which we might expect leisure to vary between different social groups. In order to examine the importance of these sorts of issues we carried out a number of multivariate analyses to identify the relative importance of a range of characteristics in predicting whether or not a person *frequently* takes part in a particular leisure activity.[1] The advantage of this approach over simple cross-tabular comparisons of different groups is that it helps us assess the relative importance of a range of different characteristics (such as age, sex, income and educational background) while taking account of their relationship with each other. This is an important advantage, as many of the characteristics we are interested in are themselves interrelated – for example, education and income. Multivariate analysis will help us understand better which characteristics are most strongly related to a person's leisure choices. Nonetheless, we will illustrate our findings with some simple bivariate analysis. Further details about the multivariate analysis we used can be found in the appendix to this chapter.

We included 10 characteristics in each of our analyses, selected to help us explore the relative importance of the issues outlined in the preceding paragraphs. The results are shown in Table 8.3. The first column in the table lists the different characteristics that emerged as significant in predicting frequent participation in *at least* three of the 11 leisure activities listed (we have excluded taking part in physical activities for now and will return to them later). The second column then describes the specific groups of interest, and the third column lists the leisure activities which this group of interest was significantly more or less likely to undertake frequently.

Age is the most important predictor of leisure choices, as it emerges as significant in eight out of our 11 models, far more so than any other characteristic. With one exception (reading books), older groups tend to be *less* likely than younger ones to do the activities in question frequently. For example, people aged 35 and over are less likely than 18–24 year olds to go to the cinema frequently; this applies to just five per cent of 35–44 year olds, compared with 23 per cent of 18–24 year olds[2] (and a similar proportion of 25–34 year olds). While nearly three-quarters (73 per cent) of 18–24 year olds see friends frequently, this applies to just one third (33 per cent) of the 65 plus age group. And, despite frequent interest in 'silver surfers', only a fifth (21 per cent) of 55–64 year olds and a ninth (11 per cent) of the 65 plus age group are frequent computer users, compared with 51 per cent of 25–34 year olds. Similar variations exist in relation to playing board games, listening to music, visiting relatives or going to sports events. These findings are likely to reflect a variety of different factors. Some will no doubt be linked to lifecycle factors; for instance, having less time or inclination to spend time with friends. But others may (also) reflect the different opportunities available to particular age groups, or a feeling that particular leisure activities are not really 'for them'. In particular, the fact that computer use among the 45 plus age group is significantly lower than it is among young people reflects a well-documented 'digital divide' between the generations in Britain (Curtice and Norris, 2007).

A few other characteristics are significantly linked to frequency of participation in a number of different leisure activities. Sex is an important predictor of participation in four. Women are more likely to visit relatives frequently or to be avid readers; a third (33 per cent) of women read books frequently, compared with just a fifth (21 per cent) of men. Meanwhile, men are more likely to go to sports events or use a computer frequently. So, while over a third (36 per cent) of men are frequent computer users, the same is true of just over a quarter (27 per cent) of women. To some extent these findings reflect very traditional notions of 'male' and 'female' roles. Thus, women traditionally have been, and remain, more likely than men to keep in touch with relatives (Park and Roberts, 2002), while the public sports arena has long been largely dominated by men. Similarly, well-documented differences between male and female access to computers and the internet, though less stark than differences relating to age, clearly remain (Curtice and Norris, 2007).

Two socio-economic factors also appear to shape people's leisure choices. As we predicted, education matters, with graduates being particularly distinctive in their leisure activities. They are significantly more likely than non-graduates to read books frequently, attend cultural events, use a computer or go to the cinema. So, while four in ten (40 per cent) of graduates read books frequently, the same is true of a quarter (24 per cent) of non-graduates. This tallies well with other research, in finding that the better educated engage more often with more 'traditional' and 'high' culture leisure pursuits (Gayo-Cal, 2006). Education does not, however, predict frequent television viewing (meaning that graduates and non-graduates do not differ significantly in this respect). A person's household income also has an impact, even once we take account of the higher earning power of graduates. We assessed this by allocating people to one of four roughly equal groups depending on their annual household income, with those in the lowest quartile having a household income of less than £12,000 a year and those in the top quartile having one of £38,000 or more.[3] Income emerges as important in relation to three activities. For one, computer use, the activity is much more likely among those in higher income groups; over half (54 per cent) of those in the top income quartile are frequent computer users in their leisure time, three times the proportion found among the bottom income quartile (16 per cent). By contrast, those in the richest quartile are less likely than those in the poorest one to visit relatives frequently (17 and 34 per cent respectively). This is likely to reflect the fact that frequent contact with kin will at least partly depend on geographical proximity, with more socio-economically advantaged groups tending to be the most geographically mobile (Park and Roberts, 2002).[4] It is notable that income is *not* a significant predictor of frequent cinema-going (which involves payment), or attendance at cultural or sporting events (many of which will require payment as well).

The only other characteristic linked to significant variations in the extent to which people do three or more leisure activities frequently is relationship status; whether or not someone lives with a partner. In all cases, those with partners are *less* likely to do the activity in question frequently: going to cultural events, visiting friends and listening to music. This characteristic is significant even once the age of the respondent is taken into account, so it does not reflect the fact that single people tend to be younger than people in relationships. So it is likely to reflect the fact that those without partners have more motivation and/or time to do these things than do people with partners.

Table 8.3 Characteristics associated with frequent participation in three or more different leisure activities

Age	Age 25 and over *less* likely than 18–24 year olds to …	… visit friends
	Age 35 and over *less* likely than 18–24 year olds to …	… visit relatives, play board games, listen to music, go to cinema
	Age 45 and over *less* likely than 18–24 year olds to …	… use computer, go to sports events[*]
	Age 45 and over *more* likely than 18–24 year olds to …	… read books
Sex	Women *more* likely than men to …	… read books, visit relatives
	Women *less* likely than men to …	… go to sports events, use computer
Education	Graduates *more* likely than non-graduates to …	… read books, attend cultural events, use computer, go to cinema
Relationship	People living with partner *less* likely than those without to …	… attend cultural events, visit friends, listen to music
Income	Top quartile *more* likely than bottom quartile to …	… use computer
	Second highest quartile *less* likely than bottom quartile to …	… read books
	Top quartile *less* likely than bottom quartile to …	… visit relatives

[*] People aged 45–54 and 65 plus were significantly more likely than 18–24 year olds to go to sports events on a frequent basis (for this activity, 55–64 year olds did not differ significantly from 18–24 year olds)

Five other characteristics were important in predicting frequency in participation in just one or two leisure activities, and so are not shown in the table. Employment status (whether or not a person is in paid work) makes a difference in two cases, with those who are not in work being more likely than those who are to watch TV or do handicrafts on a frequent basis. This no doubt reflects the fact that those who are not in work will tend to have more free time to spend on leisure activities than those who are in work. Ethnicity is a significant predictor of frequent cinema going (29 per cent of those from ethnic minorities interviewed are frequent cinema–goers, compared with just eight per cent of white respondents) and watching television (where the opposite relationship applied, with white respondents being more frequent viewers than ethnic minorities – 78 and 62 per cent respectively). The reasons behind this are not clear and the small number of ethnic minorities in our sample means that the figures should be treated with caution, although the popularity of cinema could reflect the importance of 'Bollywood'.[5] Religious belief is associated with the two most 'sociable' leisure activities, visiting friends and relatives, which are both more frequent among the religious than the non-religious.

Perhaps surprisingly, physical proximity is important in only one instance, with people in rural areas being less likely than those in urban ones to attend sporting events frequently. However, it is notable that there is no significant difference between rural and urban dwellers in relation to a range of other activities that might be expected to vary by area – going to the cinema, for example, or attending cultural events. Finally, having a child at home significantly predicts the frequent playing of board games, which is more common among parents than those who do not have children in the home (a finding that will come of little surprise to those with young children!).

Getting physical

So far we have seen that a small number of characteristics (age, sex, education, relationship status and income) are significantly linked to frequency of participation in a number of leisure activities. We turn now to examine whether the same characteristics are also linked to the likelihood of a person taking part in physically active leisure pursuits.

We begin by using multivariate analysis to look at the characteristics of those people who take part in physical activities "such as sports, going to the gym, or going for a walk" several times a week or more. Three characteristics are significantly linked to this level of participation. The first is education, with graduates being more likely than non-graduates to participate; this applying to 63 per cent of graduates and 51 per cent of non-graduates. To some extent, the fact that education is an important predictor of physical activity should not surprise us. After all, we have already seen that, after age, it is the second most important predictor of people's other leisure choices (and that, in all cases, graduates are more likely than non-graduates to take part in the leisure activity in question). But while we can make plausible speculations about the links between a graduate-level education and frequent museum attendance or book reading, the case is less obvious in relation to physical activity. One possibility is that education helps people have a clearer understanding of the relationship between physical activity and mental and physical well-being.

Having children in the home is also linked to higher levels of participation in physical leisure pursuits; 59 per cent of this group take part in physical activity regularly, compared to 51 per cent of those who do not live with children. This initially appears surprising, as we might expect to find that being a parent *reduces* the amount of time that people have to engage in physical activity. But this depends on how we define 'physical activity', of course. One plausible explanation for our finding is that, when answering our questions, parents are (quite legitimately) thinking of the various physical activities that they engage in while with their children, whether playing football in the park or going for a walk.

Intriguingly, those who define themselves as religious are *less* likely than the non-religious to take part in physical activity frequently (50 and 58 per cent). There are no obvious explanations for this finding. In the next discussion ethnicity emerges as associated with different levels of physical activity, and the significance of religion here might be related to that. Alternatively, it may reflect the importance of other characteristics that we have not been able to include in our model (and which are themselves related to religion). Or, taken at face value, it may suggest that other pressures affect the amount of time that religious people have to spend on physical activity (or indeed that this group have less interest in such activities).

In order to examine this issue in more detail, we can also examine responses to the question described earlier in Table 8.2. This required people to write down the name of the particular sport or physical activity they take part in most frequently. As described earlier, around six in ten people nominated an activity, while around three in ten said they never take part in any activity like this. Multivariate analysis of this question allows us to examine participation in *any* form of physical activity versus non-participation. (Details of our analyses can be found in the appendix to this chapter.) Once again, education is an important predictor, with graduates being markedly more likely than non-graduates to take part in any form of physical activity (86 and 62 per cent respectively). Employment status is also important, with those in work being more likely to do some form of activity than those who are not in work. Income also appears to matter, with 86 per cent of those in households in the highest income quartile (£38,000 or more a year) reporting that they take part, compared with 52 per cent of those in the lowest quartile. Finally, age and ethnicity are also significant. Those aged 55 and above are less likely to participate (with participation rates among the 65 plus group being particularly low, at 42 per cent), as are those from ethnic minority groups.

These findings confirm other research in suggesting that participation in physical activity tends to be skewed towards the more socially advantaged (for example, Delaney and Keaney, 2005). Education appears to be a particularly important factor, suggesting that its impact on people's leisure activities is not confined only to what can be described as 'high' culture. The fact that both employment status and income are linked with participation, even when education is taken into account, suggests that other socio-economic factors also play an important role. The significance of religion and ethnicity suggest that cultural issues cannot be ignored.

If only I had the time …

Although our findings so far tell us a lot about *who* does what, they tell us very little about the reasons *why* people's leisure choices vary and, in particular, whether they reflect choice or constraint. Take, for instance, the finding that age is a strong predictor of people's leisure activities. Does this reflect a simple difference in the priorities and interests of different age groups? Does it suggest that older groups have less time than younger ones? Or does it reflect a feeling that some activities are not suitable for older groups? To examine this, we asked:

> *To what extent do the following conditions prevent you from doing the*
> *free time activities you would like to do?*
> *... Lack of facilities nearby*
> *... Lack of money*
> *... Personal health, age or disability*
> *... Need to take care of someone*
> *... Lack of time*

As Table 8.4 shows, the biggest perceived barriers are a lack of time and money. A third say that lack of time "very much" or "to a large extent" prevents them from doing what they want in their free time, while a quarter say a lack of money has this impact. Around one in six say this about each of the three other barriers.

Table 8.4 Barriers to doing free time activities that would like to do

		Very much	To a large extent	To some extent	Not at all
Lack of time	%	14	19	29	25
Lack of money	%	11	14	30	35
Personal health, age or disability	%	10	7	19	55
Lack of facilities nearby	%	7	10	28	41
Need to take care of someone	%	7	7	13	60

Base: 906

If we look at how responses to these questions vary between different groups, we start to get a clearer sense of the constraints that govern people's leisure opportunities. The most pronounced differences are evident when we look at the extent to which *lack of time* gets in the way of leisure choices. As Table 8.5 shows, this varies considerably by both age and working status, as we might expect. In particular, it is notable that a significant proportion of people aged between 25 and 44 (indeed, a half of the 35–44 group) feel they simply do not have time to do the things they would like to. This no doubt reflects the demands of parenthood, especially parenthood of young children, as well as possible work commitments. The importance of work is evident in the last two lines of the table; those in work are over three times more likely than those who are not in work to say that a lack of time prevents them doing what they would like. Notably, men and women do *not* differ markedly in their responses to this question; around a third of each say that lack of time "very much" or "to a large extent" hinders them from doing what they would like. However, women are more likely than men to say that a lack of time hinders them "very much" (17 and 11 per cent respectively).

Table 8.5 Extent to which "lack of time" is a barrier to doing free time activities that would like to do, by age and working status

		Very much/ a large extent	Some extent	Not at all	Base
All	%	34	30	25	906
Age					
18–24	%	40	41	13	60
25–34	%	51	32	10	154
35–44	%	54	31	8	168
45–54	%	35	32	21	161
55–64	%	16	32	41	157
65+	%	7	15	53	206
Working status					
In work	%	48	33	12	487
Not in work	%	15	25	43	419

Time 'poverty' could of course reflect a number of factors. We have already seen that work commitments form a part of the equation. But domestic commitments are also likely to matter. This is demonstrated by the responses of different age groups to the question as to whether needing "to take care of someone" inhibits a person's leisure choices. Among 35–44 year olds, the proportion who say this prevents them from doing what they would like stands at 27 per cent, far higher than that found among any other age group. Women are also more likely than men to cite this reason (18 and 10 per cent respectively). So domestic and caring duties are clearly an important constraint on what people are able to do.

We have already seen that work can constrain people's leisure time. But it does, of course, also help provide the *income* that can help give people more choices as to what they do. This is very evident when we consider responses to the question of whether *lack of money* hinders people's leisure choices. Four in ten (39 per cent) of those in the lowest household income quartile say lack of money largely has this effect, compared with just one in nine (11 per cent) of those in the highest income quartile.

Personal health, age or disability is also an important factor in determining the types of leisure choices that a person makes. Not surprisingly, the importance of this varies considerably by age; four in ten (42 per cent) of people aged 65 and over cite this as having an impact on what they do, compared with just seven per cent of the 35–44 age group. There is little variation between urban and rural areas in the extent to which people cite a lack of facilities as getting in the way of their leisure choices.

These findings shed some light on our earlier discussion about the ways in which different groups vary in their leisure activities. This is particularly true in relation to age. Among older groups, personal health, age or disability is clearly perceived to be a barrier to their participation, but for younger groups, in their 30s and 40s, lack of time clearly plays a crucial role. Income is another important predictor of a person's leisure pursuits, and is also clearly perceived to be a barrier by some to doing what they would like to do.

However, in some regards these findings do not tally with those described in Table 8.3. In particular, it is notable that while 'lack of time' is cited by nearly a half of those in work as being a barrier to doing what they would like to do in their free time, whether or not someone is in work is *not* a particularly strong predictor of whether they participate frequently in different leisure activities. Perhaps 'not having the time' is simply an easy explanation to give as to why we do not do all the things we would like to do in our free time?

Socially divided leisure?

These findings suggest that leisure activities in Britain are clearly structured along social lines, with some groups being markedly more likely to participate in particular pursuits. Three characteristics in particular stand out as important: age (with younger groups being more likely than older ones to engage in a variety of leisure activities); gender (with women being more likely than men to engage in some activities, while less likely to engage in others); and education (with graduates being particularly distinctive in their leisure choices). We now turn to see whether, and how, this matters.

The social significance of our leisure choices

At the start of this chapter we explored a variety of arguments as to how leisure choices might affect an individual's physical and mental well-being, as well as their 'social capital'. We begin by focusing on just two of the individual benefits often mentioned as stemming from people's leisure choices – health and happiness. Throughout we will need to avoid inferring a causal relationship from any associations we find; after all, perhaps those who are healthier are simply more likely to do physical exercise (rather than exercise 'causing' good health). We can, however, draw inferences from our findings, and examine the extent to which they support or refute assertions made by those with an interest in these issues. In all cases, further details of our analyses can be found in the appendix to this chapter.

The individual benefits of leisure

We begin by considering how much *enjoyment* people get from their leisure activities. To do this, we asked people to indicate how much enjoyment they got out of four different activities. Table 8.6 shows the results, concentrating only upon those who did the particular activity in question frequently. Probably the most important finding is that watching television (the most common way of spending one's free time), is associated with far *lower* levels of enjoyment than any of the other activities we asked about. Only 37 per cent of frequent television watchers say they get a "great deal of enjoyment" from it (while nearly a quarter say they get "none" or "not much enjoyment"). This compares with 82 per cent of those who get together with friends and 85 per cent of those who read books. So, while television might represent an easy and instant leisure pursuit, it is not one that gives people the same levels of enjoyment and satisfaction as more active pursuits. It is also notable that socialising and reading are associated with higher enjoyment than taking part in physical activity, with just over a half saying they get a great deal of enjoyment from participation in exercise.

Table 8.6 Enjoyment obtained from participation in different leisure activities

		None, not much	Some, fair amount	A great deal	Base
Reading books	%	1	14	85	248
Getting together with friends	%	7	12	82	332
Taking part in physical activities	%	5	39	56	188
Watching TV, DVDs, videos	%	23	41	37	666

Base: all who do relevant activity frequently

The fact that most people do *not* report getting a great deal of enjoyment out of taking part in physical activities prompts the obvious question as to why they are engaging in this form of leisure in the first place. To assess this, we asked people how important four different motivating factors were when it came to taking part in sports or games: "for physical or mental health"; "to meet other people"; "to compete against others"; and "to look good". Among those who engage in these forms of activity, the most important motivation for taking part is, by some distance, the physical and mental health benefits. These are mentioned as being "very important" by 48 per cent and "somewhat important" by 34 per cent. By comparison, the opportunity for socialising that sports and physical activity provide is cited as "very important" by just 15 per cent and "somewhat important" by 41 per cent. So it is clear that, for those who do participate in physical activity, the consequences for their mental and physical good health are a crucial motivating factor.

We turn now to examine the evidence that people's choices of leisure activity have an impact upon their mental and physical well-being. We will do this by focusing upon people's self-reported health and happiness, and seeing how these vary according to characteristics we have already discussed (such as education, sex and age) and people's choices of leisure activity. Because we already know that the leisure choices of different groups vary enormously we will once again use multivariate analysis that allows us to take account of these relationships.

We measured health and happiness by asking:

In general, would you say your health is excellent, very good, good, fair, poor?

If you were to consider your life in general these days, how happy or unhappy would you say you are, on the whole?
[Very happy, fairly happy, not very happy, not at all happy?]

Overall, 13 per cent of people describe their health as "excellent", and 33 per cent as "very good". A similar proportion, 31 per cent, say it is "good", while 20 per cent feel their health is either "fair" or "poor". Although perceptions of one's own health are not the same as more 'objective' measures, they are important indicators of general health (Craig and Mindell, 2007). As we might expect, certain types of people tend to feel healthier than others. Women are more likely to say they are healthier than men, and younger people (aged 18 to 24) are more likely to feel healthier than older groups. There is also a clear socio-economic pattern, with more advantaged groups, such as graduates or those on higher incomes, tending to feel healthier than less advantaged groups.

We found three leisure activities to be associated with health. Perhaps least surprisingly, those who undertake frequent physical exercise are more likely than those who do not to feel healthier. Over half (52 per cent) of those who do physical exercise frequently describe their health as "excellent" or "very good", compared with 43 per cent of those who don't frequently exercise. We also found evidence that spending a lot of time watching television might have a negative impact on health; those who watch television frequently report lower levels of health than those who watch less often. Nearly six in ten (59 per cent) of people who don't frequently watch television say their health is excellent or good, compared with 43 per cent of frequent watchers. Finally, we found that those who meet friends frequently are more likely to feel healthier than those who do not. This is in line with work by Taylor *et al.* (2002) who report that leisure activities which facilitate socialising and friendships are associated with improved physical and mental health and well-being due to the increased levels of social support that these activities provide.

Just over three in ten people (31 per cent) say that they are "very happy" these days, while 58 per cent say they are "fairly happy". Only seven per cent say that they are "not very" or "not at all" happy. Women tend to be happier than men, and living with a partner is also associated with higher levels of happiness. This is in line with other work in the area (Galloway *et al.*, 2006). Just one leisure activity was associated with happiness. Consistent with the literature, we found that those who do frequent physical exercise are more likely to feel happier than those who do less exercise. So, while 35 per cent of those who exercise frequently describe themselves as very happy, this applies to only 28 per cent of those who exercise less often.

The collective benefits of leisure

In this section we will examine whether there is an apparent link between any of the leisure activities we have described so far and social capital. Social capital can be measured in a number of different ways. The Office for National Statistics (Harper and Kelly, 2003) recommends a framework which distinguishes between a number of different dimensions: social participation; civic participation; social networks and social support; and reciprocity and trust, and we have been guided by this in our approach to this issue.[6]

Social participation and civic engagement represent key dimensions of social capital which we combine for the purposes of this chapter. We measured them by asking people about their participation in five different 'associations or groups', ranging from sports and cultural groups to civic or political organisations.[7] Just under six in ten (57 per cent) had participated in at least one. Three socio-economic characteristics were linked with social participation in at least one of these organisations in the last year: education, religion and employment status (with graduates, the religious and those in work being more likely than their counterparts to have participated in at least one of these groups). So, too, were *four* leisure activities. Those who frequently do physical exercise, meet friends, or go to watch sporting events are *more* likely to have participated in at least one of these social groups.[8] However, frequent television watchers are *less* likely to have participated, only 54 per cent having done so in the last year, compared with 66 per cent of less frequent television watchers.

It is notable that the three activities positively associated with participation are all very active ones, requiring effort and engagement from their participants, in contrast to television viewing, which is arguably the most passive as well as the most common of our leisure pursuits. Perhaps Glover and Hemingway were correct when they observed that "passivity in leisure may destroy the relational basis for social capital just as readily as active forms build it up" (2005: 398). In *Bowling Alone*, Putnam identifies the growth of television as a major cause of declining civic engagement and social connectedness in contemporary America (Putnam, 1995). However, it is important not to infer a causal relationship from the associations we have found; perhaps those with higher levels of civic engagement are simply too busy to watch television (rather than frequent television watching 'causing' social disengagement).

For our measure of social networks and support, we created a combined measure from the two 'sociable' leisure activities we initially described in Table 8.2: getting together with friends and getting together with relatives. Earlier we saw that a number of socio-demographic and socio-economic characteristics are associated with the extent to which people meet up with friends and relations. Three of the most important, age, sex and religion, still apply to our combined measure (with younger age groups, women and the religious having more frequent contact with friends and relations than older groups, men or the non-religious).[9] We also found an association between frequency of contact with social networks and six different leisure activities: physical exercise, playing games, listening to music, attending sporting events, going to the cinema and watching television. In each case, those who do the leisure activity in question frequently are more likely than those who do not to be in frequent contact with friends and family. Unlike the leisure activities that emerge as significantly associated with civic or social participation, these six span a range of dimensions, from the highly active (physical exercise) to the more passive (listening to music), from the necessarily sociable (playing games or attending sporting events) to the potentially more solitary (watching television). And here at last is some comfort for frequent television watchers, who are more likely than less frequent viewers to stay in close contact with other people.

Does leisure matter?

So far we have seen that people's leisure choices *are* significantly associated with health, happiness, and three key dimensions of social capital: social participation, civic participation, and social networks and social support. In most, but not all cases, more 'active' pursuits appear to be linked to a positive outcome (whether good health, happiness, social and civic participation, and so forth). In two cases, health and social/civic participation, frequent television viewing appears to have a negative association, with frequent viewers being less likely to describe themselves as healthy or to have joined in with the activities of different groups.

Of course, none of these findings prove that a particular leisure activity *causes* social or civic engagement (or even happiness or good health). After all, it is plausible that those who are already socially engaged and interested (or indeed happy and healthy) are more likely to get involved in leisure pursuits that reflect or cater to these interests. Nonetheless, it is clear that, even once important social and demographic characteristics (such as age, education and sex) are taken into account, people's leisure choices do appear significantly linked to their physical and mental well-being, as well as the extent to which they are connected to others via voluntary groups and other forms of social engagement. Even if the causality of this relationship is unclear, it is likely to be a mutually self-reinforcing one whereby a person's leisure pursuits reflect and reinforce existing interests and outlooks. However, it is notable that leisure does *not* appear to be linked to people's social trust, a key measure of social capital. So leisure alone is thus not a significant driver of the extent to which a person has trust in others, even if it might help develop their social networks and social engagement. This is in line with previous research exploring the relationship between social trust and sport (Delaney and Keaney, 2005). In this sense, then, the importance of people's leisure activities appears more clear–cut when it comes to its individual benefits (such as health or happiness) rather than in relation to more nebulous social benefits to do with social capital and trust.

Conclusions

We began this chapter by outlining the variety of leisure activities that people in Britain do in their spare time. Some are very passive, while others are more active, either physically or mentally. The most common activities tend to be home-based ones, though not necessarily always done alone. Our most frequent leisure activity is the most passive – watching television, something that nearly three-quarters of us do every day (overall nine in ten watch television at least several times a week).

Not surprisingly, we found considerable variation between groups when it came to what they do in their spare time. Age explained the most variation – seven of the leisure activities we looked at are done significantly less often by older groups than by younger ones (there was one exception to this rule, reading books, which is done more frequently by older groups than younger ones). Gender is linked to significant differences in people's leisure choices. There is also a clear socio-economic dimension, with both education and income being linked to different levels of participation, the general rule being that the more 'socially advantaged' tend to be more likely to participate in a variety of forms of leisure, including physical or sporting activity. A variety of reasons are likely to underpin these differences. The importance of age reflects two: 'time poverty' among those in their 30s and 40s (many of whom will be working parents), and the constraints of health conditions among older groups. The fact that socio-economic factors matter is less straightforward to explain. To some extent, they reflect the fact that leisure choices can depend upon money and access to resources; that computer use is more common in richer homes than it is in poorer ones is not particularly surprising. But leisure also appears to be shaped by something less tangible than income alone, as suggested by the importance of education in helping explain people's leisure choices. This points towards the importance of what can be called *cultural capital* and the impact that education, particularly university-level education, has on the decisions people make about how to spend their free time. This applies as much to physical activity (which is done more frequently by graduates than non-graduates) as to more 'elite' pursuits (such as attending cultural events).

A large number of claims have been made about the beneficial effects that particular leisure pursuits can have upon participants – upon their health and mental well-being, most obviously, but also upon their 'connectedness' into social networks. More collective benefits are also apparent, whether as a consequence of a happier and healthier society, or as a result of the generation and promotion of the social capital that helps bind individuals together. Our findings do suggest there is a link between the sorts of leisure activities people do in their spare time and a number of these attributes (although a causal relationship cannot be inferred from this). In particular, frequent physical exercise is significantly linked to good health and happiness, as well as to social participation and social networks (both of which are important dimensions of social capital). Other leisure activities are also important; sociable activities are also associated with good health, social participation and social networks. However, the links between leisure and some elements of social capital are not clear-cut; we found no significant association between different leisure activities and social trust, an important component of social capital.

Only one leisure activity is consistently *negatively* linked to many of these phenomena: frequent television watching. Those who watch television frequently have significantly lower levels of self-rated health and are less likely to have participated in various social groups in the previous year. This suggests that efforts to promote alternative – or additional – ways of spending our free time could well be fruitful. 'Doing' more, and viewing less, may well benefit us all.

Notes

1. The definition of 'frequently' we use varies according to the leisure activity. We defined frequent TV watching as being daily, along with frequent reading, listening to music or using a computer. Getting together with relatives is described as frequent if it happens on a weekly basis or more often, as is getting together with friends or doing physical exercise. Finally, we define going to the cinema several times a month or more as being frequent, along with attending cultural events, playing cards or board games, going to sporting events, or doing handicrafts.
2. There are only 60 18–24 year olds in the sample and therefore the results for this group should be treated with caution.
3. The categories for the income variable were as follows: bottom quartile (annual gross household income of less than £12,000); next quartile (£12,000 to £25,999); next quartile (£26,000 to £37,999); top quartile (£38,000 plus).
4. There also appears to be a negative relationship between income and frequent reading, with those in the second highest income quartile being significantly *less* likely to read books frequently than those in the bottom quartile. However, the fact that this income group alone stands out (that there is no significant difference between any other income group and the bottom quartile) is odd and suggests that this finding should be treated with caution.
5. There are only 61 ethnic minority respondents in the sample, compared with 843 white respondents.

6. The ONS recommend a fifth dimension to social capital (perceptions of the local neighbourhood), which we are not able to address in this chapter.
7. The question wording was as follows:

    In the last 12 months, how often have you participated in the activities of one of the following associations or groups? [A sports group; a cultural group; a church or other religious organisation; a community-service or civic group; a political party or organization]

8. The fact that watching sporting events appears as significant here no doubt reflects the fact that sports groups were included in our list of associations or groups.
9. Ethnicity also appears in the sociability model, although the small number of ethnic minority respondents in our sample means this finding should be treated with caution.

References

Bunting, M. (2004), *Willing slaves: how the overwork culture is ruling our lives*, London: HarperCollins

Craig, R. and Mindell, J. (2007), *General health and function: the health of older people. Health Survey for England 2005*, volume 1, London: *National Centre for Social Research*

Craig, R. and Mindell, J. (2008), *Cardiovascular disease and risk factors in adults. Health Survey for England 2006*, volume 1, London: *National Centre for Social Research*

Curtice, J. and Norris, P. (2007), 'Isolates or socialites? The social ties of internet users', in Park, A., Curtice, J., Thomson, K., Phillips, M. and Johnson, M. (eds.), *British Social Attitudes: the 23rd Report*, London: Sage

Delaney, L. and Keaney, E. (2005), *Sport and social capital in the United Kingdom: statistical evidence from national and international survey data*, London: IPPR

Donovan, N. and Halpern, D. (2002), *Life Satisfaction: the state of knowledge and implications for government*, London: Strategy Unit

Dumazedier, J. (1967), *Towards a society of leisure*, New York: Free Press

Galloway, S., Bell, D., Hamilton, C. and Scullion, A. (2006), *Quality of Life and Wellbeing: Measuring the Benefits of Culture and Sport: A Literature Review and Thinkpiece*, Edinburgh: Scottish Executive Social Research

Gayo-Cal, M. (2006), 'Leisure and participation in Britain', *Cultural Trends*, **15(2)**: 175–192

Gershuny, J. and Fisher, K. (2000), 'Leisure', in Halsey, A. with Webb, J. (eds.), *Twentieth-Century British Social Trends*, Basingstoke: Macmillan Press

Glover, T.D. and Hemingway, J.L. (2005), 'Locating leisure in the social capital literature', *Journal of Leisure Research*, **37(4)**: 387–401

Harper, R. and Kelly, M. (2003), *Measuring social capital in the United Kingdom*, London: Office for National Statistics, available at http://www.statistics.gov.uk/socialcapital/downloads/harmonisation_steve_5.pdf

Keaney, E. (2006), *From access to participation: cultural policy and civil renewal*, London: IPPR

Lader, D., Short, S. and Gershuny, J. (2006), *The Time Use Survey, 2005: How we spend our time*, London: HMSO

Mulgan, G. and Wilkinson, H. (1995), 'Well-being and time', in Mulgan, G. and Wilkinson, H. (eds.), *The time squeeze*, London: DEMOS

Pagano, I.S. (2006), 'Dynamic modelling of the relations between leisure activities and health indicators', *Journal of Leisure Research*, first quarter, 2006

Park, A. and Roberts, C. (2002), 'The ties that bind', in Park, A., Curtice, J., Thomson, K., Jarvis, L. and Bromley, C. (eds.), *British Social Attitudes: the 19th Report*, London: Sage

Putnam, R. (1995), 'Bowling alone: America's declining social capital', in *Journal of Democracy*, **61**: 65–78

Putnam, R. (1996), 'Who killed civic America', *Prospect*, March: 66–72

Rojek, C., Shaw, S.M. and Veal, A.J. (eds.) (2006), *A handbook of leisure studies,* ,Basingstoke: Palgrave Macmillan

Sport England (1999), *The value of sport to the health of the nation*, London: Sport England, available at http://www.sportengland.org/text/health.pdf

Schor, J. (1992), *The overworked American: the unexpected decline of leisure*, New York: Basic Books

Taylor, Dickenson and Klein (2002), cited in Glover, T.D. (2008), 'Friendships developed subsequent to a stressful life event: the interplay of leisure, social capital and health', *Journal of Leisure Research*, second quarter, 2008

Acknowledgements

The *National Centre for Social Research* is grateful to the Economic and Social Research Council (grant number RES-501-25-5001) for the financial support which enabled us to ask the *International Social Survey Programme* (ISSP) questions reported in this chapter. Further details about ISSP can be found at www.issp.org.

Appendix

The following tables show the results of the linear and logistic regression analyses which were referenced in the text of this chapter. Ten demographic variables were included in each model (age, sex, whether living with a partner, whether have children in household, work status, rural/urban area, religion, education level, income, ethnicity). Models three, four, five and seven also included twelve leisure activities (watching TV, going to the cinema, reading, meeting friends and relatives, playing games, listening to music, doing physical exercise and handicrafts, attending sporting and cultural events and using computers). Models one and two included these leisure activities minus physical exercise and model six excluded meeting friends and relatives.

Only variables that were significantly associated with the dependant variable at the ninety-five per cent level are included in the results presented below and the significance levels are indicted. In each table the category in brackets is the reference category or comparison group.

Positive coefficients indicate a positive correlation with the dependent variable; negative coefficients indicate a negative correlation.

Model 1: Frequency of physical exercise

The first model looked at the frequency of physical exercise, based on responses to the following question:

> *How often do you do each of the following activities in your free time?*
> *... Take part in physical activities such as sports, going to the gym, going for a walk?*
> *[Daily, several times a week, several times a month, several times a year or less often, never]*

Respondents were divided into two groups. Those who said they did physical exercise *daily* or *several times a week* were classified as participating in physical activities frequently. All cases where the respondent said they took part in physical exercise *several times a month, several times a year or less often*, or *never* were classed as non-frequent exercisers. The dependent variable in this logistic regression model was frequent participation in physical exercise.

Table A.1 Logistic regression (dependent variable frequent participation in physical exercise), by education, religion and household composition

	Coefficient	Standard error
Education (non-graduate)		
Graduate	0.49*	.20
Religion (non-religious)		
Religious	-0.44**	.15
Household composition (no children in home)		
Children in home	0.32*	.14
Base	*794*	

* = significant at 95% level; ** = significant at 99% level

Model 2: Sport played most often variable

This model is an alternative way of examining participation in physical activity. It is derived from a question which asked:

> *What sport or physical activity do you take part in most frequently? (If you do not take part in any sport or physical activity, please tick the box provided below)*

A space was provided for people to write which sport or physical activity they took part in most often. A box was provided for people to tick who did not take part in any physical activity. Responses were used to create two groups of respondents; participants in physical exercise and non-participants. The dependent variable in this logistic regression model was participation in physical exercise.

Table A.2 Logistic regression (dependent variable participation in physical exercise), by work status, age, sex and household composition

	Coefficient	Standard error
Work (not in paid work)		
In paid work	0.54**	0.20
Age (18–24)		
25–34	-0.28	0.37
35–44	-0.77*	0.36
45–54	-0.89*	0.37
55–64	-1.39**	0.37
65+	-1.51**	0.37
Sex (male)		
Female	-0.57**	0.15
Household composition (does not live with partner)		
Lives with partner	-0.49**	0.18
Base	*840*	

* = significant at 95% level; ** = significant at 99% level

Model 3: Health regression

Health was measured using a question which asked for respondents to rate their own general health:

In general, would you say your health is… excellent, very good, good, fair, poor?

These responses were used to place respondents on a scale of self-rated health from poor health through to excellent health. The dependent variable in this linear regression model was self-rated health, as the value of the variable increases it represents increasing health (from poor health to excellent health).

Table A.3 Linear regression (dependent variable self-rated health), by social and demographic characteristics and leisure activities

	Coefficient	Standard error
Work (not in paid work)		
In paid work	0.28**	0.10
Education (non-graduate)		
Graduate	0.33**	0.09
Sex (male)		
Female	0.15*	0.07
Annual household income (under £12,000)		
£12,000 to under £26,000	0.29**	0.11
£26,000 to under £38,000	0.37**	0.14
£38,000 and over	0.47**	0.13
Age (18–24)		
25–34	-0.30	0.18
35–44	-0.23	0.17
45–54	-0.44*	0.17
55–64	-0.44*	0.18
65+	-0.20	0.18
Physical exercise (does not take part in frequent physical exercise		
Takes part in frequent physical exercise	0.18*	0.08
Watching TV (does not watch TV frequently)		
Watches TV frequently	-0.25**	0.09
Meeting friends (does not meet friends frequently)		
Meets friends frequently	0.20*	0.08
Base	*668*	

* = significant at 95% level; ** = significant at 99% level

Model 4: Happiness regression

Respondents were asked to rate how happy they were with their lives in general in the following question:

> *If you were to consider your life in general these days, how happy or unhappy would you say you are, on the whole?*
> *[Very happy, fairly happy, not very happy, not at all happy]*

This range of responses was used to create a scale of self-rated happiness which ranged from being not at all happy through to very happy. The dependent variable in this linear regression model was self-rated happiness, as the value of the variable increases it represents increasing happiness (from not being happy at all up to being very happy).

Table A.4 Linear regression (dependent variable self-rated happiness), by social and demographic characteristics and leisure activities

	Coefficient	Standard error
Household composition (does not live with partner)		
Lives with partner	0.23**	0.05
Sex (male)		
Female	0.11*	0.05
Physical exercise (does not take part in frequent physical exercise		
Takes part in frequent physical exercise	0.15**	0.04
Base	*858*	

* = significant at 95% level; ** = significant at 99% level

Model 5: Social participation regression

Respondents were asked about participation in a number of different social groups:

> In the last 12 months, how often have you participated in the activities of one of the following associations or groups?
> ... A sports group
> ... A cultural group
> ... A church or other religious organisation
> ... A community-service or civic group
> ... A political party or organisation
> [At least once a week, at least once a month, several times, once or twice, never]

In order to measure social participation respondents were divided into two groups, participants and non-participants. If a respondent reported that they had participated in *any* of these activities *at all* in the past 12 months they were classified as participants. Those respondents that said they had *never* participated in *any* of these groups they were coded as non-participants. The dependent variable in this logistic regression model was participation in at least one group.

Table A.5 Logistic regression (dependent variable participation in at least one group), by social and demographic characteristics and leisure activities

	Coefficient	Standard error
Education (non-graduate)		
Graduate	0.94	0.23**
Religion (non-religious)		
Religious	0.88	0.17**
Work (not in paid work)		
In paid work	0.44	0.18*
Physical exercise (does not take part in frequent physical exercise		
Takes part in frequent physical exercise	0.53	0.17**
Meeting friends (does not meet friends frequently)		
Meets friends frequently	0.36	0.18*
Watching TV (does not watch TV frequently)		
Watches TV frequently	-0.48*	0.24
Sports spectator (does not go to sporting events as a spectator frequently)		
Goes to sporting events as a spectator frequently	0.73*	0.30
Base	*731*	

* = significant at 95% level; ** = significant at 99% level

Model 6: Social networks regression

When asking about which activities people participate in during their leisure time we asked how frequently people meet with their friends and relatives:

> *How often do you do each of the following activities in your free time?*
> *... Get together with relatives?*
> *... Get together with friends?*
> *[Daily, several times a week, several times a month, several times a year or less often, never]*

Responses to each of these questions were placed on two scales, one for friends and one for relatives, which ranged from *never* to *daily*. The responses to these two variables were then added together to create one scale to represent frequency of meeting friends and relatives (ranging from infrequently through to frequently). The dependent variable in this linear regression model was frequency of contact with friends and family, as the value of the variable increases it represents increasing contact with friends and family (from no contact at all up to daily contact with both friends and family).

Table A.6 Linear regression (dependent variable frequency of contact with friends and family), by social and demographic characteristics and leisure activities

	Coefficient	Standard error
Age (18–24)		
25–34	-0.48*	0.23
35–44	-0.70**	0.23
45–54	-0.66**	0.24
55–64	-1.12**	0.24
65+	-0.92**	0.24
Religion (non-religious)		
Religious	0.28**	0.11
Ethnicity (non-white)		
White	0.44*	0.18
Sex (male)		
Female	0.38**	0.11
Physical exercise (does not take part in frequent physical exercise		
Takes part in frequent physical exercise	0.38**	0.12
Watching TV (does not watch TV frequently)		
Watches TV frequently	0.33**	0.11
Playing games (does not play games frequently)		
Plays games frequently	0.47**	0.14
Listening to music (does not listen to music frequently)		
Listens to music frequently	0.31**	0.11
Sports spectator (does not go to sporting events as a spectator frequently)		
Goes to sporting events as a spectator frequently	0.47**	0.17
Going to cinema (does not go to the cinema frequently)		
Goes to the cinema frequently	0.52*	0.21
Base	*808*	

* = significant at 95% level; ** = significant at 99% level

Model 7: Trust regression

Respondents were asked a question in order to measure levels of social trust:

> Generally speaking, would you say that people can be trusted or that
> you can't be too careful in dealing with people?
> [People can almost always be trusted, people can usually be trusted;
> you usually can't be too careful in dealing with people; you almost
> always can't be too careful in dealing with people]

Respondents were then placed on a scale to measure social trust which ranged from little trust (those who said *you almost always can't be too careful in dealing with people*) to high trust (those who responded with *people can almost always be trusted*). The dependent variable in this linear regression model was social trust, as the value of the variable increases it represents increasing levels of trust (from very little trust up to high levels of trust).

Table A.7 Linear regression (dependent variable social trust), by education, age and household income

	Coefficient	Standard error
Education (non-graduate)		
Graduate	0.27**	0.06
Age (18–24)		
25–34	0.30*	0.14
35–44	0.36*	0.14
45–54	0.48**	0.15
55–64	0.63**	0.13
65+	0.52**	0.14
Annual household income (under £12,000)		
£12,000 to under £26,000	0.15*	0.07
£26,000 to under £38,000	0.19*	0.08
£38,000 and over	0.25**	0.09
Base	*684*	

* = significant at 95% level; ** = significant at 99% level

9 Is Britain a respectful society?

Elizabeth Clery and Janet Stockdale[*]

Now is a good time to explore public attitudes towards trust and respect in Britain. There is a widely held perception among policy makers, academics and social commentators that social trust has eroded in recent decades, perhaps as part of a wider decline in social capital. These developments have been linked to a range of social problems including high levels of crime and anti-social behaviour (see, for example, Hall, 1999). The existence of a lack of respect among some sections of society has also increasingly been cited as an underlying cause of these problems. In response to these concerns, the government's cross-departmental Respect Task Force was founded in 2006 and given the job of tackling anti-social behaviour as well as promoting and supporting a modern culture of respect.[1]

But how far do these perceptions of a decline in social trust and a lack of respect among a minority in society reflect the attitudes, behaviour and experiences of the public? And to what extent are social trust and respect linked to inconsiderate behaviour? While much has been written about anti-social behaviour and the factors that are associated with it (see, for example Wood, 2004), little attention has been paid to date to milder forms of behaviour, involving a lack of consideration and respect, that might be encountered in public. In this chapter we address this imbalance by focusing solely on inconsiderate behaviour and how this links with levels of trust and respect.

We begin by examining levels of social trust and respect, and seeing how these have changed over time. We then compare the levels of trust and respect reported by different groups, and the extent to which any particular groups emerge as culprits when it comes to inconsiderate behaviour. We then examine people's own experiences of, and participation in, inconsiderate behaviour in public. Finally, we assess whether low levels of social trust and respect are an underlying cause or consequence of inconsiderate behaviour, by looking at

[*] Elizabeth Clery is a Senior Researcher at the *National Centre for Social Research* and is Co-Director of the *British Social Attitudes* survey series. Janet Stockdale is Senior Lecturer in Social Psychology at the London School of Economics and Political Science (LSE).

whether those who witness inconsiderate behaviour more frequently have lower levels of trust and respect. Throughout, we focus particularly on the extent to which there is evidence that low levels of respect and social trust, and high levels of inconsiderate behaviour, are particular problems in more deprived communities.

Defining trust and respect

Before we begin, it is worth tracing the increasing prominence of the concepts of trust and respect in public discourse, and outlining the development of the view that we are witnessing a decline in social trust and an increasing lack of respect among certain social groups, both of which help explain anti-social behaviour.

Social trust has been broadly conceptualised as the individual's belief in the honesty and integrity of others, and can thus be seen as both motivating and underpinning social relationships between people. As a concept, social trust has received increasing attention over the last decade or so, often as part of a broader discussion of 'social capital' among academics and social commentators. Popularised by Robert Putnam (1995) in the United States, social capital is broadly defined as the willingness and ability of citizens to associate with, and assist, each other and to engage in common activities. The extent to which social capital exists in a society can be measured by, among other things, levels of public engagement in voluntary groups and social networks, and participation in political activities such as voting. Social trust has variably been regarded as both a key component of social capital and one of its major outcomes.

Much of the early discussion and measurement of social capital focused on the United States and generally traced a decline in social capital in the post-war years. More recently, attention has focused on Britain (Hall, 1999). Hall does not find evidence of a decline in social capital comparable to that observed in the United States, but does identify, as a significant anomaly, a fall in levels of social trust, evident since the 1950s, particularly among the working class and younger age groups. He concludes: "the one indicator of social capital that has fallen over the post-war years is that measuring the generalised trust people express in others" (Hall, 1991: 443). This perceived decline in social trust, and its implications for social capital, remain an ongoing focus of discussion and debate in the academic literature and for social commentators (see, for example, Grenier and Wright, 2004).

The concept of respect has gained prominence more recently, primarily as a result of the discussions and initiatives of policy makers and government, rather than academics. In recent years, there has been an increasing government focus on 'milder' forms of criminal activity and irritation such as vandalism, littering and noise pollution, broadly labelled as 'anti-social behaviour'. Increasingly, the existence of anti-social behaviour has been attributed to the fact that a minority of people within society, mainly those living in deprived communities, do not share the values of the majority, namely those of respect and consideration for others. For example, in outlining the causes of anti-social behaviour, Prime Minister Tony Blair in the 2006 Respect Action Plan stated that:

> What lies at the heart of this behaviour is a lack of respect for values that almost everyone in this country shares – consideration for others, a recognition that we all have responsibilities as well as rights, civility and good manners (Respect Task Force, 2006)

The idea of a 'respect agenda' emerged during the 2005 General Election campaign and culminated in the creation of the cross-departmental Respect Task Force in 2006 and the publication of a Respect Action Plan. It was intended that the Task Force would build on the government's anti-social behaviour work by tackling the key causes of anti-social behaviour, such as poor parenting, getting more agencies involved in this issue and developing new ways to challenge and change behaviour. In undertaking these activities, the Task Force came increasingly to consider milder forms of inconsiderate behaviour that are encountered in public, but which have not been traditionally considered under the umbrella of 'anti-social behaviour'.

Respect and trust in modern Britain

The *British Social Attitudes* survey has included a number of measures of social trust since the mid-1990s, in one case updating a longer time-series initiated in other surveys. So, if there has been a decline in social trust over time, we would expect this to be reflected in responses to these questions, particularly amongst more deprived groups. Unfortunately, due to its recent emergence in public discourse, the concept of respect has received little attention from survey research to date, meaning that we can not look back at how public perceptions have changed over time. So instead, we will focus on some new questions introduced in the 2007 *British Social Attitudes* survey. These will allow us to see whether there is any evidence that levels of perceived respect within society vary, and are perhaps at their lowest among those living within the most deprived communities.

Trends in social trust

We begin by examining the evidence that social trust and respect is in decline in Britain. Since 1997, the *British Social Attitudes* survey has regularly included two broad measures of social trust. Specifically, we have asked:

> *Generally speaking, would you say that most people can be trusted or that you can't be too careful in dealing with people?*

> *How often do you think that people would try to take advantage of you if they got the chance and how often would they try to be fair?*

Table 9.1 presents the responses to these questions obtained since they were first asked on the survey series in the mid-1990s. For the first question, we have also included readings from earlier surveys dating back to the 1950s. What is immediately apparent is that the findings do not endorse the widely cited long-term erosion in social trust. In fact, the proportion of the public who agree that "most people can be trusted" has remained relatively constant since the question was first asked on the *British Social Attitudes* survey in 1997, with 41 per cent indicating that this is the case. Throughout the past decade, this proportion has hovered around the 40 per cent mark. Considered in conjunction with the earlier time-series, what is particularly striking is the relative *stability* of this measure of social trust since 1981. While a much higher level of social trust was found when this question was included on the Civic Culture study in 1959, when almost three-fifths thought most people can be trusted, the 20-year gap in data collection between then and the 1981 measure makes it hard to conclude with any certainty that there has been a gradual decline in social trust since 1959, as this first reading might simply have been an anomaly. With only the first three readings available, concern was expressed in the mid-1990s that these represented the beginning of a major decline in social trust in Britain (see, for example, Hall, 1999). But our subsequent, and more regular, readings of the data clearly imply that this is not, in fact, the case.

Our second measure of social trust, focusing on the extent to which people perceive that others would try to be fair to them, rather than taking advantage, also fails to support the argument that we are witnessing a decline in social trust. The proportion of the public who think people would try to be fair "almost all" or "most of the time" has hovered at around the 60 per mark for most of the past decade, with the last two readings both being on the high side. Once again, these data do not lend support to the often-cited view that Britain is experiencing a long-term decline in social trust.

Table 9.1 Levels of social trust, 1959–2007

	1959	1981	1990	1997	1998	2000	2002	2005	2007
% say most people can be trusted	56	43	42	42	44	45	39	45	41
% say people try to be fair almost always/ most of the time	n/a	n/a	n/a	n/a	56	55	55	65	58
Base	*963*	*1167*	*1484*	*1355*	*2066*	*2293*	*2285*	*3160*	*4124*

Source: 1959 Civic Culture study; 1981 and 1990 World Values Survey
n/a = not asked

In addition to the general measures of social trust we have just described, the 2007 *British Social Attitudes* survey also included some more specific measures of social capital, focusing on the extent to which the public would feel comfortable in a number of different situations:

Suppose you found your sink was blocked, but you did not have a plunger to unblock it. How comfortable would you be asking a neighbour to borrow a plunger?

Suppose that you were ill in bed and needed someone to go to the chemist to collect your prescription while they were doing their shopping. How comfortable would you be asking a neighbour to do this?

Suppose the milkman called for payment. The bill was £5 but you had no cash. How comfortable would you be asking a neighbour if you could borrow £5?

In a sense, the extent of public comfort with these requests is likely to be influenced, at least in part, by one's trust in their neighbours; therefore, if Britain is undergoing an erosion in social trust, we might expect to see a decline on each of these measures over the past decade.

As demonstrated in Table 9.2, responses to these three questions are mixed. Traditionally, the public has always felt more comfortable asking neighbours to provide assistance that involves their time or the provision of non-financial resources; there has always been considerably more anxiousness associated with the request to borrow money from a neighbour, a trend which persists in 2007.

Table 9.2 Trust in neighbours, 1998–2007

% who would feel comfortable …	1998	2000	2003	2005	2007
… asking a neighbour to borrow £5	34	38	33	33	34
… asking a neighbour to borrow a plunger	85	85	83	82	82
… asking a neighbour to collect your prescription while out shopping	78	80	73	71	69
Base	*2068*	*2293*	*3305*	*3151*	*3094*

The proportion of those feeling "very" or "fairly comfortable" about asking a neighbour to borrow £5 has remained relatively constant, at around one third, while the proportion feeling comfortable asking to borrowing a plunger has declined slightly over the past decade, although the majority, more than four-fifths, remain comfortable with this idea. Meanwhile, the proportion who feel comfortable asking a neighbour to collect a prescription whilst out shopping has declined significantly, down by nine percentage points since 1998. These figures suggest that, over recent years, the public has become slightly less comfortable about asking a neighbour for a favour that involves time and effort. Of course, this may simply reflect the fact that people do not know their neighbours as well as they used to, rather than necessarily being symptomatic of a decline in social trust. In any case, given the presence of a significant decline on just one of our three measures, these data do not offer wholehearted support for the view that social trust in Britain has eroded.

Variations in social trust

Discussions of a decline in social trust have tended to focus on the more deprived sections of society, for whom this development has been regarded as having been particularly pronounced and problematic. Focusing on data up to 1990, Hall concluded that social trust in Britain had declined particularly among the working classes and younger age groups. He regarded this as being a consequence of both a 'period effect' (whereby trust had declined across all groups in society) and a 'generational effect' (with the youngest age group being less likely than their predecessors to exhibit social trust) (see Hall, 1999).

We have already seen that our key measure of social trust has remained relatively stable over recent years. But this tells us nothing about whether levels of social trust vary between different groups. So we turn now to examine whether levels are particularly low amongst younger and more deprived groups.

Clearly, deprivation is a multi-faceted concept and cannot be encapsulated by one single measure. So we included in our analysis a range of measures which might be expected to be linked to deprivation, including household income, occupational class[2] and education, as well as a range of demographic characteristics. Five characteristics, presented in Table 9.3, emerged as being significantly linked to levels of social trust – the individual's age, their household income, whether they live in a rural or urban location, their occupational class and their educational level. The characteristics that most clearly relate to deprivation are associated with the most extreme differences. So, while almost six in ten of graduates think "most people can be trusted", the same is true of just one in three of those without any qualifications. More than half of those whose household income puts them into the highest income quartile agree with this proposition; as do only a third of those in the lowest income quartile. Similar variations are evident when we look at levels of social trust among different occupational groups, with more affluent and middle-class groups having far higher levels of trust than those in more routine manual jobs. Other differences are less pronounced but still significant; as Hall's work predicts, younger people have lower levels of trust than older ones. And those in urban locations are significantly less likely than those in rural locations to think that most people can be trusted.

Table 9.3 Social trust for different social and demographic groups

Social and demographic groups	% say most people can be trusted	Base
All	41	4124
Age		
18–34	36	929
35–49	42	1192
50–64	47	978
65+	45	1020
Location		
Urban	40	3253
Rural	48	838
Highest educational qualification		
Degree	59	711
Higher education below degree	48	392
A level	44	545
O level	34	696
CSE	34	259
None	33	1061
Household income		
Highest income quartile (£44,000 and above)	53	764
Lowest income quartile (less than £12,000)	33	1040
Occupational class		
Professional	58	1016
Intermediate	40	1661
Routine	33	1279

Logically, some of these characteristics are likely to be linked to one another; for instance, those with few educational qualifications are more likely to have jobs in the lowest occupational category, or to be older. Similarly, those living in rural locations may be more likely to be older, so the higher levels of social trust in those areas may simply be a consequence of their different age profile. To take account of this, we used multivariate analysis (logistic regression) to establish which characteristics best *independently* predict levels of social trust, once their relationships with one another have been taken into account.

All of the characteristics discussed above, with the exception of location, were found independently to predict levels of social trust (further details of the model we generated can be found in the appendix to this chapter). The disappearance of location from the model is likely to be due to the fact that differences in levels of social trust between those living in rural and urban settings are caused by the distinct social and demographic characteristics of the populations of these two types of area. The fact that both household income and occupation *remain* significant predictors of social trust clearly points towards the importance of material deprivation. Moreover, the importance of education suggests that the *less* material aspects of deprivation might also influence a person's social trust (reflecting, for example, the fact that education gives people opportunities to acquire and use more advanced knowledge and cognitive skills).

These enduring differences are consonant with the idea that those who feel more anonymous or alienated (because of their age or occupation) and those with less access to economic security and, perhaps, less advanced cognitive skills (because of their lack of educational qualifications) feel less able to trust others. This may reflect the realities of their lives; the fact that they live and work in environments where trusting others is not the norm and where doing so may be counter-productive, or even, dangerous. So, while *British Social Attitudes* data do not give weight to, and in some instances challenge, the premise that Britain is experiencing an ongoing decline in social trust, they do offer support to the widely held view that low levels of social trust are a particular issue for more deprived social groups.

Experiencing respect: a divided Britain?

How can we best measure people's perceptions of the levels of 'respect' that exist in Britain today? It is essential to recognise that people's answers might vary considerably depending upon whether we ask about the respect they encounter in their own day-to-day lives, as opposed to their perceptions of the general levels of respect that exist in Britain as a whole. After all, a range of factors will potentially influence an individual's perceptions of the levels of respect that exist in different spheres – their own lived experiences and those of their acquaintances, their ideas of what constitutes 'respectful' behaviour, information about respect gleaned from other sources such as politicians and the media, and so on. These different influences might have a greater or lesser influence on perceptions of respect, depending on the sphere being asked about. For this reason, we asked the public to indicate their views about three different statements:

> *In Britain, people generally treat each other with respect and consideration in public*

> *In your neighourhood, people generally treat each other with respect and consideration in public*

> *And thinking now of all the people you come across in your day to day life, how many would you say generally treat you with respect and consideration in public?*

The responses obtained are presented in Tables 9.4a and 9.4b. They clearly indicate that perceived levels of respect depend crucially on the level of abstraction in the question. When asked about one's own specific neighbourhood and one's day-to-day life, perceptions are fairly positive; almost three-quarters agree that people in their neighbourhoods "generally treat each other with respect and consideration", and eight in ten think that "everyone" or "most people" they come across in their day-to-day life treat them with respect and consideration. But when asked about Britain as a whole, the impression is far more gloomy; only four in ten agree that people generally treat others with respect and around the same proportion disagree. The findings also endorse the view that a lack of respectful and considerate behaviour is a phenomenon regularly experienced by a significant minority of the British public. One in eight (13 per cent) indicate that people in their neighbourhoods generally do *not* treat others with respect and consideration, and around a quarter say that at least some people in their day-to-day lives do not treat them with respect.

Table 9.4a Perceptions of respect and consideration in public

People generally treat each other with respect and consideration		Agree	Neither	Disagree	Base
In Britain	%	40	21	39	3094
In your neighbourhood	%	73	14	13	3094

Table 9.4b Personal experience of respect and consideration in public

		Everyone/ most people	Some people	A few people/ No one	Base
How many people in day-to-day life treat you with respect and consideration	%	79	16	6	3094

People's perceptions of the levels of respect that exist within Britain as a whole are likely to be formed, to some extent, by their own experiences in public. This is borne out by the fact that those who think people in Britain treat each other with respect and consideration are also more likely to say this is the case in their own neighbourhoods and that most people do this in their day-to-day lives. But this relationship cannot explain the large discrepancy shown in the tables above between people's general and specific perceptions. This is likely to reflect, at least partly, the fact that people tend to be more positive about things that they have direct experience of, or encounter regularly, than they are about more abstract or general issues. (So, for example, they tend to be more positive about their GP than about the NHS in general, or about their MP than politicians in general.) It is also likely that the increasing prominence of 'respect' as a concept within government and media discourse has created a perception that it is an important concern elsewhere in Britain, even if it is not something that worries people in their own neighbourhood. For this reason, we will focus in the remainder of this chapter upon people's perceptions of respect in their own immediate lives and neighbourhoods, rather than on their general perceptions about Britain as a whole.

Who feels treated respectfully?

We have seen that a significant minority of people feel they are not treated with respect or consideration. So we now turn to consider whether this minority, as is often assumed, consists largely of people living in the most deprived communities, or whether there are other characteristics associated with experiencing a lack of respectful and considerate behaviour on a regular basis. Several characteristics emerge as being strongly associated with experiencing disrespectful and inconsiderate behaviour in public. People in urban areas have far more negative perceptions than those who live in rural locations. Almost nine in ten (86 per cent) of those in rural areas agree that most people in their neighbourhoods treat each other with respect and consideration, compared to just seven in ten (71 per cent) of people in urban environments. Similar differences exist in response to our question about the respect people encounter in their day-to-day lives. These may reflect the fact that urban environments are less conducive to respectful behaviour, perhaps given the greater concentration of people they contain, or it may reflect the fact that these settings contain higher proportions of particular social groups that are less likely to report respectful behaviour.

Income also emerges as being strongly associated with experiences of respect and consideration, with those in the highest quartile of household incomes reporting far more positive experiences; 81 per cent of this group agree that people in their neighbourhoods generally treat each other with respect and consideration, compared to 70 per cent of those in the lowest income quartile. Again, a similar difference can be observed in relation to perceptions of respectful behaviour in individuals' day-to-day lives. Those in higher occupational groups also tend to express more positive attitudes, with more than eight in ten of those in professional occupations (83 per cent), three in four of those in intermediate occupations (75 per cent) and around two in three (65 per cent) of those in routine occupations indicating that, in their neighbourhoods, people treat one another with respect.

Two demographic characteristics also appear to make a difference. Younger age groups are much less likely to report experiencing respectful and considerate behaviour than older age groups; 68 per cent of those aged between 18 and 34 agree that "everyone" or "most people" in their daily lives treat them with respect and consideration, compared to almost nine-tenths (88 per cent) of those aged over 65. A similar difference occurs in relation to marital status.

Single people are the least likely to perceive respectful and considerate behaviour, while those who are married or widowed are the most likely to do so.

We carried out two multivariate analyses (linear regression) to establish which of these characteristics *independently* predicts people's perceptions of the respect they encounter in their day-to-day life and in their local neighbourhood. The two models are presented in the appendix to this chapter. Five of the six factors highlighted above – age, location, income, occupation and marital status – were found to predict levels of respect within the individual's neighbourhood, while the same set of variables predict experiences of respect within the individual's day-to-day life.

The more negative experiences of people in urban locations, the young, lower occupational groups and those with lower incomes are likely to reflect the pressures associated with urban life and a lack of access to economic resources, as well as the ways in which young people interact, both with their age group and with older people in Britain today. These findings endorse, to some extent, the view that a lack of respect is a particular problem in certain communities (for instance, urban centres containing a preponderance of people in routine manual occupations or with low incomes). However, the importance of age suggests that, to some extent, a perceived lack of respect may also be an issue for younger age groups across all sections of society, not just the most deprived. It is interesting to note that age explains the greatest proportion of variance in levels of respect in the individual's day-to-day life while living in an urban or rural location explains the greatest proportion of variance in perceptions of respect within the individual's neighbourhood. So, while we have seen that the most deprived groups are less likely to perceive respectful behaviour in their own lives, this is clearly a greater issue among a group that cuts across all socio-economic groupings in society – the young.

Young people and inconsiderate behaviour

So far we have found that certain groups are far less likely to report respectful behaviour in their neighbourhoods and day-to-day lives than others. Perhaps this reflects the fact that they have the most contact with groups whose behaviour is particularly disrespectful or inconsiderate? To explore this, we now consider the characteristics of those who are seen to be particularly at fault. We asked:

> *Do you think there are particular groups of people in Britain who tend to treat others with a lack of respect and consideration in public?*

For those who agreed, we asked a follow-up question:

> *Which groups do you think tend to treat others in Britain with a lack of respect and consideration in public?*

The vast majority of the public, almost nine in ten (87 per cent) indicate that there *are* particular groups of people in Britain who treat others with a lack of respect and consideration. The variation in this percentage associated with membership of particular social and demographic groups is negligible; all sections of society largely hold this view.

As shown in Table 9.5, young people clearly emerge as the main group seen to behave with a lack of respect and consideration in public. Two-thirds of people view young people as at fault in this regard, with no other group coming close. Other groups seen as lacking respect and consideration for others are minority ethnic groups, immigrants and less well-educated people – each selected by around a fifth of respondents. Groups identified by at least ten per cent of the public as showing a lack of respect for others are rich people, old people and those who are unemployed.

Table 9.5 Groups identified as treating others with a lack of respect and consideration in public (groups selected by 10 per cent or more)

Groups who don't treat others with respect and consideration in public	% choosing group
Young people	67
Minority ethnic groups	20
Immigrants	20
Less well-educated people	20
Rich people	16
Old people	14
Unemployed people	10
Base	2705

We have already seen that people in more deprived social groups are more likely than others to perceive a lack of respect and consideration in society and in their own lives. So it is interesting to find that the group defined as the main perpetrator is a demographic one, rather than being defined by social characteristics such as income or educational level. While minorities of the public identify a range of other groups as problematic – such as immigrants, less well-educated people and unemployed people – the discrepancy between these proportions and the overwhelming majority who identify young people is stark. So, while the government's Respect Agenda was founded on the premise that a lack of respect and consideration exists in a minority of primarily deprived communities, these data suggest that the public perceive this problem to be more widely spread across society and not confined simply to particular communities. Of course, it could be concluded that young people feature so prominently here because older age groups are inherently less tolerant of their lifestyles and behaviour, perhaps because they differ so radically to their own. Interestingly, however, younger respondents – those aged 18–34 – are no less likely than other age groups to see young people as problematic, with 66 per cent indicating that this is the case, suggesting that the association in the minds of the public between a lack of respect and young people does not only reflect prejudice against the young. However, it is important to bear in mind that respondents define for themselves what is meant by "young people"; many of those mentioning young people as responsible for inconsiderate behaviour in public might well be thinking of teenagers rather than the young adults, aged 18–34, whose views are captured as part of this survey.

Inconsiderate behaviour

Our consideration of public attitudes to trust and respect in Britain so far has prompted us to challenge the commonly perceived erosion of social trust, while adding support to the view that levels of respect in society vary substantially between different groups. They also indicate that a lack of respect is a problem for particular social and demographic groupings. However, while our findings support the assumption that a lack of social trust and respect are particular issues for deprived communities, they also highlight the fact that age is an important dimension; the lower levels of social trust and perceived respect reported by younger groups suggest that, to some extent, these problems are ones which face society as a whole, rather than a minority of mainly deprived communities.

But how do public experiences of behaviour that involves a lack of respect and consideration tally with and inform these attitudes? Are those groups seen to behave with lack of respect most often the same as those that admit to more regularly undertaking inconsiderate behaviour in public? Do the groups that most regularly experience inconsiderate behaviour have lower levels of social trust and perceive a greater lack of respect in society? Answering these questions will allow us to examine whether experiences of inconsiderate behaviour are linked to levels of social trust and respect. This should help us test the assumption that increasing levels of trust and respect might reduce inconsiderate behaviour.

Experience of inconsiderate behaviour

We begin by examining experiences of inconsiderate behaviour in public. To do this, we asked respondents how often they experience a range of inconsiderate behaviours:

How often in the last 12 months have you seen someone…

… deliberately jumping a queue?
… making a rude and offensive gesture in public?
… deliberately pushing past you roughly in public?
… swearing or shouting aggressively at a stranger in public?
… deliberately dropping litter?

As shown in Table 9.6, people experience a range of inconsiderate behaviours in public on a fairly regular basis. The most common example is deliberately dropping litter; six in ten see someone deliberately doing this at least once or twice a fortnight. More than four in ten see someone making a rude and offensive gesture with this regularity, and around a third see queue-jumping and swearing or shouting at a stranger this often. In total, all five inconsiderate behaviours are reported as being encountered at least once every six months by six in ten people or more. However, experiences of inconsiderate behaviour in public are clearly not uniform. Substantial minorities of the public rarely or never witness these behaviours; a fifth have not seen anyone jump a queue in the last year, and nearly a quarter have not had someone push past them roughly in public.

Table 9.6 Experiences of inconsiderate behaviour in the last 12 months

		Frequency of witnessing behaviour			
		At least once or twice a fortnight	At least once or twice every six months	Less often	Never
Deliberately jumping a queue	%	33	32	15	20
Making a rude and offensive gesture	%	44	33	11	13
Deliberately pushing past you roughly	%	26	32	20	23
Swearing or shouting aggressively at a stranger	%	32	37	15	16
Deliberately dropping litter	%	59	25	8	9

Base: 3094

To explore which sections of the public are more and less likely to experience these behaviours, we created a scale based upon the number of the behaviours listed in Table 9.6 that respondents had seen at least once or twice a fortnight in the past year. Overall, slightly less than half (47 per cent) had not witnessed *any* of the behaviours that often. One in seven (15 per cent) had experienced one behaviour, while 11 per cent had encountered two, 10 per cent three, and nine per cent four of the listed behaviours. Eight per cent had encountered all five behaviours this often. The average number of negative behaviours witnessed at least once a fortnight was 1.9.

A range of social and demographic characteristics were associated with encountering inconsiderate behaviour in public. Many should be familiar from our earlier discussions in this chapter – most notably age, location, educational level, occupational class and household income. But sex and marital status also emerged as significant predictors as well. Those who experience inconsiderate behaviour most frequently are more likely to be young, male, single, to live in an urban location, have few educational qualifications, have a routine occupation and a low income. As before, many of these characteristics are linked to one another and so we used multivariate analysis (logistic regression) to establish which factors *independently* predict experiences of inconsiderate behaviour, once their relationship with all the characteristics are taken into account. Just three stand out as significantly predicting the number of inconsiderate behaviours experienced regularly by an individual – their age, whether they live in an urban or rural location and their sex. This is illustrated in Figure 9.1, which shows the average number of experiences of inconsiderate behaviour witnessed per fortnight for these different groups.

We have already seen that young people are perceived to be a group amongst whom disrespectful and inconsiderate behaviour is particularly common. While this perception might not specifically relate to those aged between 18 and 34, people in this, the youngest age group in our survey, are also more likely than older age groups to feel they are regularly not treated respectfully in their own neighbourhoods and in their daily lives. Here we see that actual experience of inconsiderate behaviour is far higher among the young than among older groups. Young people aged between 18 and 34 encounter on average more than twice as many types of inconsiderate behaviour as those experienced by people aged 65 and over. Of course, this will largely reflect the places that young people visit (and, perhaps, the fact that they are likely to socialise in places frequented by other young people). However, it does confirm that young people should be seen not only as the perpetrators, but also as key victims of inconsiderate behaviour. Marital status did not emerge as significant in our model, suggesting that those who are single are more likely to encounter inconsiderate behaviour primarily as a result of the fact that they are more likely to be in the youngest age group.

Interestingly, while men and women do not differ in their perceptions of social trust or respect, men are more likely to witness inconsiderate behaviour than women. The reasons for this are unclear. One possibility is that our results are skewed by the fact that three of the five behaviours are directly aggressive and might be more likely to be experienced by men. But men are also more likely than women to report experiencing the less obviously 'aggressive' behaviours (queue-jumping and dropping litter), so this explanation does not appear very helpful. So we are left to conclude that our finding reflects the tendency of men to spend time in public settings where inconsiderate behaviour is more common. This seems a plausible explanation; after all, young men have long been the most likely victims of violent crime (Kershaw *et al.*, 2008).

Our analysis also finds that people in urban locations are more likely to experience inconsiderate behaviour than those living in rural communities. This could reflect a number of issues. Clearly residents of large towns and cities simply have more opportunities than those elsewhere to encounter people, maximising their opportunities of experiencing inconsiderate behaviour. But, beyond this, perhaps the stresses and strains of urban life also tend to produce more aggressive or inconsiderate behaviour than is found in less densely populated parts of Britain? Finally, it might also reflect the fact that urban-dwellers more regularly encounter strangers, rather than people known to them and with whom they might have a reciprocal relationship (and therefore treat considerately).

Figure 9.1 Experiences of inconsiderate behaviour at least once a fortnight (mean number of behaviours), by social and demographic characteristics

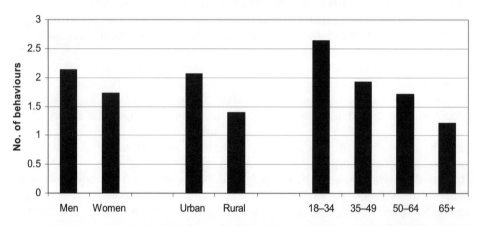

It is perhaps surprising that no characteristics linked to a person's socio-economic position emerged as significant in our model. There is often an assumption that anti-social behaviour is a particular problem in less well-off communities; indeed the government's Respect Task Force has adopted an approach of focusing on specific individual communities where there are perceived to be particular problems. But in comparison our data suggest that the impact of mild forms of inconsiderate behaviour, as opposed to anti-social behaviour, whilst occurring mainly in urban communities, is in fact far wider and less strongly associated with deprivation than might be assumed.

Behaving inconsiderately

The obvious corollary of the public's regular experiences of inconsiderate behaviour in Britain is that considerable numbers of people must *themselves* engage in these sorts of negative acts. It is, however, notoriously difficult to get an accurate picture of these sorts of behaviour. There is an extensive literature demonstrating that people tend to represent their own behaviour in an overly positive light in surveys, due to both selective memory and issues of social desirability (see, for example, Schaeffer, 2000). For instance, an individual may want to present themselves in the best possible light to an interviewer, which might discourage accurate reporting of involvement in inconsiderate behaviour.

For this reason, we included questions about any inconsiderate behaviour respondents might have undertaken in a self-completion booklet. But despite this precaution, only small proportions of the public admit to personally undertaking any of the five inconsiderate behaviours illustrated in Table 9.6. One fifth (22 per cent) indicate they had made a rude and offensive gesture in public at some point in the last year, whilst a similar proportion (21 per cent) had deliberately dropped litter. Self-reported levels of the other inconsiderate behaviours were lower; minorities of between one and two-tenths indicate that they have jumped a queue in the last year (19 per cent), sworn or shouted at a stranger in public (14 per cent) or pushed past someone roughly (11 per cent). Moreover, the minority of the public who *do* admit to having behaved inconsiderately indicate that they undertake this behaviour infrequently. Whilst making a rude and offensive gesture and deliberately dropping litter were the most widely reported negative behaviours admitted by the public, more than four times as many respondents reported having witnessed, compared to having done themselves, one of these things in the past year.

Of course, we should not expect levels of self-reported and witnessed behaviour to match. One example of inconsiderate behaviour could be seen by a large number of individuals, and a small number of individuals regularly behaving inconsiderately would inevitably result in a larger number of individuals witnessing inconsiderate behaviour on a regular basis. However, we strongly suspect that our findings considerably under-report the proportion of people who themselves engage in inconsiderate behaviour. Nonetheless, it is certainly worth examining *who* admits to behaving inconsiderably in public and examining how this tallies with the public's perception of those groups who are most to blame. It is to this task that we now turn.

As noted previously, young people were cited as the primary group at fault when it comes to behaving disrespectfully and inconsiderately. This is substantiated by people's reporting of their own behaviour. While 33 per cent of people admit to having undertaken any of our five negative behaviours in the past year, this proportion varies from 45 per cent of those aged between 18 and 34, to just 16 per cent of those aged over 65. This adds weight to the perception that inconsiderate behaviour is more often undertaken by younger groups. On the other hand, 40 per cent of men, compared to 26 per cent of women, report having undertaken inconsiderate behaviour, while 45 per cent of those who are single claim that this is the case. These figures suggest that those groups that we identified as being the most likely to witness inconsiderate behaviour are also the most likely to undertake it themselves. It therefore seems likely that there are certain public settings, frequented mainly by men, those who are single and in the youngest age group, where the undertaking, and therefore the witnessing of, inconsiderate behaviour is much more common. Due to the association of these demographic characteristics with experiences of witnessing and undertaking inconsiderate behaviour, we cannot simply conclude that inconsiderate and disrespectful behaviour is a problem for a minority of deprived communities; this evidence suggests that it cuts across the whole of society.

Trust, respect and inconsiderate behaviour

So far, we have established that experiences of witnessing and undertaking inconsiderate behaviour vary widely between different groups. Those groups seen as being more likely to behave inconsiderately are also more likely to experience this behaviour themselves. They also correspond to some extent with the groups we earlier identified as having particularly low levels of social trust and perceived respect – the young, single and urban-dwellers. This suggests that experiences of inconsiderate behaviour may be linked to social trust and respect, a linkage often assumed by policy makers who have, for instance, cited increasing respect in society as a method for reducing the incidence of anti-social behaviour (Respect Task Force, 2006).

We examine this in Table 9.7, which presents the average number of inconsiderate behaviours witnessed regularly according to people's social trust and their perceptions of respect (both in their day-to-day life, and in their local neighbourhood).

Table 9.7 Experiences of inconsiderate behaviour at least once a fortnight, by levels of social trust and perceived respect

	Mean number behaviours witnessed	Base
People generally treat each other with respect and consideration in public – in respondent's neighbourhood		
Strongly agree	1.4	502
Agree	1.7	1817
Neither	2.3	391
Disagree	2.8	288
Strongly disagree	3.4	84
How many people generally treat you with respect and consideration in public in day-to-day life		
Everyone	1.2	455
Most people	1.8	2038
Some people	2.6	444
A few people/No one	3.1	149
Social trust (I)		
Most people can be trusted	1.6	1730
Can't be too careful in dealing with people	2.2	2340
Social trust (II)		
People are fair almost all of the time	1.4	366
People are fair most of the time	1.7	1277
People try to take advantage most of the time	2.5	570
People try to take advantage almost all of the time	2.6	125

Both measures of respect appear to be linked to experiences of inconsiderate behaviour, with those who encounter inconsiderate behaviour regularly perceiving lower levels of respect.[3] For instance, those who "strongly agree" with the proposition that, in their neighbourhoods, "people generally treat each other with respect and consideration in public", reported experiencing 1.4 inconsiderate behaviours in the past fortnight, half the rate (2.8 behaviours) reported by those who "disagree" with the statement. Similarly, those who indicate that "everyone" in their day-to-day lives treats them with respect and consideration in public report just 1.2 inconsiderate behaviours in the past fortnight, compared to the 3.1 behaviours experienced by those who indicate that "a few people" or "no one" treats them in this way. A similar pattern emerges in relation to social trust, with those exhibiting the lowest levels of social trust being more likely to experience inconsiderate behaviours on a regular basis. Those members of the public who felt that "most people can be trusted" reported an average of 1.6 negative behaviours at least once a fortnight, compared to an average of 2.2 for those who stated that "you can't be too careful in dealing with people". A similar difference was observed on the second general measure of social trust, focusing on the extent to which people will try to treat you fairly.

Clearly, then, a relationship exists between public experiences of inconsiderate behaviour and levels of social trust and perceived respect. However, the direction of this relationship is not necessarily clear. Perhaps those who experience inconsiderate behaviour more often have lower levels of social trust and perceived respect as a result, because their experiences have coloured their perceptions of the behaviour and intentions of the public as a whole. Conversely, it could be that those with lower levels of social trust and perceived respect are more likely to identify, recall and report instances of inconsiderate behaviour, as this tallies with and enforces their existing views of public behaviour. But in either case, the frequently held assumption that increasing levels of social trust and respect should lead to a reduction in levels of inconsiderate behaviour, and *vice versa*, appears to be borne out. Clearly, levels of social trust and respect, and experiences of inconsiderate behaviour, are closely linked to one another.

Conclusions

By reviewing public attitudes and experiences in relation to social trust, respect and inconsiderate behaviour, we have sought to establish how far they endorse the commonly held perceptions of government, social commentators and academics, perceptions which have in many cases underpinned current thinking and social policy. The picture that we have obtained is mixed. Certainly, our data do not lend support, and in some cases appear to contradict, the widely held view that Britain is experiencing an erosion in social trust. But they do confirm the view that low levels of social trust are a particular issue for the youngest and more deprived groups in society. However, these minorities are not simply located within more deprived communities; their characteristics (particularly in relation to age and location) suggest that the issue cross-cuts society as a whole.

While official views of social trust and respect and those of the public are far from identical, both share the assumption that underpins much current policy; there is a link between levels of social trust and respect, and levels of inconsiderate behaviour in society. So, while current policies and thinking in relation to social trust and respect may need to shift and broaden their focus, their basic assumptions – that an increase in social trust and respect would generate a reduction in inconsiderate behaviour or *vice versa* – does find support among public attitudes and experiences.

Notes

1. In October 2007, as part of the machinery of government changes, the Youth Taskforce was created from the Respect Task Force and the Targeted Youth Support team in the recently created Department for Children, Schools and Families. The Youth Taskforce built on the work of the Respect programme by working to improve opportunities for young people, to prevent problems and tackle the root causes of anti-social behaviour.
2. The 'professionals' category include those in higher managerial and professional occupations, as well as in lower professional and higher technical occupations. 'Intermediate workers' includes lower managerial jobs, supervisors, small employers and the self-employed. 'Routine' includes lower technical occupations, semi-routine and routine jobs. Further information about NS-SEC, the classification schema upon which this is based can be found in Appendix I of this report.
3. A similar relationship between respect and experience of inconsiderate behaviour is also apparent when looking at the respondent's views about levels of respect in Britain as a whole; those who disagree report experiencing more inconsiderate events.

References

Grenier, P. and Wright, K. (2004), 'Social capital in Britain: an update and critique of Hall's analysis', London School of Economics, Centre for Civil Society, Working Paper **14**

Hall, P. (1999), 'Social Capital in Britain', *British Journal of Political Science*, **29(3)**: 417–461

Kershaw, C., Nicholas, S. and Walker, A. (2008), *Crime in England and Wales 2007/8: Findings from the British Crime Survey and police recorded crime*, available at http://www.homeoffice.gov.uk/rds/pdfs08/hosb0708.pdf

Putnam, R. (1995), 'Bowling alone: America's declining social capital', in *Journal of Democracy*, **6(1)**: 65–78

Respect Task Force (2006), *Respect Action Plan*, available at http://www.crimereduction.homeoffice.gov.uk/antisocialbehaviour/antisocial behaviour54.htm

Schaeffer, N. (2000), 'Asking questions about threatening topics: a selective overview', in Stone, A., Turkkan, J., Bachrach, C., Jobe, C., Kurtzman, H. and Cain, V. (eds.), *The Science of Self-Report: Implications for research and practice*, Mahwah: Erlbaum

Wood, M. (2004), *Perceptions and experiences of anti-social behaviour: findings from the 2003–2004 British Crime Survey*, Home Office Online Report 49/04, available at http://www.homeoffice.gov.uk/rds/pdfs04/rdsolr4904.pdf

Acknowledgements

The *National Centre for Social Research* is grateful to the Respect Task Force (now the Youth Taskforce) for their financial support which enabled us to ask the questions reported in this chapter, although the views expressed are those of the authors alone.

Appendix

The following tables show the results of the linear and logistic regression analyses which were referenced in the text of this chapter. Positive coefficients indicate a positive correlation with the dependent variable; negative coefficients indicate a negative correlation.

Model 1: Social trust

Table A.1 Logistic regression (dependent variable whether respondent thinks "most people can be trusted"), by social and demographic characteristics

Predictor variables	Social and demographic characteristics
Nagelkerke R^2	.092
Age (increase by one year)	.018**
Location (urban)	
Rural	.116
Household income (increase by one income band)	.053**
Highest educational qualification (degree)	
Higher education below degree	-.237
A level	-.061
O level	-.500**
CSE	-.343*
Foreign qualification	-.503
No qualification	-.633**
Occupational class (professional)	
Intermediate	-.435**
Routine	-.494**
Base	3471

* = significant at 95% level; ** = significant at 99% level

Model 2: Perceptions of respect

Two linear regressions were run. The dependent variable in Model A was agreement/disagreement with the view that in the respondent's neighbourhood, people generally treat each other with respect and consideration in public; as the value of the variable increased it represented increasing disagreement with this statement. The dependent variable in Model B was the proportion of people perceived by the respondent to treat them with respect and consideration in public in their day-to-day life, as the value of the variable increased it represented a decreasing proportion of people who treated the respondent with respect.

Table A.2 Linear regression (dependent variables perceptions of respect), by social and demographic characteristics

Predictor variables	Model A	Model B
	Respondent's neighbourhood	Respondent's day-to-day life
Nagelkerke R^2	.094	.065
Age (increase by one year)	-.008**	-.008**
Location (urban)		
Rural	-.357**	-.102**
Household income (increase by one income band)	-.016**	-.010**
Highest educational qualification (degree)		
Higher education below degree	.014	.004
A level	.048	.009
O level	.036	-.047
CSE	.090	-.050
Foreign qualification	-.141	-.222
No qualification	.085	.008
Marital status (married)		
Cohabiting	.132*	-.016
Separated or divorced	.141*	-.062
Widowed	-.019	-.150*
Single	.138*	.005
Occupational class (professional)		
Intermediate	.095*	.059
Routine	.234**	.178**
Base	3094	3094

* = significant at 95% level; ** = significant at 99% level

Model 3: Experiences of inconsiderate behaviour

Table A.3 Logistic regression (dependent variable respondent has witnessed any type of inconsiderate behaviours in public in the past fortnight), by social and demographic characteristics

Predictor variables	Social and demographic characteristics
Nagelkerke R^2	.092
Age (increase by one year)	-.024**
Sex (male)	
Female	-.465**
Location (urban)	
Rural	-.469**
Household income (increase by one income band)	-.008
Highest educational qualification (degree)	
Higher education below degree	.132
A level	-.108
O level	.013
CSE	.224
Foreign qualification	-1.207**
No qualification	-.023
Marital status (married)	
Cohabiting	.107
Separated or divorced	.228
Widowed	-.232
Single	.191
Occupational class (professional)	
Intermediate	.101
Routine	.145
Base	*2645*

* = significant at 95% level; ** = significant at 99% level

Appendix I
Technical details of the survey

In 2007, the sample for the *British Social Attitudes* survey was split into four sections: versions A, B C and D, each made up a quarter of the sample. Depending on the number of versions in which it was included, each 'module' of questions was thus asked either of the full sample (4,124 respondents) or of a random quarter, half or three-quarters of the sample. The structure of the questionnaire can be found at www.natcen.ac.uk/bsaquestionnaires.

Sample design

The *British Social Attitudes* survey is designed to yield a representative sample of adults aged 18 or over. Since 1993, the sampling frame for the survey has been the Postcode Address File (PAF), a list of addresses (or postal delivery points) compiled by the Post Office.[1]

For practical reasons, the sample is confined to those living in private households. People living in institutions (though not in private households at such institutions) are excluded, as are households whose addresses were not on PAF.

The sampling method involved a multi-stage design, with three separate stages of selection.

Selection of sectors

At the first stage, postcode sectors were selected systematically from a list of all postal sectors in Great Britain. Before selection, any sectors with fewer than 500 addresses were identified and grouped together with an adjacent sector; in Scotland all sectors north of the Caledonian Canal were excluded (because of the prohibitive costs of interviewing there). Sectors were then stratified on the basis of:

- 37 sub-regions;
- population density with variable banding used, in order to create three equal-sized strata per sub-region; and
- ranking by percentage of homes that were owner-occupied.

Four hundred and four postcode sectors were selected, with probability proportional to the number of addresses in each sector.

Selection of addresses

Twenty-two addresses were selected in each of the 404 sectors. The issued sample was therefore 404 x 22 = 8,888 addresses, selected by starting from a random point on the list of addresses for each sector, and choosing each address at a fixed interval. The fixed interval was calculated for each sector in order to generate the correct number of addresses.

The Multiple-Occupancy Indicator (MOI) available through PAF was used when selecting addresses in Scotland. The MOI shows the number of accommodation spaces sharing one address. Thus, if the MOI indicates more than one accommodation space at a given address, the chances of the given address being selected from the list of addresses would increase so that it matched the total number of accommodation spaces. The MOI is largely irrelevant in England and Wales, as separate dwelling units generally appear as separate entries on PAF. In Scotland, tenements with many flats tend to appear as one entry on PAF. However, even in Scotland, the vast majority of MOIs had a value of one. The remainder were incorporated into the weighting procedures (described below).

Selection of individuals

Interviewers called at each address selected from PAF and listed all those eligible for inclusion in the *British Social Attitudes* sample – that is, all persons currently aged 18 or over and resident at the selected address. The interviewer then selected one respondent using a computer-generated random selection procedure. Where there were two or more 'dwelling units' at the selected address, interviewers first had to select one dwelling unit using the same random procedure. They then followed the same procedure to select a person for interview within the selected dwelling unit.

Weighting

The weights for the *British Social Attitudes* survey correct for the unequal selection of addresses, dwelling units (DU) and individuals and for biases caused by differential non-response. The different stages of the weighting scheme are outlined in detail below.

Selection weights

Selection weights are required because not all the units covered in the survey had the same probability of selection. The weighting reflects the relative selection probabilities of the individual at the three main stages of selection: address, DU and individual. First, because addresses in Scotland were selected using the MOI, weights were needed to compensate for the greater probability of an address with an MOI of more than one being selected, compared to an address with an MOI of one. (This stage was omitted for the English and Welsh data.) Secondly, data were weighted to compensate for the fact that a DU at an address that contained a large number of DUs was less likely to be selected for inclusion in the survey than a DU at an address that contained fewer DUs. (We use this procedure because in most cases where the MOI is greater than one, the two stages will cancel each other out, resulting in more efficient weights.) Thirdly, data were weighted to compensate for the lower selection probabilities of adults living in large households, compared with those in small households.

At each stage the selection weights were trimmed to avoid a small number of very high or very low weights in the sample; such weights would inflate standard errors, reducing the precision of the survey estimates and causing the weighted sample to be less efficient. Less than one per cent of the sample was trimmed at each stage.

Non-response model

It is known that certain subgroups in the population are more likely to respond to surveys than others. These groups can end up over-represented in the sample, which can bias the survey estimates. Where information is available about non-responding households, the response behaviour of the sample members can be modelled and the results used to generate a non-response weight. This non-response weight is intended to reduce bias in the sample resulting from differential response to the survey.

The data was modelled using logistic regression, with the dependent variable indicating whether or not the selected individual responded to the survey. Ineligible households[2] were not included in the non-response modelling. A number of area-level and interviewer observation variables were used to model response. Not all the variables examined were retained for the final model: variables not strongly related to a household's propensity to respond were dropped from the analysis.

The variables found to be related to response were; Government Office Region (GOR), population density (population in private households according to the Census 2001 divided by the area in hectares), condition of the local area and relative condition of the address and whether there were entry barriers to the selected address. The full model is given in Table A.1.

The model shows non-response increases if there are barriers to entry (for instance, if there are locked gates around the address or an entry phone) and if the general condition of the address and area is good. Response is lower in areas where there is a higher population density and lower if the address is in the West Midlands, London, the South East or South West.

Table A.1 The final non-response model

Variable	B	S.E.	Wald	df	Sig.	Odds
Population density	-0.003	0.001	19.3	1	0.00	0.997
Govt Office Region			60.1	10	0.00	
North East	0.43	0.11	16.4	1	0.00	1.54
North West	0.04	0.08	0.3	1	0.58	1.05
Yorks. and Humber	0.17	0.08	3.9	1	0.05	1.18
East Midlands	0.02	0.09	0.0	1	0.83	1.02
West Midlands	-0.23	0.08	8.0	1	0.00	0.79
East of England	-0.04	0.08	0.2	1	0.65	0.96
London	-0.08	0.09	0.7	1	0.39	0.93
South East	-0.07	0.07	0.9	1	0.35	0.93
South West	-0.17	0.08	4.2	1	0.04	0.84
Wales	-0.05	0.10	0.3	1	0.59	0.95
Scotland					*(baseline)*	
Barriers to address			10.3	1	0.00	
No barriers	0.20	0.06	10.3	1	0.00	1.22
One or more					*(baseline)*	
Condition of the area			70.3	2	0.00	
Mainly good	0.33	0.10	10.2	1	0.00	1.39
Mainly fair	0.03	0.10	0.1	1	0.76	1.03
Mainly bad					*(baseline)*	
Relative condition of the address			40.8	2	0.00	
Better	0.65	0.10	40.3	1	0.00	1.91
About the same	0.34	0.08	17.6	1	0.00	1.40
Worse					*(baseline)*	
Constant	-0.36	0.14	6.3	1	0.01	0.70

Notes:
The response is 1 = individual responding to the survey, 0 = non-response
Only variables that are significant at the 0.05 level are included in the model
The model R^2 is 0.02 (Cox and Snell)
B is the estimate coefficient with standard error **S.E.**
The **Wald**-test measures the impact of the categorical variable on the model with the appropriate number of degrees of freedom **df**. If the test is significant (**sig.** < 0.05), then the categorical variable is considered to be 'significantly associated' with the response variable and therefore included in the model

The non-response weight is calculated as the inverse of the predicted response probabilities saved from the logistic regression model. The non-response weight was then combined with the selection weights to create the final non-response weight. The top and bottom one per cent of the weight were trimmed before the weight was scaled to the achieved sample size (resulting in the weight being standardised around an average of one).

Calibration weighting

The final stage of the weighting was to adjust the final non-response weight so that the weighted respondent sample matched the population in terms of age, sex and region.

Table A.2 Weighted and unweighted sample distribution, by GOR, age and sex

	Population	Unweighted respondents	Respondents weighted by selection weight only	Respondents weighted by un-calibrated non-response weight	Respondents weighted by final weight
Govt Office Region	%	%	%	%	%
North East	4.4	5.6	5.2	4.3	4.4
North West	11.6	11.9	11.6	11.5	11.6
Yorks. and Humber	8.7	9.5	9.6	8.8	8.7
East Midlands	7.4	8.0	8.1	7.8	7.4
West Midlands	9.0	8.2	8.5	9.3	9.0
East	9.5	8.9	9.4	9.3	9.5
London	12.8	9.7	9.8	11.2	12.8
South East	14.0	14.5	14.8	14.9	14.0
South West	8.8	9.0	8.6	8.9	8.8
Wales	5.0	5.2	5.0	4.9	5.0
Scotland	8.8	9.5	9.2	9.0	8.8
Age & sex	%	%	%	%	%
M 18–24	6.0	3.2	4.8	4.9	6.0
M 25–34	8.3	6.9	7.6	7.9	8.3
M 35–44	9.7	8.2	8.2	8.2	9.7
M 45–54	8.2	7.5	8.2	8.2	8.2
M 55–59	4.1	3.7	3.7	3.6	4.1
M 60–64	3.3	3.7	3.9	3.8	3.3
M 65+	8.8	10.9	10.1	10.0	8.8
F 18–24	5.8	3.7	4.6	4.8	5.8
F 25–34	8.3	8.7	8.5	8.8	8.3
F 35–44	9.8	11.7	11.4	11.4	9.8
F 45–54	8.3	9.2	10.0	9.9	8.3
F 55–59	4.2	4.0	4.0	3.9	4.2
F 60–64	3.5	4.7	4.4	4.3	3.5
F 65+	11.7	13.9	10.6	10.4	11.7
Base	*46,158,090*	*4124*	*4124*	*4124*	*4124*

Only adults aged 18 and over are eligible to take part in the survey; therefore the data have been weighted to the British population aged 18+ based on the 2006 mid-year population estimates from the Office for National Statistics/General Register Office for Scotland.

The survey data were weighted to the marginal age/sex and GOR distributions using raking-ratio (or rim) weighting. As a result, the weighted data should exactly match the population across these three dimensions. This is shown in Table A.2.

The calibration weight is the final non-response weight to be used in the analysis of the 2007 survey; this weight has been scaled to the responding sample size. The range of the weights is given in Table A.3.

Table A.3 Range of weights

	N	Minimum	Mean	Maximum
DU and person selection weight	4124	0.55	1.00	2.19
Un-calibrated non-response weight	4124	0.40	1.00	2.58
Final calibrated non-response weight	4124	0.35	1.00	3.65

Effective sample size

The effect of the sample design on the precision of survey estimates is indicated by the effective sample size (neff). The effective sample size measures the size of an (unweighted) simple random sample that would achieve the same precision (standard error) as the design being implemented. If the effective sample size is close to the actual sample size, then we have an efficient design with a good level of precision. The lower the effective sample size is, the lower the level of precision. The efficiency of a sample is given by the ratio of the effective sample size to the actual sample size. Samples that select one person per household tend to have lower efficiency than samples that select all household members. The final calibrated non-response weights have an effective sample size (neff) of 3,347 and efficiency of 81 per cent.

All the percentages presented in this report are based on weighted data.

Questionnaire versions

Each address in each sector (sampling point) was allocated to either the A, B, C or D portion of the sample. If one serial number was version A, the next was version B, the third version C and the fourth version D. Thus, each interviewer was allocated seven or eight cases from each of versions A, B, C and D. There were 2,222 issued addresses for each version.

Fieldwork

Interviewing was mainly carried out between June and September 2007, with a small number of interviews taking place in October and November.

Fieldwork was conducted by interviewers drawn from the *National Centre for Social Research*'s regular panel and conducted using face-to-face computer-assisted interviewing.[3] Interviewers attended a one-day briefing conference to familiarise them with the selection procedures and questionnaires.

The mean interview length was 68 minutes for version A of the questionnaire, 75 minutes for version B and 66 minutes for versions C and D.[4] Interviewers achieved an overall response rate of between 51.5 and 53.1 per cent. Details are shown in Table A.4.

Table A.4 Response rate[1] on *British Social Attitudes*, 2007

	Number	Lower limit of response (%)	Upper limit of response (%)
Addresses issued	8888		
Out of scope	873		
Upper limit of eligible cases	8015	100.0	
Uncertain eligibility	254	3.2	
Lower limit of eligible cases	7761		100.0
Interview achieved	4124	51.5	53.1
Interview not achieved	3637	45.4	46.9
Refused[2]	2888	36.0	37.2
Non-contacted[3]	287	3.6	3.7
Other non-response	462	5.8	6.0

1 Response is calculated as a range from a lower limit where all unknown eligibility cases (for example, address inaccessible, or unknown whether address is residential) are assumed to be eligible and therefore included in the unproductive outcomes, to an upper limit where all these cases are assumed to be ineligible (and are therefore excluded from the response calculation)

2 'Refused' comprises refusals before selection of an individual at the address, refusals to the office, refusal by the selected person, 'proxy' refusals (on behalf of the selected respondent) and broken appointments after which the selected person could not be recontacted

3 'Non-contacted' comprises households where no one was contacted and those where the selected person could not be contacted

As in earlier rounds of the series, the respondent was asked to fill in a self-completion questionnaire which, whenever possible, was collected by the interviewer. Otherwise, the respondent was asked to post it to the *National Centre for Social Research*. If necessary, up to three postal reminders were sent to obtain the self-completion supplement.

A total of 546 respondents (13 per cent of those interviewed) did not return their self-completion questionnaire. Version A of the self-completion questionnaire was returned by 88 per cent of respondents to the face-to-face interview, version B by 85 per cent, version C by 86 per cent and version D by 87 per cent. As in previous rounds, we judged that it was not necessary to apply additional weights to correct for non-response to the self-completion questionnaire.

Advance letter

Interviewers were supplied with letters describing the purpose of the survey and the coverage of the questionnaire, which they posted to sampled addresses before making any calls.[5]

Analysis variables

A number of standard analyses have been used in the tables that appear in this report. The analysis groups requiring further definition are set out below. For further details see Stafford and Thomson (2006). Where there are references to specific question numbers, the full question text, including frequencies, can be found at www.natcen.ac.uk/bsaquestionnaires.

Region

The dataset is classified by the 12 Government Office Regions.

Standard Occupational Classification

Respondents are classified according to their own occupation, not that of the 'head of household'. Each respondent was asked about their current or last job, so that all respondents except those who had never worked were coded. Additionally, all job details were collected for all spouses and partners in work.

With the 2001 survey, we began coding occupation to the new Standard Occupational Classification 2000 (SOC 2000) instead of the Standard

Occupational Classification 1990 (SOC 90). The main socio-economic grouping based on SOC 2000 is the National Statistics Socio-Economic Classification (NS-SEC). However, to maintain time-series, some analysis has continued to use the older schemes based on SOC 90 – Registrar General's Social Class, Socio-Economic Group and the Goldthorpe schema.

National Statistics Socio-Economic Classification (NS-SEC)

The combination of SOC 2000 and employment status for current or last job generates the following NS-SEC analytic classes:

- Employers in large organisations, higher managerial and professional
- Lower professional and managerial; higher technical and supervisory
- Intermediate occupations
- Small employers and own account workers
- Lower supervisory and technical occupations
- Semi-routine occupations
- Routine occupations

The remaining respondents are grouped as "never had a job" or "not classifiable". For some analyses, it may be more appropriate to classify respondents according to their current socio-economic status, which takes into account only their present economic position. In this case, in addition to the seven classes listed above, the remaining respondents not currently in paid work fall into one of the following categories: "not classifiable", "retired", "looking after the home", "unemployed" or "others not in paid occupations".

Registrar General's Social Class

As with NS-SEC, each respondent's Social Class is based on his or her current or last occupation. The combination of SOC 90 with employment status for current or last job generates the following six Social Classes:

I	Professional etc. occupations	
II	Managerial and technical occupations	'Non-manual'
III (Non-manual)	Skilled occupations	
III (Manual)	Skilled occupations	
IV	Partly skilled occupations	'Manual'
V	Unskilled occupations	

They are usually collapsed into four groups: I & II, III Non-manual, III Manual, and IV & V.

Socio-Economic Group

As with NS-SEC, each respondent's Socio-Economic Group (SEG) is based on his or her current or last occupation. SEG aims to bring together people with jobs of similar social and economic status, and is derived from a combination of employment status and occupation. The full SEG classification identifies 18 categories, but these are usually condensed into six groups:

- Professionals, employers and managers
- Intermediate non-manual workers
- Junior non-manual workers
- Skilled manual workers
- Semi-skilled manual workers
- Unskilled manual workers

As with NS-SEC, the remaining respondents are grouped as "never had a job" or "not classifiable".

Goldthorpe schema

The Goldthorpe schema classifies occupations by their 'general comparability', considering such factors as sources and levels of income, economic security, promotion prospects, and level of job autonomy and authority. The Goldthorpe schema was derived from the SOC 90 codes combined with employment status. Two versions of the schema are coded: the full schema has 11 categories; the 'compressed schema' combines these into the five classes shown below.

- Salariat (professional and managerial)
- Routine non-manual workers (office and sales)
- Petty bourgeoisie (the self-employed, including farmers, with and without employees)
- Manual foremen and supervisors
- Working class (skilled, semi-skilled and unskilled manual workers, personal service and agricultural workers)

There is a residual category comprising those who have never had a job or who gave insufficient information for classification purposes.

Industry

All respondents whose occupation could be coded were allocated a Standard Industrial Classification 2003 (SIC 03). Two-digit class codes are used. As with Social Class, SIC may be generated on the basis of the respondent's current occupation only, or on his or her most recently classifiable occupation.

Party identification

Respondents can be classified as identifying with a particular political party on one of three counts: if they consider themselves supporters of that party, as closer to it than to others, or as more likely to support it in the event of a general election. The three groups are generally described respectively as *partisans*, *sympathisers* and *residual identifiers*. In combination, the three groups are referred to as 'identifiers'. Responses are derived from the following questions:

> *Generally speaking, do you think of yourself as a supporter of any one political party? [Yes/No]*

> *[If "No"/"Don't know"]*
> *Do you think of yourself as a little closer to one political party than to the others? [Yes/No]*

> *[If "Yes" at either question or "No"/"Don't know" at 2nd question]*
> *[Which one?/If there were a general election tomorrow, which political party do you think you would be most likely to support?]*

> *[Conservative; Labour; Liberal Democrat; Scottish National Party; Plaid Cymru; Green Party; UK Independence Party (UKIP)/Veritas; British National Party (BNP)/National Front; RESPECT/Scottish Socialist Party (SSP)/Socialist Party; Other party; Other answer; None; Refused to say]*

Attitude scales

Since 1986, the *British Social Attitudes* surveys have included two attitude scales which aim to measure where respondents stand on certain underlying value dimensions – left–right and libertarian–authoritarian.[6] Since 1987 (except 1990), a similar scale on 'welfarism' has been asked. Some of the items in the welfarism scale were changed in 2000–2001. The current version of the scale is listed below.

A useful way of summarising the information from a number of questions of this sort is to construct an additive index (Spector, 1992; DeVellis, 2003). This approach rests on the assumption that there is an underlying – 'latent' – attitudinal dimension which characterises the answers to all the questions within each scale. If so, scores on the index are likely to be a more reliable indication of the underlying attitude than the answers to any one question.

Each of these scales consists of a number of statements to which the respondent is invited to "agree strongly", "agree", "neither agree nor disagree", "disagree" or "disagree strongly".

The items are:

Left–right scale

> Government should redistribute income from the better off to those who are less well off. *[Redistrb]*

> Big business benefits owners at the expense of workers. *[BigBusnN]*

> Ordinary working people do not get their fair share of the nation's wealth. *[Wealth]*[7]

> There is one law for the rich and one for the poor. *[RichLaw]*

> Management will always try to get the better of employees if it gets the chance. *[Indust4]*

Libertarian–authoritarian scale

> Young people today don't have enough respect for traditional British values. *[TradVals]*

> People who break the law should be given stiffer sentences. *[StifSent]*

> For some crimes, the death penalty is the most appropriate sentence. *[DeathApp]*

> Schools should teach children to obey authority. *[Obey]*

> The law should always be obeyed, even if a particular law is wrong. *[WrongLaw]*

> Censorship of films and magazines is necessary to uphold moral standards. *[Censor]*

Welfarism scale

> The welfare state encourages people to stop helping each other. *[WelfHelp]*

> The government should spend more money on welfare benefits for the poor, even if it leads to higher taxes. *[MoreWelf]*

> Around here, most unemployed people could find a job if they really wanted one. *[UnempJob]*

> Many people who get social security don't really deserve any help. *[SocHelp]*

> Most people on the dole are fiddling in one way or another. *[DoleFidl]*

> If welfare benefits weren't so generous, people would learn to stand on their own two feet. *[WelfFeet]*

Cutting welfare benefits would damage too many people's lives. *[DamLives]*

The creation of the welfare state is one of Britain's proudest achievements. *[ProudWlf]*

The indices for the three scales are formed by scoring the leftmost, most libertarian or most pro-welfare position as 1 and the rightmost, most authoritarian or most anti-welfarist position as 5. The "neither agree nor disagree" option is scored as 3. The scores to all the questions in each scale are added and then divided by the number of items in the scale, giving indices ranging from 1 (leftmost, most libertarian, most pro-welfare) to 5 (rightmost, most authoritarian, most anti-welfare). The scores on the three indices have been placed on the dataset.[8]

The scales have been tested for reliability (as measured by Cronbach's alpha). The Cronbach's alpha (unstandardised items) for the scales in 2007 are 0.80 for the left–right scale, 0.81 for the 'welfarism' scale and 0.74 for the libertarian–authoritarian scale. This level of reliability can be considered "very good" for the left–right and welfarism scales and "respectable" for the libertarian–authoritarian scale (DeVellis, 2003: 95–96).

Other analysis variables

These are taken directly from the questionnaire and to that extent are self-explanatory (see www.natcen.ac.uk/bsaquestionnaires). The principal ones are:

Sex (Q. 44)
Age (Q. 45)
Household income (Q. 1443)
Economic position (Q. 817)
Religion (Q. 1166)
Highest educational qualification obtained (Qs. 1299–1300)
Marital status (Qs. 138–144)
Benefits received (Qs. 1363–1436)

Sampling errors

No sample precisely reflects the characteristics of the population it represents, because of both sampling and non-sampling errors. If a sample were designed as a random sample (if every adult had an equal and independent chance of inclusion in the sample), then we could calculate the sampling error of any percentage, p, using the formula:

$$s.e. \ (p) = \sqrt{\frac{p(100 - p)}{n}}$$

where n is the number of respondents on which the percentage is based. Once the sampling error had been calculated, it would be a straightforward exercise to calculate a confidence interval for the true population percentage. For example, a 95 per cent confidence interval would be given by the formula:

$$p \pm 1.96 \text{ x s.e. } (p)$$

Clearly, for a simple random sample (srs), the sampling error depends only on the values of p and n. However, simple random sampling is almost never used in practice because of its inefficiency in terms of time and cost.

As noted above, the *British Social Attitudes* sample, like that drawn for most large-scale surveys, was clustered according to a stratified multi-stage design into 286 postcode sectors (or combinations of sectors). With a complex design like this, the sampling error of a percentage giving a particular response is not simply a function of the number of respondents in the sample and the size of the percentage; it also depends on how that percentage response is spread within and between sample points.

The complex design may be assessed relative to simple random sampling by calculating a range of design factors (DEFTs) associated with it, where:

$$\text{DEFT} = \sqrt{\frac{\text{Variance of estimator with complex design, sample size n}}{\text{Variance of estimator with srs design, sample size n}}}$$

and represents the multiplying factor to be applied to the simple random sampling error to produce its complex equivalent. A design factor of one means that the complex sample has achieved the same precision as a simple random sample of the same size. A design factor greater than one means the complex sample is less precise than its simple random sample equivalent. If the DEFT for a particular characteristic is known, a 95 per cent confidence interval for a percentage may be calculated using the formula:

$$p \pm 1.96 \text{ x } \textit{complex sampling error } (p)$$

$$= p \pm 1.96 \text{ x DEFT x } \sqrt{\frac{p(100 - p)}{n}}$$

Calculations of sampling errors and design effects were made using the statistical analysis package STATA.

Table A.5 gives examples of the confidence intervals and DEFTs calculated for a range of different questions. Most background variables were fielded on the whole sample, whereas many attitudinal variables were asked only of a half or quarter of the sample; some were asked on the interview questionnaire and some on the self-completion supplement.

Table A.5 Complex standard errors and confidence intervals of selected variables

	% (p)	Complex standard error of p	95% confidence interval	DEFT	Base
Classification variables					
Q230	**Party identification (full sample)**				
Conservative	24.6	0.9	22.9–26.3	1.28	*4124*
Labour	34.1	1.0	32.2–36.0	1.29	*4124*
Liberal Democrat	9.3	0.6	8.2–10.3	1.23	*4124*
Q1154	**Housing tenure (full sample)**				
Owns	71.6	1.0	69.7–73.5	1.37	*4124*
Rents from local authority	9.9	0.7	8.6–11.2	1.42	*4124*
Rents privately/HA	17.0	0.8	15.5–18.5	1.31	*4290*
Q1166	**Religion (full sample)**				
No religion	45.6	1.1	43.5–47.8	1.41	*4124*
Church of England	20.9	0.7	19.4–20.3	1.17	*4124*
Roman Catholic	9.0	0.6	7.9–10.1	1.22	*4124*
Q1234	**Age of completing continuous full-time education (full sample)**				
16 or under	55.2	1.0	53.2–57.2	1.30	*4124*
17 or 18	16.8	0.6	15.5–18.0	1.10	*4124*
19 or over	24.2	0.9	22.5–25.9	1.29	*4124*
Q223	**Home internet access (full sample)**				
Yes	67.5	0.9	65.7–69.3	1.24	*4124*
No	32.5	0.9	30.7–34.3	1.24	*4124*
Q1155	**Urban or rural residence (full sample)**				
A big city	9.2	0.8	7.7–10.7	1.66	*4124*
The suburbs or outskirts of a big city	25.4	1.5	22.5–28.3	2.18	*4124*
A small city/town	45.5	2.1	41.4–49.6	2.70	*4124*
Country village	16.8	1.5	13.9–19.6	2.49	*4124*
Farm/home in the country	2.3	0.4	1.4–3.2	1.90	*4124*
Attitudinal variables (face-to-face interview)					
Q246	**Benefits for the unemployed are … (3/4 sample)**				
… too low	25.9	1.0	23.9–27.9	1.29	*3094*
… too high	54.3	1.2	52.1–56.6	1.29	*3094*
Q578	**Trusts drs. to put needs of NHS before interests of hosp. (1/2 sample)**				
Always	10.8	0.8	9.3–12.3	1.1	*2022*
Most of the time	53.1	1.4	50.3–55.8	1.3	*2022*
Some of the time	29.0	1.2	26.6–31.3	1.2	*2022*
Just about never	5.5	0.6	4.3–6.7	1.2	*2022*

table continued on next page

		% (p)	Complex standard error of p	95% confidence interval	DEFT	Base
Q621	**In neighbourhood, people generally treat each other with respect and consideration in public (3/4 sample)**					
	Agree strongly	15.2	0.7	13.8–16.6	1.13	3094
	Agree	58.0	1.1	55.8–60.1	1.21	3094
	Neither agree nor disagree	13.5	0.8	11.9–15.1	1.31	3094
	Disagree	9.8	0.6	8.6–10.9	1.12	3094
	Disagree strongly	3.1	0.4	2.3–3.9	1.27	3094
Q1133	**Views on pre-marital sex (1/4 sample)**					
	Always wrong	5.9	0.8	4.3–7.6	1.13	1030
	Mostly wrong	5.3	0.8	3.7–7.0	1.19	1030
	Sometimes wrong	11.8	1.1	9.6–14.0	1.12	1030
	Rarely wrong	9.9	1.0	8.0–11.8	1.06	1030
	Not wrong at all	61.7	1.8	58.2–65.3	1.20	1030

Attitudinal variables (self-completion)

		% (p)	Complex standard error of p	95% confidence interval	DEFT	Base
A44a **B32a**	**Government should redistribute income from the better off to those who are less well off (full sample)**					
C31a **D33a**	Agree strongly	7.1	0.5	6.2–8.1	1.16	3578
	Agree	24.6	0.9	22.9–26.3	1.18	3578
	Neither agree nor disagree	28.8	0.8	25.2–28.6	1.12	3578
	Disagree	29.8	0.9	28.2–31.3	1.03	3578
	Disagree strongly	7.2	0.5	6.2–8.2	1.16	3578
A20a **B13a**	**Would worry if housing for those with mental health problems was opened near own home (3/4 sample)**					
C13a	Agree strongly	11.0	0.7	9.5–12.4	1.21	2665
	Agree	28.2	1.0	26.2–30.2	1.18	2665
	Neither agree nor disagree	32.4	1.0	30.3–34.4	1.14	2665
	Disagree	19.7	0.8	18.1–21.3	1.06	2665
	Disagree strongly	4.3	0.5	3.4–5.1	1.15	2665
A26a **B19a**	**Schools that fail to attract enough pupils should be closed and the teachers lose their jobs (1/2 sample)**					
	Agree strongly	1.3	0.3	0.7–1.9	1.07	1753
	Agree	9.9	0.8	8.3–11.5	1.17	1753
	Neither agree nor disagree	23.0	1.1	20.9–25.1	1.05	1753
	Disagree	48.8	1.3	46.3–51.3	1.06	1753
	Disagree strongly	10.0	0.8	8.5–11.6	1.09	1753
A6	**Prefers to be with other people or on their own in free time (1/4 sample)**					
	Most of the time with other people	23.9	1.7	20.6–27.4	1.22	906
	More with other people than alone	39.4	1.7	36.1–42.8	1.05	906
	More alone than with other people	21.6	1.6	18.4–24.7	1.18	906
	Most of the time alone	5.3	0.8	3.7–7.0	1.10	906

The table shows that most of the questions asked of all sample members have a confidence interval of around plus or minus two to three per cent of the survey percentage. This means that we can be 95 per cent certain that the true population percentage is within two to three per cent (in either direction) of the percentage we report.

Variables with much larger variation are, as might be expected, those closely related to the geographic location of the respondent (for example, whether they live in a big city, a small town or a village). Here, the variation may be as large as five or six per cent either way around the percentage found on the survey. Consequently, the design effects calculated for these variables in a clustered sample will be greater than the design effects calculated for variables less strongly associated with area. Also, sampling errors for percentages based only on respondents to just one of the versions of the questionnaire, or on subgroups within the sample, are larger than they would have been had the questions been asked of everyone.

Analysis techniques

Regression

Regression analysis aims to summarise the relationship between a 'dependent' variable and one or more 'independent' variables. It shows how well we can estimate a respondent's score on the dependent variable from knowledge of their scores on the independent variables. It is often undertaken to support a claim that the phenomena measured by the independent variables *cause* the phenomenon measured by the dependent variable. However, the causal ordering, if any, between the variables cannot be verified or falsified by the technique. Causality can only be inferred through special experimental designs or through assumptions made by the analyst.

All regression analysis assumes that the relationship between the dependent and each of the independent variables takes a particular form. In *linear regression*, it is assumed that the relationship can be adequately summarised by a straight line. This means that a one percentage point increase in the value of an independent variable is assumed to have the same impact on the value of the dependent variable on average, irrespective of the previous values of those variables.

Strictly speaking the technique assumes that both the dependent and the independent variables are measured on an interval-level scale, although it may sometimes still be applied even where this is not the case. For example, one can use an ordinal variable (e.g. a Likert scale) as a *dependent* variable if one is willing to assume that there is an underlying interval-level scale and the difference between the observed ordinal scale and the underlying interval scale is due to random measurement error. Often the answers to a number of Likert-type questions are averaged to give a dependent variable that is more like a continuous variable. Categorical or nominal data can be used as *independent* variables by converting them into dummy or binary variables; these are variables where the only valid scores are 0 and 1, with 1 signifying membership of a particular category and 0 otherwise.

The assumptions of linear regression cause particular difficulties where the *dependent* variable is binary. The assumption that the relationship between the dependent and the independent variables is a straight line means that it can produce estimated values for the dependent variable of less than 0 or greater than 1. In this case it may be more appropriate to assume that the relationship between the dependent and the independent variables takes the form of an S-curve, where the impact on the dependent variable of a one-point increase in an independent variable becomes progressively less the closer the value of the dependent variable approaches 0 or 1. *Logistic regression* is an alternative form of regression which fits such an S-curve rather than a straight line. The technique can also be adapted to analyse multinomial non-interval-level dependent variables, that is, variables which classify respondents into more than two categories.

The two statistical scores most commonly reported from the results of regression analyses are:

A measure of variance explained: This summarises how well all the independent variables combined can account for the variation in respondent's scores in the dependent variable. The higher the measure, the more accurately we are able in general to estimate the correct value of each respondent's score on the dependent variable from knowledge of their scores on the independent variables.

A parameter estimate: This shows how much the dependent variable will change on average, given a one-unit change in the independent variable (while holding all other independent variables in the model constant). The parameter estimate has a positive sign if an increase in the value of the independent variable results in an increase in the value of the dependent variable. It has a negative sign if an increase in the value of the independent variable results in a decrease in the value of the dependent variable. If the parameter estimates are standardised, it is possible to compare the relative impact of different independent variables; those variables with the largest standardised estimates can be said to have the biggest impact on the value of the dependent variable.

Regression also tests for the statistical significance of parameter estimates. A parameter estimate is said to be significant at the five per cent level if the range of the values encompassed by its 95 per cent confidence interval (see also section on sampling errors) are either all positive or all negative. This means that there is less than a five per cent chance that the association we have found between the dependent variable and the independent variable is simply the result of sampling error and does not reflect a relationship that actually exists in the general population.

Factor analysis

Factor analysis is a statistical technique which aims to identify whether there are one or more apparent sources of commonality to the answers given by respondents to a set of questions. It ascertains the smallest number of *factors* (or dimensions) which can most economically summarise all of the variation found in the set of questions being analysed. Factors are established where respondents who give a particular answer to one question in the set, tend to give the same answer as each other to one or more of the other questions in the set. The technique is most useful when a relatively small number of factors are able to account for a relatively large proportion of the variance in all of the questions in the set.

The technique produces a *factor loading* for each question (or variable) on each factor. Where questions have a high loading on the same factor, then it will be the case that respondents who give a particular answer to one of these questions tend to give a similar answer to the other questions. The technique is most commonly used in attitudinal research to try to identify the underlying ideological dimensions which apparently structure attitudes towards the subject in question.

International Social Survey Programme

The *International Social Survey Programme* (ISSP) is run by a group of research organisations, each of which undertakes to field annually an agreed module of questions on a chosen topic area. Since 1985, an *International Social Survey Programme* module has been included in one of the *British Social Attitudes* self-completion questionnaires. Each module is chosen for repetition at intervals to allow comparisons both between countries (membership is currently standing at over 40) and over time. In 2007, the chosen subject was Leisure Time and Sports, and the module was carried on the A version of the self-completion questionnaire (Qs. 1.1–1.18).[9]

Notes

1. Until 1991 all *British Social Attitudes* samples were drawn from the Electoral Register (ER). However, following concern that this sampling frame might be deficient in its coverage of certain population subgroups, a 'splicing' experiment was conducted in 1991. We are grateful to the Market Research Development Fund for contributing towards the costs of this experiment. Its purpose was to investigate whether a switch to PAF would disrupt the time-series – for instance, by lowering response rates or affecting the distribution of responses to particular questions. In the event, it was concluded that the change from ER to PAF was unlikely to affect time trends in any noticeable ways, and that no adjustment factors were necessary. Since significant differences in efficiency exist between PAF and ER, and because we considered it untenable to continue to use a frame that is known to be biased, we decided to adopt PAF as the sampling frame for future *British Social Attitudes* surveys. For details of the PAF/ER 'splicing' experiment, see Lynn and Taylor (1995).

2. This includes households not containing any adults aged 18 and over, vacant dwelling units, derelict dwelling units, non-resident addresses and other deadwood.

3. In 1993 it was decided to mount a split-sample experiment designed to test the applicability of Computer-Assisted Personal Interviewing (CAPI) to the *British Social Attitudes* survey series. CAPI has been used increasingly over the past decade as an alternative to traditional interviewing techniques. As the name implies, CAPI involves the use of lap-top computers during the interview, with interviewers entering responses directly into the computer. One of the advantages of CAPI is that it significantly reduces both the amount of time spent on data processing and the number of coding and editing errors. There was, however, concern that a different interviewing technique might alter the distribution of responses and so affect the year-on-year consistency of *British Social Attitudes* data.

   Following the experiment, it was decided to change over to CAPI completely in 1994 (the self-completion questionnaire still being administered in the conventional way). The results of the experiment are discussed in *The 11th Report* (Lynn and Purdon, 1994).

4. Interview times recorded as less than 14 minutes were excluded, as these timings were likely to be errors.

5. An experiment was conducted on the 1991 *British Social Attitudes* survey (Jowell *et al.*, 1992) which showed that sending advance letters to sampled addresses before fieldwork begins has very little impact on response rates. However, interviewers do find that an advance letter helps them to introduce the survey on the doorstep, and a majority of respondents have said that they preferred some advance notice. For these reasons, advance letters have been used on the *British Social Attitudes* surveys since 1991.

6. Because of methodological experiments on scale development, the exact items detailed in this section have not been asked on all versions of the questionnaire each year.

7. In 1994 only, this item was replaced by: Ordinary people get their fair share of the nation's wealth. *[Wealth1]*

8. In constructing the scale, a decision had to be taken on how to treat missing values ('Don't knows,' 'Refused' and 'Not answered'). Respondents who had more than two missing values on the left–right scale and more than three missing values on the libertarian–authoritarian and welfarism scales were excluded from that scale. For respondents with just a few missing values, 'Don't knows' were recoded to the midpoint of the scale and 'Refused' or 'Not answered' were recoded to the scale mean for that respondent on their valid items.

9. See www.natcen.ac.uk/bsaquestionnaires.

References

DeVellis, R.F. (2003), *Scale Development: Theory and Applications* (2nd Edition), Applied Social Research Methods Series, 26, Thousand Oaks, CA: Sage

Jowell, R., Brook, L., Prior, G. and Taylor, B. (1992), *British Social Attitudes: the 9th Report*, Aldershot: Dartmouth

Lynn, P. and Purdon, S. (1994), 'Time-series and lap-tops: the change to computer-assisted interviewing', in Jowell, R., Curtice, J., Brook, L. and Ahrendt, D. (eds.), *British Social Attitudes: the 11ᵗʰ Report*, Aldershot: Dartmouth

Lynn, P. and Taylor, B. (1995), 'On the bias and variance of samples of individuals: a comparison of the Electoral Registers and Postcode Address File as sampling frames', *The Statistician*, **44**: 173–194

Spector, P.E. (1992), *Summated Rating Scale Construction: An Introduction, Quantitative Applications in the Social Sciences*, 82, Newbury Park, CA: Sage

Stafford, R. and Thomson, K. (2006), *British Social Attitudes and Young People's Social Attitudes surveys 2003*: Technical Report, London: National Centre for Social Research

Appendix II
Notes on the tabulations in chapters

1. Figures in the tables are from the 2007 *British Social Attitudes* survey unless otherwise indicated.
2. Tables are percentaged as indicated by the percentage signs.
3. In tables, '*' indicates less than 0.5 per cent but greater than zero, and '−' indicates zero.
4. When findings based on the responses of fewer than 100 respondents are reported in the text, reference is made to the small base size.
5. Percentages equal to or greater than 0.5 have been rounded up (e.g. 0.5 per cent = one per cent; 36.5 per cent = 37 per cent).
6. In many tables the proportions of respondents answering "Don't know" or not giving an answer are not shown. This, together with the effects of rounding and weighting, means that percentages will not always add to 100 per cent.
7. The self-completion questionnaire was not completed by all respondents to the main questionnaire (see Appendix I). Percentage responses to the self-completion questionnaire are based on all those who completed it.
8. The bases shown in the tables (the number of respondents who answered the question) are printed in small italics. The bases are unweighted, unless otherwise stated.

Subject index